# ENGAGING AMBIENCE

# ENGAGING AMBIENCE

*Visual and Multisensory Methodologies and Rhetorical Theory*

**BRIAN McNELY**

UTAH STATE UNIVERSITY PRESS
*Logan*

© 2024 by University Press of Colorado

Published by Utah State University Press
An imprint of University Press of Colorado
1580 North Logan Street, Suite 660
PMB 39883
Denver, Colorado 80203-1942

All rights reserved

 The University Press of Colorado is a proud member of the Association of University Presses.

The University Press of Colorado is a cooperative publishing enterprise supported, in part, by Adams State University, Colorado State University, Fort Lewis College, Metropolitan State University of Denver, University of Alaska Fairbanks, University of Colorado, University of Denver, University of Northern Colorado, University of Wyoming, Utah State University, and Western Colorado University.

ISBN: 978-1-64642-587-7 (hardcover)
ISBN: 978-1-64642-588-4 (paperback)
ISBN: 978-1-64642-589-1 (ebook)
https://doi.org/10.7330/9781646425891

Library of Congress Cataloging-in-Publication Data

Names: McNely, Brian, 1973– author.
Title: Engaging ambience : visual and multisensory methodologies and rhetorical theory / Brian McNely.
Description: Logan : Utah State University Press, [2024] | Includes bibliographical references and index.
Identifiers: LCCN 2023035261 (print) | LCCN 2023035262 (ebook) | ISBN 9781646425877 (hardcover) | ISBN 9781646425884 (paperback) | ISBN 9781646425891 (ebook)
Subjects: LCSH: Visual communication—Research. | Rhetoric—Philosophy—Research. | Information visualization. | Academic writing—Methodology.
Classification: LCC P93.5 .M37 2024 (print) | LCC P93.5 (ebook) | DDC 302.2/2—dc23/eng/20231206
LC record available at https://lccn.loc.gov/2023035261
LC ebook record available at https://lccn.loc.gov/2023035262

Cover photograph © Brian McNely

# CONTENTS

*List of Figures*     vii

*Acknowledgments*     ix

### PART I: PICTURING WRITING AND RHETORIC

Introduction: Attending to Attention     5
Salience/Ambience | Empirical Rhetorics: Showing Up for What Shows Up | Unbracketing and Unforgetting

1. Picturing Writing: Visibility, *Techne*, *Poiesis*     27
   Picturing Writing | Persistent Tensions | "Actual Writing" | *Techne*: Productive Tension | Visibility, *Techne*, *Poiesis* | This-Now-Here-Ness

2. Realist Visibilities, Imaginative Praxiographies     58
   Realist Rhetorics | Ontological Constitution | "Excessive Inclusion" | Ambience and Ambivalence | Doing Visual Research | Empirical Rhetorics: Three Praxiographies

### PART II: LIGHTENING AND CLEARING

3. Topographies and Trajectories of Writing     87
   Visual Ethnography at Investigation and Foresight | Factorial Rhetorics | The Meaning and Enigma of Visibility | From Known Contingency to Experienced Permanence

4. The Ineffable in the Tangible     117
   Eucharistic Adoration and Multisensory Research | Building, Gathering, Dwelling | Kneeling in Public | Concealment and Withdrawal | Things by Which We Dwell

5. Walks, Talks, *Gelassenheit*     149
   Nigel | Autoethnography and Ambient Attunement | Turning and Tuning to Everydayness | Mutual Vulnerability, *Gelassenheit* | Commuting in Releasement | "The [Body] at Three Miles an Hour"

### CODA

6. Writing with Light     191
   Writing with Light | Clearings, Openings, Lightenings | One Last Photo

*References*     211
*Index*     221
*About the Author*     227

# FIGURES

1.1. Lauren storyboarding gameplay and user interface elements    29
1.2. Picturing collaborative writing as a spatial, embodied, material, intra-active practice    31
1.3. Overview of project-related writing work shared by Valerie    38
3.1. Focus group table with "thinking tools" and participant jottings    99
3.2 Privacy toplight exercise from focus group session    100
3.3. Conference room whiteboard with a key interstitial genre: the project outline    102
3.4. Open-plan office space at Investigation and Foresight    104
3.5. "DO NOT ERASE": Conference room whiteboard with semi-stable project outline    106
3.6. Mike and Jenn's office space, with Mike's personal whiteboard in the background    115
4.1. Incenser used during a Eucharistic Procession    119
4.2. Adoration chapel, with a tabernacle in the foreground    120
4.3. Eucharistic Exposition: a monstrance on the altar in the sanctuary    121
4.4. A young person kneels and makes the sign of the cross as a Eucharistic Procession moves down the street    132
4.5. Mark leading a Eucharistic Procession through the city    133
4.6. Mark (with monstrance) leading a benediction at the base of the university bell tower    134
5.1. Wind and waves    173
5.2. Traces    175
5.3. Subtle reclamations    176
5.4. Subtle reclamations    177
5.5. Subtle reclamations    177
5.6. Subtle reclamations    178
5.7. Sounds and rhythms    180
5.8. Sounds and rhythms    181
5.9. Openings at three miles per hour    184
5.10. Openings at three miles per hour    185
6.1. Lie Down in the Light    192
6.2. One last photo    209

# ACKNOWLEDGMENTS

This book began in 2012 with a long literature review.

In 2010 and 2011 I'd been devouring research in visual anthropology, visual sociology, and material cultures research—mostly ethnographic studies that used photography, videography, and participant drawing to better understand social life. I wondered why we weren't using such methods in rhetoric and writing, and I had a hunch that the term *visual rhetoric* meant, in practice, something like "rhetorical criticism of visual phenomena." It seemed as though scholars in my field weren't using technologies of visual *production* and were rarely doing *empirical studies* of or with visual phenomena.

That long literature review, encompassing more than 150 articles published in rhetoric and writing's major journals between the early 1980s and 2012, confirmed my suspicions: as a subfield of rhetoric and writing, *visual rhetoric* was overwhelmingly (but not exclusively) practiced as rhetorical criticism. Approaches using photography and videography in fieldwork were outliers—just a handful of projects amid a veritable library of criticism. There were, at the time, *zero* studies in the field's major journals that used visual ethnography. But making this argument in public scholarship was challenging. Despite the comprehensiveness of the literature review, early versions of the work in this book were often rejected, and other pieces of my research at that time were published in subfields adjacent to rhetoric and writing—in communication design, for example.

Thankfully, the field has come around a bit since 2012. There are now many fine books and articles that have sought and developed empirical approaches to visual rhetoric. Despite the many speedbumps along the way, there were always folks who believed in my approach and supported my work.

First and foremost, I am deeply grateful to all the participants in my fieldwork; without their generosity and candor I would not be able to do this kind of research. I am also indebted to the colleagues who have helped me carry out several of the ethnographic projects detailed in this book: Paul Gestwicki, Ann Burke, Bridget Gelms, Elmar Hashimov, Jennifer Stewart, and Brad King.

I am thankful, too, for the many colleagues who have helped me think through the ideas in this book. Randall Monty is the first person with whom I share new ideas and draft prose, and I am grateful for his sage advice and tactful feedback. I have benefited from the wisdom of so many others throughout the long process of developing this book. I thank Helen Foster, Beth Brunk-Chavez, Jenny Rice, Michael Pennell, Jim Ridolfo, Jan Fernheimer, Clay Spinuzzi, Christa Teston, Bill Hart-Davidson, Laurie Gries, Jeff Grabill, Jeff Rice, Jody Shipka, Nathaniel Rivers, and Jason Kalin. I am *so* thankful for Rachael Levay, who believed in this book from the start, who patiently worked with me through many ups and downs, and who provided tireless encouragement and support. And I'm indebted to the peer reviewers, whose generosity and collegiality helped make this a much better work than it would have been without them.

Thanks, most of all, to Jennifer, who always supports me no matter what.

# ENGAGING AMBIENCE

# PART I

*Picturing Writing and Rhetoric*

# Introduction
## ATTENDING TO ATTENTION

Humans have never been lone arbiters of persuasion. Rhetorical theory has turned toward things, moods, sensations, feelings, environments, and their combined effects as the ground and grounding of suasive events. As Scot Barnett and Casey Boyle (2016, 1) have argued, "Things provoke thought, incite feeling, circulate affects, and arouse in us a sense of wonder."

How do things do this? And how and why does the doing matter? How and why, to interpolate Karen Barad (2007), does matter come to matter in rhetoric?

One way to address to such questions is with thought experiments. Pick some *thing*, *any* thing, and work through its suasive potential. The Norwegian novelist and essayist Karl Ove Knausgaard has done something similar (*Autumn* [2017a], *Winter* [2017b], and *Summer* [2018c]), defamiliarizing and making strange the things with which we live our everyday lives—from rubber boots and winter sounds to frogs, chewing gum, piss, and Flaubert novels. Somehow, after reading his short chapters on chestnut trees or hollow spaces, you see those things anew.

Knausgaard makes the familiar strange at human scale—he muses on what things do to other things and non-human organisms and what they do to, for, with, and through *us*. He's sometimes nostalgic and anthropomorphic; he reads memories and desires into things in ways that might give scholars pause. Yet things provoke thought, and humans tend to think at human scale, even when thinking through non-human things (a tendency not without problems; see Pilsch 2017). Things, too, "incite feeling, circulate affects"—what we typically see as non-cognitive suasion. And all this may be immanent, all at once—affecting us, conditioning us, spilling over into our words, thoughts, acts, and comportments. How? Follow me in a brief thought experiment: let's consider desks.

Desks are flat surfaces that stabilize things and actions and ideas.

Although flat and smooth, the surface of a desk may be angled—as in the medieval desks of my imagination (stoked by images from popular culture) whereupon tonsured monks in heavy earthen-hued robes labored to copy manuscripts on thin sheets of vellum. Or they may be rotated and evacuated, as in the contemporary desk-and-chair combos that populate classrooms around the world. Some desks look like tables, but tables are not always desks. Most desks are rectangular. Some desks have nooks and hollows and cubbies—perhaps a smooth, thin groove along one edge to prevent pencils and pens from rolling to the floor. A hinge that opens onto a hidden space for storing books, erasers, binder clips, sandwiches, juice boxes. A built-in shelf at the edge—like a dollhouse row of Brooklyn brownstones shorn of their facades—for tucking paperclips, stamps, bills, and receipts inside the walls of its apartments.

The flat, smooth surfaces of desks are kept in place and elevated by any number of innovations—poles we call "legs," adjustable trestles, blocks of tooled and joined wood or metal that contain drawers or hollow cubbies—almost always with a large open space in the middle for a chair, feet, legs, or a curled cat. Some desks have cranks or motors with gears so one can adjust the height; some desks are for standing at rather than sitting. Some desks hide their surfaces and cubbies under a curved wooden canopy that rolls down along grooved walls at its sides, like the corrugated metal door of a bodega storefront, closed for the night.

The etymology of *desk* dates from the fourteenth century, from the medieval Latin *desca*, a table on which one writes. A common contemporary German word for desk is *Schreibtisch*, which fuses *schreiben* (to write) with *Tisch* (table) and thus preserves the connection between desk and writing. The French *escritoire* carries a similar connection and describes a particular kind of writing space with doors and drawers that resembles an armoire.

The notion that writing was an activity accomplished on a special kind of table—*desk* as a new species of the genus *table*, family *furniture*—seems to have coincided with medieval writing and, later, with the emergence of the printing press. Desks, in concept and material form, solidified in the seventeenth and eighteenth centuries, alongside, perhaps, a dominant (Western) cultural conception of writers and writing. Our modern era has spawned desk jobs and deskwork, cubicle farms with desk jockeys, paper pushers and ergonomics and desktop computers. Desks have become places, destinations, anchors. Desks have their own gravity—they pull together myriad things, concepts, compartments. Desks keep things in place and function as launching pads for ideas that sometimes travel around the world.

\* \* \*

I am sitting at a desk, at home, facing a window and a dawning autumn day. My desk is a large rectangle of thick tempered glass with rounded, matte edges. It sits atop two adjustable wooden trestles, each of which has four angled legs that form large As because each trestle has a horizontal shelf, a few inches above the floor. On the left shelf is a wire wastebasket—empty because I am writing on a Thursday and have taken out the garbage ahead of tomorrow's weekly pickup. In front of the wastebasket is a small plastic organizer I have carried with me, from one place to the next, for over twenty years. In its narrow, smoky black corridors lay a checkbook (used once each month to pay the rent and for virtually nothing else); stamps; a letter opener I can't recall having ever used; two pens; library cards; a few business cards I found in one of my dad's desk drawers after he died; return address stickers; a sad, reedy notepad; and credit cards rarely swiped in the flesh. On the right shelf is a folded towel I use in the early mornings, after running, to wipe sweat from my face and neck.

I like a clean desk, but I'm hemmed in by companions—some of which I need, some of which I loathe, some of which I am anxious to process and internalize and move away as soon as possible. To my left are three separate piles of books at different heights, like stout, nondescript office buildings in any city center housing insurance companies, banks, and more infernal insurance companies. Towering above is a sleek white pillar of index cards, more than 1,200 of them, each with a word in German on one side and a word or two in English on the other. I have been slowly digitizing them, the desk skyscraper shrinking day by day. Behind the little MacBook on which I type is a pile of printed journal articles; these need to be annotated, my handwritten notes and underlinings added to a research database and tagged for use as scholarly support in my writing.

To my right is a volume of Nabokov's early novels; I resent this book, have been trudging through it joylessly. It's a grudge match. I can't wait to shove this book down the narrow metal throat of my library's book return chute. Next to Nabokov are a small glass teapot and a ceramic teacup, both empty and sitting on a folded paper towel that is inelegant but functional. Toward the back of the desk are framed photographs—my three kids in various poses and places, my wife and me dressed in 1940s film-noir garb for a party in downtown Albuquerque, me and my two daughters on the beach in Carlsbad, California, one brisk, seabreezy evening when they were little. My camera—a Nikon 35Ti from the mid-1990s—sits in its faux-leather case, next to six rolls of exposed film in gray plastic cylinders awaiting their journey to the lab.

At this desk, I have struggled to finish this book. Two days ago, I scrapped a fieldwork vignette I had planned to use. Sitting here over the last few weeks, I've read and edited and smoothed the prose in the chapters I've drafted and revised. I've eaten here, read here, annotated here. My gaze has been here, peering into this screen as I type, but it has also been pulled toward my companions—my camera; the film I want to develop; a photo of my youngest daughter flat on her back at three or four years old, smiling from the fine mesh surface of a trampoline; the fucking Nabokov book.

A social theorist could read much into these descriptions of my desk, and indeed, there is much to glean. My desk, the things it holds, and my descriptions say much about me. It's trite, but my desk and these things support my writing, literally and otherwise. Reading meaning from these descriptions would be to extract salience—a move typical of rhetorical theorists, as Thomas Rickert (2013) argues. To extract salience is to make a point; it is also to miss a point. As Knausgaard (2018b, loc. 8603) has it, "designation is another kind of disappearance." Something is pulled out, foregrounded, pointed to, probed, and so many other somethings fade into the haze of an arbitrarily defined background.

The things with which I have surrounded myself, sometimes intentionally, sometimes haphazardly, all condition my rhetorics—from the straightforward composition of this sentence to the ways I conceptualize myself as a writer, scholar, and human being. I am sometimes acutely aware of the effects of these things, but most often I am not. Sometimes salience is clear, but often there is none I can identify. I pay bills here, eat yogurt and bananas and cheese sticks here like a toddler strapped into a high chair. This glass surface, seemingly impermeable, is nonetheless embedded with memories, laden with affects, piled with inscrutable, numberless variables. I fall into the screen, into my document, my desk's deskness invisible to my machinations but no less crucial, despite my myopia.

There is a different form of myopia at play, too: how can I know how these things truly affect me? In what ways is their effect on me combinatorial, factorial, exponential, ineffable? How often does my gaze switch from the screen to the piles of books or to the photos of my kids? What causes me to check out and daydream? How can I ever see myself among my things, from outside myself? Is finding salience possible or even desirable? Isn't salience always a guess, an assessment, a sentence passed down? Thought experiments take us only so far. I am still connected to and immersed in the things that surround me, even as I attempt to make them strange.

\* \* \*

If rhetoric is originary, immanent in one's material environs, and ambient, how should we go about studying it systematically—with something more rigorous than thought experiments? This is a key question for contemporary empirical researchers in rhetoric, writing, communication, and related fields.

This book offers a set of approaches for addressing this question, connecting new materialist theories of rhetoric to empirical methodologies that enliven and extend such theories. It helps scholars operationalize and extend new materialist, affective, and ambient perspectives on rhetoric and writing by considering how we engage (and are engaged by) what surrounds us, in systematic, rigorous, and theoretically nuanced ways. It offers approaches to rhetorical study that meet the warp, weft, and welter of being and communicating in a world full to bursting with all manner of suasive and affective actors, moods, and comportments.

*Engaging Ambience* reexamines what we know about methodology and theory, about reality and imagination, about visuality and visibility, and about *techne* and *poiesis*.

### SALIENCE/AMBIENCE

In Edmund Husserl's phenomenology, bracketing is a preliminary move, something one does before analysis in the hopes of unpacking experience, free of cultural bias. Bracketing is a nice idea, but it is effectively impossible. In the more common sense of "setting aside," bracketing is anathema to studies of ambience. As Husserl's student, Martin Heidegger realized early on the impossibility of bracketing—in a phenomenological or colloquial sense. And I cannot bracket—set aside—the problems Heidegger presents to contemporary rhetorical theory.

Heidegger joined the Nazi party in 1933. He was an anti-Semite. He turned his back on Husserl, who was Jewish. He was largely silent after World War II and tried to explain away his Nazi party membership in an infamous interview with *Der Spiegel*, published—at his request—posthumously.

I draw on Heidegger's work throughout this book because many of my sources draw from, build on, and push back against Heideggerian philosophy. My own arguments continue those scholarly conversations and, I hope, offer new understandings of what Heidegger has to say about rhetorical theory. I cannot reconcile Heidegger's personal and political views with his philosophy. They cannot be untangled or bracketed. From my perspective, a theory of ambient rhetoric calls for unbracketing, an idea suggested by Heidegger's early work.

In his first lecture after World War I, Heidegger began publicly to think beyond the phenomenology of his mentor, Husserl. "The Idea of Philosophy and the Worldview Problem" (Safranski 1998) considered our *experience* of reality prior to any *appropriation*—before we layer our values, worldviews, and biases on material phenomena. It suggests that our experience is always already an intra-active enactment. At first blush, this sounds like classical phenomenology; but Heidegger was concerned with the nature of *experience itself,* or the *attitude* of experience—inclusive of what we bring to it—rather than a phenomenological bracketing of values and worldviews. He tries, therefore, to *unbracket* both materiality and subjectivity.

He was interested in *how* this happens, how these interactions unfold, here and now, absent some metaphysical synthesis or theoretical apparatus. He asks: "Do we experience reality before we arrange it for ourselves in a scientific, or value-judging, or worldview approach" (Safranski 1998, 93). And he uses the lectern before him to consider how we experience the lectern's lecternness. This should sound familiar.

In his biography of Heidegger, Rüdiger Safranski quotes from the lecture extensively, for the lectern acts as the argument's "hinge." What we see in the lectern are not various material parts that resolve, somehow, into "lectern" as concept. Instead, Heidegger says, "I see the lectern at a single stroke" (Safranski 1998, 94). The lectern is part of its material, historical, and cultural context, all at once. The lectern—and any related elements: a book lying atop its angled surface, its height, the lighting in the room, its orientation—"presents itself to me," Heidegger says, as something here and now and of one suasive bundle (95).

Heidegger cannot *bracket* his own history of visits to lectures, his interactions with previous lecterns, his sense of Western elocution, or his religious training. Bracketing is impossible, for the lectern presents itself with this bundle of learned histories and ways of being immanent *in its thingness* and not something exclusively in Heidegger's head. The idea that things are *presented to us* in an *attitude of everyday experience* is crucial, for it shifts the locus of agency from humans perceiving and apprehending an inert world to an intra-action of human apprehension and the world's active disclosures: "Living in an environment, it means to me everywhere and always, it is all of this world, it is worlding," Heidegger argues (Safranski 1998, 95). *Worlding,* Safranski notes, is the first of Heidegger's many neologisms.

*Worlding*, so crucial throughout Heidegger's oeuvre, emerges from a methodological-theoretical move: *unbracketing*. Worlding involves an "environmental something" that resolves into focus and "presents itself to me from an immediate environment" (Safranski 1998, 95). The lectern—and all its ambient *somethings*—arrives directly, "without any mental detour via a grasping of things" (95).

*Salience* comes later; worlding is *ambient*.

When we see the lectern, "we unexpectedly slide into a different order that is no longer the order of perceiving" (Safranski 1998, 95). Instead, we see a *bundle* of things, material and imagined. Heidegger argues that we should engage phenomena unbracketed, attending to our attention. Safranski adds: "The lectern is 'worlding' therefore means: I am experiencing the significance of the lectern, its function, its location in the room, its lighting, and the little episodes that are associated with it (an hour ago someone else was standing here; my recollection of the road I had to cover to get here; my irritation at standing here at the lectern listening to this incomprehensible stuff, and so on). The lectern 'is worlding' means it assembles a whole world, in terms of time and space" (96). "In the beginning," Safranski says, "there is 'worlding,' one way or another" (96).

Yet because of familiarity, much of the bundle is withdrawn in everyday apprehension. Worlding thus describes "that which normally we do not recognize because it is too close to us" (Safranski 1998, 95). Nearness means we regularly take things for granted *as disclosive and agentive things*—we overlook or misjudge or willingly evade (Heidegger 2010) a thing's capacity to "provoke thought, incite feeling, circulate affects, and arouse in us a sense of wonder" (Barnett and Boyle 2016, 1). We bracket unintentionally.

We simply do not *see* the ways things present themselves to us in everyday life, their myriad potential disclosures. We are only able to see such disclosures by focusing attention on our attention to them, a theme in Heidegger's work that grows stronger after his "Worldview Problem" lecture (see Heidegger 2010). We must perform some act or series of acts—thinking through the experience of encountering a lectern, performing a thought experiment on desks or Flaubert novels or winter sounds—and simultaneously attend to our attention to gather some sense of how we experience phenomena as an interchange of suasive disclosure and apprehension.

Thought experiments are useful but insufficient. We need other ways of attending to our attention, other ways of seeing ourselves with our everyday things from outside the compartments and affects that are always already embedded and entangled with our understanding. We need ways of re-seeing, or seeing differently, the disclosures of everyday things, their worlding.

Worlding suggests that within phenomena—things, smells, caresses; desks, lecterns, winter sounds—"an entire life situation" may be immanent (Safranski 1998, 96). "We do not experience every Something as 'worlding' so powerfully, but every Something 'worlds' to some extent," Safranski argues (96). This is the rub. The disclosures of things in our everyday environs emerge not from premise-free subject-object relations; instead we find ourselves presented with worldings—responding to them, interacting with them, embracing our fundamental entanglement with them (97; see Barad 2007).

In Heidegger's later work, worlding is not mere presence, a bundle of things that are simply there. It is also not "merely an imagined framework added by our representation to the sum of such given things" (Heidegger 2013, 43). Instead, "the world worlds, and is more fully in being than the tangible and perceptible realm in which we believe ourselves to be home" (43). The "world" does not simply stand before us as something we perceive and can bracket from previous experience; instead, the world *worlds* in and through our very *inquiry* into being (43).

Heidegger's perspective on the world and worlding is congruent with Steven Shaviro's (2014) understanding of the universe of things: being and interacting is more than we can grasp and describe; the more-than-human world is here, disclosing, worlding, whether we pay attention or not, whether we grasp disclosures or not, whether we "bracket" or not. We don't always see or think about a lectern or a desk or a person walking behind us; rather, we *feel* their worlding. The world "is more fully in being" than we often realize, Heidegger argues (2013, 43); the world worlds even when we do not or cannot perceive its worlding. The world's worlding is often non-correlational, nonobjective, pre-reflective, *presentative*, or *given* (Serres 2016) rather than re*p*resentative. R*e*presentation is what humans do. We sometimes glimpse worlding, however; Proust's involuntary memory is a canonical example.

*  *  *

For Heidegger, experience of the lectern is framed by what we *see*. Yet *seeing* is an imprecise term, shorthand for something more complex than visual perception. Indeed, Heidegger explicitly demonstrates how visual perception is so embedded in everyday apprehension as to be *invisible* to us: "What do I see: brown surfaces intersecting at right angles? No, I see something different—a box, moreover a biggish box, with a smaller built upon it. No, that's not it at all, I see the lectern at which I am to speak. You see the lectern from which you are spoken to" (Safranski 1998, 94). It feels odd to devolve *seeing* to the level of perception, to describe the lectern as brown surfaces at right angles or a desk's grooves and cubbies and articulated hinges. It feels odd because this is precisely what we do not mean by *seeing*. Instead, *seeing* often means something like sensing, feeling, grasping. None of these other gerunds evoke sight; they all evoke *touch*. Heidegger *sees* the lectern, but he means the opposite of *perceives*—the physiological work of rods and cones and reflected light waves.

He means, instead, that we *feel* something in the lectern—we become immersed in a whole world. In rhetorical studies, we typically use the word *visual* to mean the opposite of visual facticity and the *perception* of visual phenomena. Indeed, though we rarely use the term, we tend to be much more interested in *visibility*, a concept that is thoroughly material-social-historical-suasive. When we talk about visual rhetoric we are, above all, interested in what we *feel*, what we experience in our encounters with visual phenomena, in a Heideggerian sense of seeing: a worlding. We *see*, which is to say that we feel and hear and touch and take in the world with our eyes and with our bodies. Safranski (2017, 302) quotes Goethe's "Roman Elegies": "See with a feeling eye, feel with a seeing hand."

Roland Barthes connects photography and the sense of touch in both primary uses of the word—the notion that something could be affective, and the notion that one experiences something beyond the ocular, that interactions with photographs are somehow haptic and tactile as well. A photograph "is literally an emanation of the referent. From a real body, which was there, proceed radiations which ultimately *touch me*, who am here . . . the photograph of the missing being, as Sontag says, *will touch me like the delayed rays of a star*" (Barthes 1981, 80–81, emphasis added). There are chemical, physiological, material, haptic, and affective affordances connecting referents, photography, photographs, and viewers all at once. When we view a photograph, we feel the light emanating from a real somewhere, and at the same time we *see*, perhaps, an entire world, in the Heideggerian sense: "at a single stroke" (Safranski 1998, 94).

Barthes (1981, 82) describes a family photograph as a "treasury of rays which emanated from [his] mother as a child, from her hair, her skin, her dress, her gaze, on that day." One effect of these emanations is the knowledge that what is pictured was irrefutably *real* (82). The two-way gaze—of Barthes into the photograph, of his mother into the lens—is, even decades later, an enacting material reality. Ordinary scenes depicted in photographs yield a "reality in a past state: at once the past and the real" (82). More than any other visual medium, photography "offers an immediate presence to the world—a co-presence" (84). A photograph "does not necessarily say what is no longer, but only and for certain what has been" (85). A photograph may thus "ratify what it represents," in a way writing cannot (85). In photographs, "The past is as certain as the present, what we see on paper is as certain as what we touch" (88).

In *Mythologies*, Barthes (1977, 90) argued that "touch is the most demystifying of all senses" while acknowledging that the sense of sight "is the most magical." Yet as Shawn Michelle Smith (2014, 29) has shown, affect, feeling, and touch in and through photography were among Barthes's central concerns—the intersection of demystification and magic. Affect, Barthes says, is precisely "what I didn't want to reduce"; he approached photography not as a theme but as a wound: "I *see*, I *feel*, hence I notice, I observe, and I think" (1981, 21, emphasis added). Smith (2014, 29) argues that "Barthes seeks to forestall the scholarly leap from perception to observation, to linger in the in-between moment of feeling, and to make his critical work account for his emotional response."

Barthes proposed an affective approach to photography, one that was premised on the tactile aspects of seeing, one premised *on touch*. His theory of photography hinges on the *punctum*, on the affective *wound* in any given photograph: "the images that move him 'touch' him violently, 'prick' and 'pierce,' and 'bruise' him" (Smith 2014, 34). According to Smith, "Barthes's entire understanding of photography is remarkably tactile; his experience of viewing is one of being touched"; "all attentive viewing is an exchange of touching for Barthes" (34). Seeing photographs is an affective exchange, touching, worlding unbracketed. Worlding may be *felt*: in our skin, in our throats, with our hands and bellies and eyes.

And Barthes has company. In bas-relief, Gilles Deleuze (2002, 99) saw "the most rigid link between the eye and the hand . . . which allows the eye to function like the sense of touch; furthermore, it confers, and indeed imposes, upon the eye a tactile or rather *haptic* function." Deleuze argued that in "the different regimes of color" is found "a properly visual sense of touch, or a haptic sense of sight" (123). For John Berger (1977, 8), "To touch something is to situate oneself in relation to it." We situate ourselves with attentive *looking*, he argues; to look is to touch. The most distinguishing characteristic of oil painting is its "special ability to render the tangibility, the texture, the lustre the solidity of what it depicts" (88). As Michel Serres (2016, loc. 3012) has it, "The painter makes us see through touch." We sense, we see, we feel with our eyes.

In *Blind Spot*, Teju Cole deftly evokes visual synesthesia. He recounts the parable of Doubting Thomas: "Christ advises Thomas to surrender the sensual faculty in favor of the cognitive. But his hand, guiding Thomas's hand, says something different" (Cole 2017, 90). Christ asks if Thomas believed because he had *seen*. Thomas's *seeing*, however, was haptic: he saw Christ, he *felt* his wounded side, and a world opens. Cole describes (and pictures) an ordinary tableau in rural New York: "This dreamwork bricolage comes by an arrangement of the eye, not of the hands" (228). And yet, the photograph evokes the hands-on: "An object is used. A thing is seen" (228). A few pages later he writes "how streaked we are by what we see" (230). For Cole, "Color is the sound an object makes in response to light": "with my eyes I begin to hear what I see" (232). We sense, we see, we hear, we feel with our eyes.

These ideas are certainly not new to scholars in rhetoric. We see and feel with our whole bodies, and *visual* rhetoric is always already *multisensory* rhetoric. As Casey Boyle, James J. Brown Jr., and Steph Ceraso (2018, 253) argue, "Theories that focus on the visual are also affected and influenced by other senses. Even at its visual foundations, digital rhetoric was a multisensory enterprise." They remind us that "by attending to rhetorical encounters as multisensory events we are afforded an experience of resonance between and among a host of relations" (254).

But how do we attend to rhetorical encounters as multisensory events, empirically? How do we identify which relations matter and how they matter? One approach is to get closer to the things that are near us, by literally and figuratively *picturing* them. Visual and multisensory methodologies and methods offer empirical ways of *unbracketing* the world. They demonstrate how we can build conceptions of ambience and composites of worlding rather than creating the critical distance of salience. They cultivate nearness—dwelling with the things and practices that condition the everyday rhetorics we see, hear, feel, and touch.

### EMPIRICAL RHETORICS: SHOWING UP FOR WHAT SHOWS UP

New materialist, affective, and ambient theories have transformed understanding of rhetoric's foundations—*what* rhetoric is, *where* rhetoric is, *how* rhetoric emerges, and what, where, and how rhetoric *might be* in the future.

Recent scholarship explores concepts that have traditionally received comparatively little attention: affect and emotion (Ingraham 2017; Rice 2012; Walsh et al. 2017), sound (Ceraso 2018; Hawk 2018), energy (Ingraham 2018), embodiment (Chávez 2018; Hawhee 2015), things and objects (Barnett and Boyle 2016; Gries 2015), non-human animals (Davis 2010; Hawhee 2016), plants and trees (Davis 2017; Jones 2019; Rickert 2017; Walsh et al. 2017), accidents (Stormer 2020), and, most encompassing of all, ambience (Rickert 2013, 2017; Yarbrough 2018). In such work, rhetoric is something *in* the world rather than *on* the world (Ingold 2008), a phenomenon always already in things and added to things, immanent and invented, affective and cognitive, processual and fixed, salient and ambient.

These theories call for new methodologies—as Laurie E. Gries (2015, 5) argues, "new materialism is also a methodological project." Complexity—one exigence for new materialist methodologies, Gries notes—"cannot be investigated via methodologies that give too much weight to language's ability to account for reality, agency, and ontology" (6). We need instead "new kinds of empirical investigations that foreground distributed relations and attend to the nonlinear processes of materialization" (6).

We need methodologies and methods that explore ambience *empirically*—considering how desks, piles of books, smells in rooms, memories, framed photographs, lecterns, and views from windows contribute in a nonlinear fashion (alongside warrants, claims, and audiences) to our theories of rhetoric. "In arguing that rhetoric is ambient," Rickert (2013, xii) writes, "I am claiming that rhetoricity is the always ongoing disclosure of the world shifting our manner of being in that world so as to call for some response or action." This is the kind of complexity Gries identifies; this is the kind of ever-present exigence that requires new ways of approaching and studying rhetoric.

However, many proponents of new materialist and ambient theories of rhetoric have been less focused on methodological questions, despite Gries's call to action (and despite her own methodology of iconographic tracking; contributors to *Text + Field* [2017] are also notable exceptions). Empirical researchers might ask: Which methodologies are most appropriate for understanding and extending new materialist theories of rhetoric? What are the implications of such theories for how we understand and undertake empirical studies of rhetoric, writing, and communication writ large? How might we study the potentially overwhelming variables found in theories of rhetoric that assume the world's originary affectability? How can one credibly bound an empirical study of rhetoric if rhetoric is boundless?

As Clay Spinuzzi (2003) has argued, methods entail the specific ways we investigate phenomena. In any given empirical study, we might use multiple methods, and those methods may change or be exchanged as we trace phenomena across participants, across scenarios, and across instances of fieldwork (see also McNely 2013a). Methods are tools—sometimes we need a wrench, and sometimes pliers will do. But methodologies *embody* theories—the practical working out of theory. Methodologies are several orders of magnitude more complex than methods—they create the very frameworks in which different methods are brought together and used. Methodologies include, therefore: our overriding theoretical perspectives; our value commitments as researchers, scholars, and empathic human beings; and the broader philosophies that bear upon a specific approach (see Spinuzzi 2003, 7).

Methodologies are not *appended to* theories. They *enact* theories, values, and philosophies; enliven theoretical understanding; and reciprocally extend the development of theory. In short, methodologies are ways of *doing* theory, such that theory and practice are inseparable and mutually constitutive. *Engaging Ambience* presents empirical methodologies for *doing* new materialist and ambient theories of rhetoric. Its purpose is to explore and demonstrate systematic means for understanding how matter comes to matter in rhetoric. The book offers methodologies and methods for the empirical study of rhetoric conceived as originary, immanent, and enveloping. It builds from and extends methodological innovations (Barnett 2016; Gries 2015; McKinnon, Asen, Chávez, and Howard 2017; McNely 2019; McNely, Gestwicki, Gelms, and Burke 2013; Rule 2018, 2019) that are central to the field's turn to things, affects, and ambience.

\* \* \*

In her introduction to *The Body Multiple* (2002, xi), an ethnography of atherosclerosis in one Dutch hospital, Annemarie Mol sketches the book's provenance: it began decades ago, during "long-gone Thursdays" in which she had philosophy classes in the mornings and anatomy classes in the afternoons, where she dissected and analyzed human bodies. Her days mixed Foucault and formalin, Merleau-Ponty and pelvic cavities (x). "The remarkable materiality of it all," she says, shows up in her book: "sentences in difficult French, strange smells, my clumsiness in cutting" (xi), memories still palpable in the present.

This remarkable materiality framed her ethnographic practice: her study of atherosclerosis pays attention to, among other things, bike parking and name tags, vending-machine coffee and microscopes, gestures and sighs, tissue slices and stents, dog walking and documentation, patient stories and the sound of blood pulsing in the body as heard through a listening apparatus, "pshew, pshew" (Mol 2002, 60). Mol argues that vending-machine coffee, bike parking, and the sounds of blood flow—pshew, pshew—are inseparable from the *reality* of atherosclerosis. These elements could not be bracketed from her fieldwork. But these elements of everyday life in the hospital are not, in themselves, salient, and this is the point: *they all matter* to an ontology of atherosclerosis. Mol's novel contribution is *unbracketing*: she slows the search for salience by embracing ambience.

How? By focusing on *enactments*, on how diagnosis and treatment of atherosclerosis was *enacted* in the everyday layering of conversations with patients; diagnostic procedures; patient history records; microscopic analyses; and scalpels, corpses, sounds, arguments, and slanted medical tables. Mol (2002, 152) calls her methodology *praxiography*, an approach that "follows objects where they are being enacted in practice."

If atherosclerosis is a phenomenon with contours we can trace, understand, and discuss, she argued, "this is because it is part of a practice. It is a reality enacted" (Mol 2002, 44). But epistemological barriers persist. We cannot "know" atherosclerosis, for example, by following one surgeon or one pathologist or one patient. Further we cannot "know" atherosclerosis by consulting demographic trends and incidences of diagnosis. By focusing on enactments, Mol gave up on *knowing* to instead trace *knowledges*, which do "not reside in subjects alone, but also in buildings, knives, dyes, desks," and technologies—especially technologies of writing, recording, and inscribing (48).

Knowledges are *embedded* in practices, in technologies, in things. Mol (2002, 50) suggests that we flatten agential assessments, that it "may be a good methodological strategy to withhold from doctors and patients the subjectivity we are reluctant to grant to corpses in order to analyze embedded knowledges instead." This "may be a way out of the dichotomy between the knowing subject and the objects-that-are-known: to spread the activity of knowing widely" (50). The first step is to see the entanglements in any practice—each enactment must remain unbracketed for as long as possible (156). By tracing enactments, Mol presented stories about the assembled objects she observed: composites emerged, realities multiplied. An ontology of atherosclerosis unfolded—a composite of knowledges, practices, subjects, objects, affects, and stories.

Mol (2002, 1) describes her book as an "empirical philosophy." It is philosophy in the sense that its object of study is ontology. It is empirical because her motivating question was not "how to find the truth" but rather "how are objects handled in practice" (5). To answer the second question necessitates attentional and methodological shifts. To understand how objects are handled in practice, one must show up, pay attention to, and follow objects as they are pushed around, shared, yelled at, discarded. One must show up and observe systematically.

Such attentional and methodological shifts are a deliberate departure from "the epistemological tradition in philosophy that tried to articulate the relation between knowing subjects and their objects of knowledge" (Mol 2002, 32). For Mol, knowing is flattened, subjectivity is not granted by fiat, ontologies move and multiply. Although the philosophical object of her study—an ontology of disease—is found all over the world, the practices and objects she traced were decidedly not *everywhere* but in a very particular *somewhere* (140).

By showing up and asking "how are objects handled in practice" *here*, in this place and at this time, among these people, Mol (2002, viii) formulates "snapshot-stories" about a specific disease in a specific hospital. Her snapshot-stories slow down, thicken, and suspend enactments. Rather than carve a slice of everyday life, her snapshot-stories trace layers of ontological enactments. Together, they form a complex composite drawn from hundreds or thousands of everyday slices.

Mol's work is empirical because it is systematic, grounded in observational fieldwork, a product of showing up repeatedly to a specific place, at specific times, among specific actors, practices, and environments. It is methodologically replicable, something someone else could do in the same hospital or a different one. But her "concern with theorizing," she adds, "turns this into a philosophical book" (Mol 2002, viii). This is what she means by "empirical philosophy": it is a direct consequence of changing focus—of asking "how are objects handled in practice" or "where are knowledges embedded" or "what actors do the doing?"

Tracing enactments means being there. It means attending carefully to the actors that do the doing. It means systematic looking and documenting and unbracketing. It means paying attention to vending machines, the sounds of instruments, the ways people talk about disease, the gestures they make, their sighs, the tissues being sliced, the bodies being probed, the muscles tensing, the samples measured. It means paying attention to walking, to staircases, and to stories (Mol 2002, vii). This is how an ontology is enacted, how a world *worlds*, or, as Kathleen Stewart (2007) might say, how a *something* throws itself together.

To explore enactments empirically—and to be concerned with *theorizing* a particular ontology—we must *be there*, we must show up to see what shows up, to see *how* it shows up, to see how all the remarkable materiality in which we are immersed matters in any unfolding reality.

\* \* \*

Praxiography has as much to offer to empirical rhetorics as it did to Mol's empirical philosophy. A praxiographic approach "allows and requires one to take objects and events of all kinds into consideration when trying to understand the world" (Mol 2002, 158). "No phenomenon," Mol adds, "can be ignored on the grounds that it belongs to another discipline" (158). No phenomenon can be ignored on the grounds that it is not a subject—non-human objects of all kinds participate in and shape the emergence of any ontology.

Praxiography is a way of framing and performing ethnographic methodologies. But praxiographic studies are difficult to execute: "No entity can innocently stay the same throughout the story, unaltered between various sites. There are no invariable variables" (Mol 2002, 121). Instead, there is interdependence and interference (121). To study interdependence and interference, to document and follow invariable variables, "the practicalities" of experience must remain *unbracketed*—"in the forefront of our attention" (119).

S. Scott Graham (2015) has adapted Mol's notion of praxiography to rhetorical studies, exploring the material and discursive practices of pain management physicians. Graham and Lynda Walsh (2019, 194) also note that Mol's praxiographic emphasis on ontology identifies her with new materialisms. Praxiography creates a kind of methodological and empirical overlay in which what happens in a given *somewhere* is compared against what is claimed or assumed to be in a conceptual *everywhere*. As Graham and Walsh note, praxiography relentlessly compares knowledge claims to ontological enactments (193). "As one might expect," Graham and Walsh argue, "praxiographies frequently demonstrate a misalignment of epistemology and ontology, theory, and praxis" (193).

Mol's praxiography and empirical philosophy thus foreground the artificiality of theory/empirical practice bifurcations. Her work illustrates several key methodological-theoretical concepts that guide this book:

    a. Epistemological lines drawn between empirical work and theoretical work are ontologically problematic.

    b. Distinctions between theory and practice are often placeholders, used to extract and demonstrate salience.

    c. Distinctions between theory and methodology are similarly tenuous; Mol's praxiography is a way of engaging theory—attending to practices, objects, and environments in the midst of enactments necessitates attentional shifts that, in turn, enrich the ways a given ontology is theorized.

    d. Attentional shifts foster shifts in understandings of agency.

e. Empirical philosophy and empirical rhetoric are *realist* approaches—ontologies emerge from identifiable objects and actors, with socio-historical commitments and mores, in specific places and times, through specific practices that may be observed, apprehended, or imagined in their enacted complexity.

Rather than pry open a given epistemology with its attendant conceptual schemes and theories, Mol uses praxiography to trace an ontology and thus builds a theory of how that complex ontological object is *enacted*. Most researchers understand that epistemological lines delineate, circumscribe, and identify salience.

But in studies of ambience, those lines—like the epistemologies and conceptual schemes on which they are based—wobble, loosen, and spool from one's grasp. In empirical studies of ambient rhetorics, epistemological lines must be drawn loosely from the jump. In an ideal scenario, the methodology drives the empirical work; the empirical work points toward new theories, which drive new practices. In other scenarios, these lines are less defined, the movements among methodology, theory, and practice even more active and mutually informative. Messy, as John Law (2004) has argued.

Theory and practice are *both* ways of making things *visible*—complementary, intertwined, and recursive ways of bringing something to light, often literally. As Gries's work demonstrates, theory can be empirical and methodological. Marking *this* as theory work and *that* as practical work serves researchers interested in salience; to study ambience, we must assume from the start no clean or clear divisions between empirical work and theory work.

Even attempting to study ambience empirically is always already a theoretical-methodological undertaking. Ambient rhetorics posit certain assumptions about the world; the empirical rhetorics practiced in this book take those theories at face value and attempt to explore them in particular *somewheres*. If Rickert is correct in the notion that a worldly affectability conditions rhetorical practice, there must be a praxiological approach for studying that; in studying it, we should learn more about the theory and maybe even push it in new directions.

Our attention thus oscillates between theoretical perspectives and ontological enactments. We follow things and moods and affects that condition rhetorical practice. We do this empirical, systematic, practical work *as* rhetorical theory. Any distinctions, boundaries, and lines we draw are mere placeholders. Mol gives us an example of what can happen when we see theory as practice, practice as theory, philosophy as ethnography, ethnography as philosophy.

But to develop this kind of attentional oscillation, a different understanding of agency is needed, one that gives up on salience.

Gries's (2015, 57) definition of agency echoes Mol and builds from Barad: "Agency—an act of intervention—is not some capacity that any single image [or any other actor] has and carries with it just as it is not some capacity that any single person has. Agency is a doing, an enactment generated by a variety of components intra-acting within a particular phenomenon." If we're going to pay attention to metal tables, vending machines, patient stories, and "pshew, pshew," then we must acknowledge that none of these actors "has" agency; instead, they contribute—collectively, frictionally (Springgay and Truman 2017), diffractively (Barad 2007), factorially (see chapter 3, this volume)—to the doing in any given ontology.

We cannot make clear "cuts" about which actors have or do not have agency. As Gries (2015, 70) notes of the images she studied, "The visual things we intra-act with are both phenomena in their ongoing materialization and part of an ongoing reconfiguring of the world." These "ongoings" are "not frozen when we conduct our research" (70). Things and agency are thus "always in excess of what we can capture in our studies" (71). Agential cuts tend to make things intermediaries rather than mediators (75). As researchers, we often make agential cuts in the interest of finding salience.

Visual and multisensory methodologies and methods, consonant with Mol's praxiography, make snapshots—but of a different order. The methodological-theoretical approaches described in this book rely on an understanding of *realism* rooted in Mol's praxiography, Gries's iconographic tracking, and Barad's agential realism. Snapshots can slow things down and thicken *enactments*. They aim at complex understandings of what is *really* in a given *somewhere*, day after day, to create complex and layered *composites* of ambience rather than individual slices of salience.

Barad's agential realism assumes that reality can be documented and that the apparatuses we use to document reality are, in turn, inseparable from the reality that is enacted. It can't be any other way, for to remove the research apparatus is to create an agential cut. Many scholars in rhetoric have already explored the "agential" side of Barad's agential realism (see, for example, Barnett and Boyle 2016; Gries 2015; Rivers 2014, and others). We have written less about her "realism," however. For Barad (2007, 37), realism "is not about representations of an independent reality but about the real consequences, interventions, creative possibilities, and responsibilities of intra-acting within and as part of the world."

Realism in this sense is a form of *being there*, in a *somewhere*, inseparable from the environment, inseparable from ontological enactments, response-able (Davis 2010) as an intra-acting component of whatever happens. Praxiographic approaches for doing empirical rhetorics are not naive representations of some fixed reality that precedes their entry into the scene but rather consequential intra-actions and enactments, ways of tracing and presenting complex rhetorics, views of practice that temporarily slow down, thicken, and suspend ambient engagements—openings onto whatever is there, whatever emerges, whatever ends up mattering. These approaches don't seek salience; they seek to document, instead, *whatever shows up*.

In rhetorical studies, Scot Barnett (2016) has most directly explored the ways realist commitments in philosophy are congruent with, or divergent from, theories of rhetoric. Barnett proposed a historiographic methodology for exploring materiality in rhetoric. Gries (2015, 440; Walsh et al. 2017), too, has argued that new materialisms can help us "develop a more realistic understanding of ourselves, as human things intimately entangled with other entities from which all rhetoric comes to matter." She stresses attunement to relationality, where relations are *real*, identifiable, traceable.

These approaches have much in common with those of speculative realism (Bogost 2012; Shaviro 2014)—a non-correlational philosophy that de-centers the human subject—and object-oriented ontology (OOO; see Bryant 2011; Harman 2011, 2016, 2018; Morton 2012, 2013), "a realist position that views objects of every sort as existing prior to their relations or effects" (Harman 2016, loc. 520). In OOO, reality exists as a surplus, an enveloping ambience that may never be entirely expressed or understood (287). Although there are important differences among new materialists, speculative realists, and object-oriented ontologists (see, for example, Harman 2018; Shaviro 2014), they all share a *realist* perspective on phenomena—things *really* exist in the world, before and in excess of what we can *know* of their relations and effects. For most new materialists and (some) speculative realists, real things (material or not) and their real relations and effects can be identified, followed, and traced to some degree. Even if we concur with object-oriented ontologists who counter that all such tracings are translations and approximations, we're still in the realm of the real rather than the transcendent.

Barad's (2007, 44) realism concerns "the sense in which direct engagement with the ontology of our world is possible." Mol's (2002) praxiography demonstrates as much. In agential realism, one needs "a strong commitment to accounting for the material nature of practices and how they come to matter" (45). Barad (2007, 206) thus grounds her theory in "specific material configurations of the world." Phenomena are not merely social constructions and not merely products or handmaidens of human activity, but crucially, "neither is the world . . . independent of human practices" (206). Human practices matter in matter's differential becoming, but so do myriad non-human practices.

## UNBRACKETING AND UNFORGETTING

In Deborah Levy's *The Cost of Living* (2018), the narrator lies on her sofa in her new home, exhausted, surrounded by unpacked boxes. "An Emily Dickinson poem came to mind," she says; "I could say it flew into my mind from nowhere, but there is no such thing as nowhere" (loc. 274). *Engaging Ambience* explores empirical, systematic, theoretical, and practical approaches to the study of rhetoric and writing that are grounded in Baradian realism. This is a book about how to practice "direct engagement with the ontology of our world" in specific *somewheres* (Barad 2007, 44). I use visual and multisensory methods in a new materialist and ambient key to systematically engage "speculation, curiosity, and the concrete" (Stewart 2007, 1).

These approaches require the consistent *unbracketing* of reality and a systematic *unforgetting* inherent to visual fieldwork. Praxiographic studies of rhetoric and writing attend to whatever shows up in research sites. Drawing from work in visual anthropology, visual sociology, and material cultures research, I demonstrate how visual fieldwork is marked by an "excessive inclusion" (Pinney 2011, 89) that acts as productive ballast to field notes, interviews, and transcripts—the sifting and winnowing of attention common to traditional field methods.

Visual methods unbracket reality and unforget the "remarkable materiality" of enactments. They help us hold back salience for as long as possible so we can embrace ambience in its bewildering fullness.

Chapter 1 considers what it means to picture writing, both figuratively and literally. It argues for a stronger focus on visibilities in rhetorical scholarship and discusses ways visual methods, as *technes* for picturing writing and rhetorics, simultaneously circumscribe what can be made visible while opening fieldwork to ambient concerns. Visual methods are *technes* of *poiesis* that train our attention to visibilities, invisibilities, and absent presences. Chapter 1 connects Heidegger's notion of "this-now-here-ness" to contemporary perspectives on ambience.

Chapter 2 explores realisms, literalisms, and imagination in methodologies and methods of unbracketing and unforgetting. It draws from material rhetorics research to posit an approach to ontological constitution—how things and people and practices show up and coalesce as *real* enactments that may be traced and explored in an ambient key. Chapter 2 also situates the methodologies and methods deployed in later chapters by drawing from foundational approaches developed in related fields—namely, visual anthropology, visual sociology, and visual and material cultures research. These approaches are seldom used in rhetoric and writing scholarship, despite our decades-long focus on visual rhetorics. Chapter 2 describes how they may be productively adapted and deployed in praxiographies of rhetoric and writing.

Chapter 3 demonstrates what we can learn from picturing writing. Detailing findings from a visual ethnography of professionals in a media research firm, I use photo-elicitation as a method for making strange the familiar environments of participants' everyday rhetorics. Picturing writing revealed rich topographies: we can learn much about histories of collaboration and argument from the ways we make rhetorics *visible* to one another in everyday practice. Chapter 3 also introduces the notion of factorial rhetorics. In any enactment of *poiesis*, variables are multiple, combinatorial, historically laden, individually situated, and idiosyncratic. The products of such variables are *factorial* because they proliferate quickly and produce potentially dizzying follow-on effects. Chapter 3 traces factorial rhetorics, showing how—and through what kinds of things—rhetoric is ambient.

Chapter 4 details findings from a multi-site visual ethnography of Roman Catholic Eucharistic Adoration practices, focusing on sensory suasion. By dwelling with and attending to sensations, we can learn much about how sensory artifacts are built, how they gather and condition us, how they shape bodily and affective comportments in both presence and withdrawal, and how, through things, we are our *there*, wherever we may find ourselves. Chapter 4 illustrates empirical approaches to Heidegger's notions of building, dwelling, and gathering and Rickert's notion of ambient dwelling. These methodological attunements to ambience foster theoretical perspectives that evince the "constitutive roles of sensation in participatory, rhetorical acts" (Hawhee 2015, 13).

Chapter 5 extends discussion of sensory rhetorics by detailing findings from an autoethnography of an ordinary pedestrian commute. Central to this chapter is *Gelassenheit*, Heidegger's (1966) concept of *releasement*. Through visual and multisensory autoethnography, I demonstrate the ways releasement is both a theoretical and a practical mode of turning toward and tuning into one's ambient environs. As a theory of opening—of waiting in openness and of collapsing distances—*Gelassenheit* conditions practice and aligns one's bodily comportments to worlding. In releasement, we open outward and intra-act in a world bursting with disclosures.

In chapter 6, I consider writing and photography as ways of standing outside ourselves. For Heidegger, meditative forms of thinking help us draw nearer to what is ostensibly most distant. Heidegger demonstrates that we can effectively think with and through visual phenomena. Chapter 6 argues that both photography and writing make worlds and worlding visible and legible—they both bring forth worlds in acts of *poiesis*. They are each in their own way sublime *technes* for engaging experience, sensation, affect, and ambience. Methodological innovation, I conclude, can suggest nimble and lightened ways into novel theoretical perspectives.

# 1
## PICTURING WRITING
Visibility, *Techne*, *Poiesis*

On a sunny spring day, on the inside surface of a colonial window, on one of the small square panes in the middle of the window's grid, Lauren writes in a green, dry erase pen: "Game design is hard."

Over the next three weeks, messages and notes are written in other panes and erased. "Game design is hard" remains. It's never even smudged. "I've been using the glass," Lauren says, "partly because we have a beautiful view out there, and we're forced to take an emotional break and just enjoy the view sometimes, but . . . it's just kind of more for motivation." Similar bits of writing—about game design, about learning through failure, about tasks and designs and root beer float parties—blossomed in and around Lauren's workspace, on her desks and tables, on whiteboards and sticky notes, in notebooks, on windows.

A twenty-four-year-old visual communication major, Lauren was a member of a student-led software development studio formed as part of a unique curriculum at a research university in the midwestern United States. Lauren worked with twelve other students to imagine, design, plan, test, and develop a web-based educational game for their community partner—the state's preeminent public museum. They spent over forty hours each week in a renovated, university-owned mansion on almost three acres a mile from campus. Most students earned fifteen credit hours for their participation. But Lauren earned just nine credit hours in the program, known at the university as an "immersive learning" experience. She was also enrolled in nine hours of traditional on-campus courses. This often caused her to feel disconnected from the group, even though her studio workload was comparable to that of her colleagues.

At the end of the semester, when studio members were frantically finishing the game *Museum Assistant*, Lauren felt more disconnected than ever, despite logging as many hours as her colleagues during the final two-week sprint. "I started to feel really unappreciated," she said during her third and final interview with my research team. "Overall,

I think I'm still proud of what we did, but . . . I don't feel the ownership, so that really makes me sad." Game design is "hard" for many reasons; for Lauren, what was most difficult was understanding how to live with the fact that many of her ideas and designs were not ostensibly *visible* in the finished game. "I feel like a lot of the things that I've done were needed at the time," she explains, "but . . . you can't see them anymore."

I led a research team of four, conducting ethnographic fieldwork among Lauren and her colleagues. We had unlimited access to their everyday work lives, from the start of the semester until shortly after the game was delivered to the state museum. We observed their arrivals in the morning, daily status meetings, coffee and tea breaks, and the languid late afternoon hours when only a handful remained—debugging, redrawing, rethinking essential details.

We conducted almost 135 hours of fieldwork across 83 site visits; we interviewed each of our participants three times, at different stages of the project; we made audio recordings of collaborative writing and programming sessions; we wrote almost 170,000 words of field notes and analytic memos; we collected over 150 team-written artifacts; and we composed 422 photographs tracing ephemeral and ad hoc writing practices and the places in which such practices occurred (see McNely, Gestwicki, Gelms, and Burke 2013). In short, we knew something important about Lauren's work, something she seemed to have forgotten: although her designs weren't apparent in the final user interface, her semester-long contributions were indeed *visibly* and *materially* inextricable from the finished game.

And we were able to *show* Lauren some of the many ways she contributed. During a two-week sprint early in the semester, it was Lauren who generated the primary storyboard from which gameplay decision points and user interface elements were developed for paper prototyping and play testing (figure 1.1). In an interview from that time, Lauren noted the importance of such work: "Everything we [the audiovisual design team] decide kind of pulls strings of the web to everything else in the game." She described the iterative, intersubjective, and intermediated enactments of game design—from deciding on a prototype, to storyboarding and play testing, to character, scene, and sound design, to digital development—and she was keenly aware of her role in such collaborations. She took pride in her work and knew that the decisions she made directly impacted software development.

Why then, at the end of the project, did Lauren feel unappreciated and sad?

*Figure 1.1. Lauren storyboarding gameplay and user interface elements. Author photo.*

As she noted in her final interview, she was upset that her work was no longer *visible*. She could not see—could not picture or conceptualize—her role. We had evidence to the contrary. The storyboard Lauren created early in the design process (figure 1.1) established gameplay norms that shaped the final game. To be sure, Lauren did not *see* her design assets; much of her art and graphic design work did not make the final user interface. But she lost sight of all the other ways her designs materially and visually shaped the final product.

We were able to trace those contributions—to *unforget* them—by repeatedly showing up, and we were able to show *her* many of those contributions when she was feeling uncertain about her role. We reminded her, too, of the other written and rhetorical work she contributed that substantively shaped the game's design: production and design notes; internal blog posts; jottings on sticky notes and whiteboards, computer displays, and walls; character sketches on tablets and wispy, crinkly sheets of pale newsprint; text messages to team members; a fifty-page design document and requirements list; notes on color schemes and style; play testing pieces and storyboards and game pitches; hallway conversations, daily status meetings, and work with the faculty mentor; notes on glass windowpanes.

"Game design is hard" *because* it is iterative, collaborative, and deeply intermediated. Lauren's contributions do not "show up" in the final design as clear and recognizable graphic design assets, but they show up clearly in our study of game design. Her contributions were not invisible because they were thrown away or because Lauren's colleagues did not value her work. Instead, her contributions were invisible because they were *baked into* the game, inextricable from the final design.

## PICTURING WRITING

In *Academic Writing as a Social Practice*, Linda Brodkey (1987) argued for a new conception of writers and writing, one that subverts the modernist image of the solitary writer, toiling in anguish and alienation. She asked readers to "see writing anew" and, in the process, to "tear ourselves away from an image that we have come to think of as the reality of writing" (57). The predominant "picture" of writing "prevents us from thinking about writing in other ways," she wrote (58). What Brodkey did not consider was that one way to see writing anew was to *literally picture writers and writing*. As my experience with Lauren demonstrates, picturing writing may be generative for scholarship in rhetoric, composition, and communication, particularly as scholars deepen understandings of rhetorical enactments as everyday social, material, embodied, intra-active practices that emerge from—and, in turn, condition—ambient environments.

Picturing writing and rhetorics creates new engagements with research participants and their communicative contexts. Picturing writing explores the intricate ways writing and rhetorics do more than simply *mediate* practice. By engaging the ambient, sensory environments of everyday writing and rhetorical practice, we diffractively trace entangled phenomena that participate in intra-active becoming (Barad 2007). Karen Barad's realism entails an "ontological inseparability of agentially intra-acting components" (33). Intra-action thus "*signifies the mutual constitution of entangled agencies*" (33, original emphasis).

To picture writing is to study complex routes and circulations of people, words, ideas, gestures, technologies, artifacts, and material environments. Each of these variables carries differential agential contributions to emergent phenomena. Picturing, sensing, listening to, and intra-acting with phenomena are simultaneous methodological and theoretical engagements with rhetorical ambience.

In figure 1.2, for example, Mike, Jenn, and Michelle (right of frame)—media researchers whose work is explored in chapter 3—collaboratively develop a slide deck for a conference. They use an ecology of artifacts (Bødker and Nylandsted Klokmose 2011), and they deploy many rhetorical means to collaboratively negotiate their understanding of their focus group research. By picturing their writing in its enactment, new and different routes through the complex, interconnected, and embodied materiality of their work are made more hyaline than written

Figure 1.2. Picturing collaborative writing as a spatial, embodied, material, intra-active practice. Author photo.

descriptions alone—for me, for other researchers, and for the participants themselves.

Visual and multisensory methods of empirical research in writing and rhetorics thus expand our ability to trace the routes, circulations, and coordinations of literate activity; they help us better explore and engage these routes in concert with research participants; and they may lead to an unforgetting of the complexity and wonder of the everyday spaces and practices of rhetoric. Picturing writing attends to attention by tracing enactments in practice.

By using visual and multisensory approaches in rhetorical studies, I am building from rich traditions of research on the everyday: from Martin Heidegger's (2010) foundational notions of everydayness and "thrownness" to Pierre Bourdieu's (1977) and Michel de Certeau's (1984) work on habitus and everyday life, through more recent research on the anthropology of everyday affects, moods, and sensory experiences from scholars such as Kathleen Stewart (2007, 2008, 2011), Tim Ingold (2000, 2008), and Sarah Pink (2012b). Picturing writing engages many of the variables that participate in and condition everyday relational ontologies.

Picturing writing and rhetorics thus engages ontological enactments—what it means to *emerge* and disclose oneself as a media researcher (chapter 3, this volume), as a religious supplicant (chapter 4), or as a pedestrian commuter (chapter 5)—*through* the practical, rhetorical activity conditioned by and embedded within ambient environs. Picturing writing and rhetorics is a provocation—a call for rethinking how we work with and theorize visuality and visibility—and an exploration of new ways of looking at and doing rhetorical research.

Surely Brodkey did not have such approaches in mind. At a minimum, when we "picture writing"—in Brodkey's formulation as a cultural construct and, in my own, as an empirical and theoretical engagement with writers and rhetors through photography, videography, and participant drawing—we see that not only is writing unequivocally and inescapably social but that it is deeply conditioned by ambience. Visual and multisensory research methods, as tactics in broader qualitative methodologies (McNely and Teston 2015), foster engagements that are idiographic and nomothetic simultaneously, literally offering new pictures of writers and writing in both senses detailed above. These approaches make rhetorical ambience visible, helping researchers trace the participation and intra-action of materials, technologies, and spaces in the constitution and performance of everyday life. These approaches invite what Helen Liggett (2003, 107) calls "constitutive participation by the writer/viewer/reader" that expound upon traditional rhetoric and writing scholarship.

In *Toward a Composition Made Whole*, Jody Shipka (2011, 134) drew on Brodkey's work to argue that researchers must render "more visible the taken-for-granted assumptions, technologies, and dimensions of composing processes that have become invisible, and so, seemingly natural over time." Although Shipka (2011, 36; see also Prior and Shipka 2003) has enriched writing research by leveraging a particular visual method—participant drawing—she argued that one of rhetoric and composition's key contemporary research challenges involves "finding ways to trace the dynamic, emergent, distributed, historical, and technologically mediated dimensions of composing practices." Our theoretical and methodological frameworks, she added, "must allow us to trace the multiple, and oftentimes overlapping, sites and spaces where composing occurs" (36).

*  *  *

Rhetoric and writing scholarship includes a decades-long focus on the visual. Why then, as Shipka suggests, might we need an even greater focus on visibility?

To answer this question is to explore what we mean by visuality and visibility and what we're *doing* when we *do* visual rhetoric. Drawing from Brodkey and Shipka, I argue that we need new ways of *looking at* and *apprehending* writing and rhetoric and thus "picturing"—in the twofold sense of conceptualizing and visually tracing—what writing and rhetorics *do* in everyday life.

In scholarship on visual rhetoric, we don't often *picture* writing or make visible the complex contexts of rhetorical practice; a common approach, instead, is to subject visual phenomena (photographs, paintings, public monuments) to analyses of rhetorical salience. Yet picturing writing and rhetoric—as an empirical engagement—offers new and complementary ways of *doing* visual rhetorics. These approaches take up Brodkey's charge to formulate new pictures of writers and rhetors by using methods, methodologies, and theoretical orientations that engage Shipka's arguments for making the complex contexts of writing and rhetorics *more visible.*

Over several years of fieldwork, I have attempted to picture writing and its ambient environs. Collectively, those research projects have yielded new pictures of writing and rhetoric that demonstrate three outcomes:

a. Visual and multisensory methodologies and methods foster granular and rich qualitative datasets about who communicates, how they communicate, why they communicate, where they communicate, and what their communication practices and environments contribute to who they *are* and who they *will be.*

b. Visual and multisensory methodologies and methods encourage different forms of participant knowing and understanding—engaging tacit ways of being and acting that are sometimes unintentionally elided by traditional fieldwork methods.

c. Visual and multisensory methodologies and methods yield new kinds of scholarly products. These approaches foster complementary ways of considering and understanding situated and embodied writing and rhetorics that explore how writers and rhetors "show up" in the world and how their writing and rhetorics constitute situated and relational ontologies (Packer 2011, 242) and forms of everyday dwelling (Heidegger 1993; Rickert 2013, 2016).

In figure 1.1, Lauren develops a storyboard to play-test an early game prototype. Her *activity* is well documented in the data record—in field notes, in analytic memos, and in Lauren's responses in semi-structured interviews. Our fieldwork documented her work and its relationship to the collaborative activity of the studio. In methodological terms, our research was both granular and well triangulated. But photographs of Lauren at work offer something else: they evoke a feeling, a mood, and a broadened understanding of her sensory environment and embodied comportments.

Figure 1.1 renders ambient details that would be difficult to evoke in field notes or interviews alone. More important, by comparing visual data against field notes, memos, and interview responses, we were able to answer questions—informed by ambient and new materialist theories of rhetoric—that would be challenging to address otherwise, such as: How do people and things and places show up and intra-act within a given environment? What things, spaces, surfaces, and moods matter, epistemologically—in the work of game development—and ontologically, in what it means to be a member of the studio? Our approach helped us intra-act with the ambient environments of game design, which influenced our understanding of its *enactment* in ways we did not anticipate and likely would not have ascertained with traditional methods alone.

Our work with Lauren demonstrates some of the ways visual and multisensory approaches help researchers engage ambience. It also demonstrates some of the ways visual phenomena work beyond critique—beyond a search for salience.

### PERSISTENT TENSIONS

To *do* empirical rhetorics is to develop praxiological approaches that engage all that shows up, holding back the search for salience for as long as possible to create new "pictures" of rhetorical enactments.

But there are persistent tensions in such approaches. For example, are new materialist and ambient methodologies consonant with terms such as *data, fieldwork,* and *representation*? Can traditional social science fieldwork be deployed with new materialist and ambient theories of rhetoric? Are broader tensions between theory and methodology productive or inhibiting? Can new ways of seeing and picturing rhetoric contribute to developments and refinements of theory? And what of the fundamental tension between salience and ambience—is not all scholarship, eventually (even this book), an argument for *some kind of* salience?

I cannot resolve these tensions for every reader, but the fact that they persist points to the value of new and creative ways of empirically investigating and enlivening contemporary rhetorical theory.

Tension, after all, may be productive. Derek Owens (2014) argues that a pairing of opposites, *coniunctio,* can foster productive tensions. He uses alchemy as a metaphor, "the bringing together of unlike materials or states of being in order to construct some alternate hybrid form" (73). The aim is to bridge disparate elements or concepts, to hold them in tension with one another—the suspension bridge works *because of* the tension—creating "a point where the binary might be left behind and some other, more interesting, complex, queered understanding . . . begins to surface" (73). Perhaps the tensions between social scientific fieldwork and new materialisms are one such *coniunctio*.

Jason Kalin and David Gruber (2022) explore some of these tensions through concepts of "epistemist" and "anti-epistemist" rhetorical methodologies. They ask: how do we reconcile traditional norms of empirical research with new materialist theories? Our methodologies, they argue, govern to some extent *what shows up for us* in any given field of study. And the things we study may withdraw from us as we study them—sometimes objects *object*. Kalin and Gruber provide a vocabulary for discussing and working with/in these tensions.

They argue, for example, that some empirical researchers in rhetoric may choose an epistemist approach to fieldwork. Such researchers would acknowledge a *coniunctio* of traditional fieldwork norms and new materialist theories. "An epistemist approach," Kalin and Gruber (2022, 141) suggest, "would license scholars to forward conclusions about getting closer to research participants' experiences," using fieldwork techniques that attempt to *know*, in some way, what participants know and do. In contrast, anti-epistemist approaches "may offer opportunities for experimentation" (131). These may not allow scholars to "get closer" to phenomena under scrutiny—to *know* phenomena, empirically—but rather to imagine *possibilities* for rhetorical theory. Anti-epistemist approaches reject the traditional social scientific notion that empirical researchers can *know* phenomena or access a thing's essence.

Kalin and Gruber's terminology applies well to the different methods and methodologies discussed in this book and the tensions that accompany them. The case study chapters are primarily epistemist in nature—I attempt to create *coniunctios* that foster productive tension, combining traditional social scientific fieldwork methods with new materialist and ambient theories. Kalin and Gruber (2022, 134) write: "We are not arguing that rhetorical method/ologies should solve the question of onto-epistemological access"—a researcher's access to any given thing's *essence*, or any firm attestation of *knowledge*. Instead, researchers should engage the tension, "resolving it at least momentarily, because how we construct the question determines what appears available to us" (134).

Their final clause is crucial: *Engaging Ambience* is all about how we construct the question of empirical research on rhetoric in the wake of ambient and new materialist theories. Indeed, because the fundamental *techne* of photography and videography fosters, to some extent, object-to-object interactions, the jump to *knowing* is suspended. These fieldwork methods (to use the vocabulary of traditional social scientific research) thicken ambient encounters and delay salience. What happens afterward may trend epistemist *or* anti-epistemist. As we'll see, visual and multisensory approaches allow researchers to both *document* ambient environs and *imagine* new possibilities for rhetorical theory.

Kalin and Gruber (2022, 129) argue that "being there" does not automatically "provide direct access to rhetorical encounters." *How* we show up and attend to field sites shapes what we encounter. The tension persists: our theoretical and methodological framing will condition, to some extent, what shows up for us and what recedes or hides from our gaze. There is no direct, unmediated, unproblematic access to the essence and ontology of any given research subject or object.

Once this and related tensions are acknowledged, what comes next? For Kalin and Gruber (2022, 130), playful invention: we should "play with/in the tensions between a real object and its sensual qualities. Playing with/in these tensions is a way to interrupt the quest for knowledge by creating and multiplying rhetorical encounters." They draw from John Muckelbauer (2020, 298), who argues that the scholar's task "has never been to understand things so much as it is to make things"—to make things that multiply, juxtapose, and illuminate rhetorical encounters and enactments.

Although my approach is largely epistemist in nature, it is also—as in the case of Lauren—inventional. *Engaging Ambience* offers new routes to understanding and new engagements with the wonderful complexity of rhetorical enactments. But it offers, too, anti-epistemist possibilities—new inventional and imaginative frameworks with which to explore rhetoric and writing. It makes new rhetorical products: what show up are encounters with ambience that readily acknowledge tensions between contemporary rhetorical theory and traditional fieldwork. Indeed, it finds these tensions productive.

## "ACTUAL" WRITING

*Transmedia Indiana* was an attempt to tell the story of one small town—New Harmony—through both historical and fictional narratives in a variety of genres, media, and digital applications. Twenty-four undergraduates, two graduate students, and two faculty members collaborated with the Indiana State Museum over one academic year, working in small, interdisciplinary teams.

The writing team, for example, developed fictional content but also cobbled together historical details that served as copy for nonfiction web pages. The audiovisual team developed podcasts, trailers, photographs, and videos—some fictional, some historical—that provided complementary perspectives. The design team included computer science students (web development) and journalism graphics students who created a style guide for websites, digital artifacts, and the layout for an interactive eBook. Together, students produced over 100 different webpages, 4 social media accounts, 51 audio files, hundreds of photographs, 19 video files, a 45,000-word interactive eBook, and in-person installations and performances.

Elmar Hashimov and I conducted ethnographic fieldwork during the entire project—from the first brainstorming sessions through the various moments when sections of the story were released publicly, culminating in a special event held at the Indiana State Museum (see Hashimov and McNely 2012). Our fieldwork was guided by socio-cultural theories—particularly writing, activity, and genre research (WAGR; see McNely 2017; Russell 2009; Spinuzzi 2010).

We were interested in the practical, everyday activities involved in planning and coordinating collaborative, multi-genre, multi-platform narratives. We collected granular data about the processes and practices of our participants, using a variety of in situ methods, including observational field notes, audio recordings of collaborative activities, semi-structured interviews with each participant, and three visual methods: still photographs, videos of collaborative writing, and researcher-created fieldwork diagrams. The visual methods helped us trace participant workflow practices, their tools in use, and their interpersonal spatial and positional arrangements during group work sessions.

Three weeks before *Transmedia Indiana* wrapped, I interviewed Valerie, a senior journalism graphics major.

> BRIAN: Can you tell me about the different forms of writing you've been doing for the project?
>
> VALERIE: Like, *actual* writing?
>
> BRIAN: Uh, yeah. Actual writing, or the kind of writing that supports other work, like sketching, storyboarding . . .
>
> VALERIE: Ah! I make lists. I actually write 'em down and stuff because I just can't—at first I liked having 'em all on the computer but now I just have so many, and there's no good way to organize it. But yeah, other than that, I haven't done a ton of writing for the project or anything, that's not really our [the design team's] thing.

I'd asked this question—what kinds of writing have you been doing?—during two previous interviews. Though I knew she was regularly interacting with requirements and asset lists that helped coordinate project planning (see McNely 2017), Valerie had never mentioned lists.

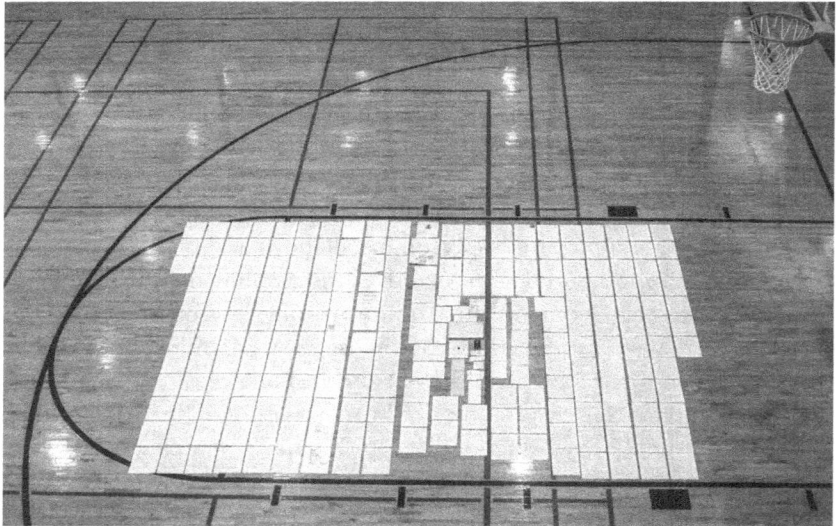

*Figure 1.3. Overview of project-related writing work shared by Valerie. Author photo.*

We'd been observing Valerie for more than seven months; we knew she was writing much more than lists. And her comment about *actual* writing was intriguing. There was a disconnect between what Valerie considered to be *actual* writing—assignments for class, essays, and reports were *actual* forms of writing—and the sheer volume of everyday writing we'd observed during the project. Her conception of *work* was tied to graphic design assets—website style templates, digital graphics, storyboards, and layout schemes. The writing team does the writing, she seemed to imply, and "that's not really [her] thing."

I asked Valerie whether she kept any of the lists she generated during the project. She had, as well as several other written artifacts. I asked if she'd be willing to share once the project was finished, and she graciously agreed. Figure 1.3 provides a glimpse of what some of Valerie's *actual* writing looks like.

Each 8½-by-11-inch page in figure 1.3 is double-sided and single-spaced; many of those pages include jottings, marginal notes, and other paratextual inscriptions (e.g., underlining, stars, circled phrases). A composite image visualizing *both* sides of those standard sheets of paper would have been more accurate, nearly doubling the space Valerie's writing would cover on the gym floor. More important, this image—shot from the running track at the campus fitness center, the only place nearby where I could "picture" Valerie's writing—visualizes only a small portion of the *actual* writing she generated during the project.

If we followed Valerie's work through the MacBook, iPad, and iPhone near the center of this image, we would see much more—hundreds of instant and text message threads among members of the design team; hundreds of project-related emails exchanged with colleagues, community partners, and professors; strings of alt-text for web-based images; a host of Google documents and spreadsheets; and hundreds of tweets and Instagram captions. Writing may not be her thing, but this overview indicates just how much writing mediated Valerie's work as a graphic designer on the *Transmedia Indiana* project.

Our study design was epistemist—we wanted to trace and better understand how writing, in all its forms, mediated a complex transmedia project. But the visual products of our work are also potentially antiepistemist. By literally picturing a portion of Valerie's *actual* writing, we momentarily interrupted the drive to *know* and the search for salience. We *made* something, too. What we made multiplied, juxtaposed, and illuminated some of the rhetorical encounters and enactments central to the *Transmedia Indiana* project.

By visualizing Valerie's work—using still photography to literally generate a new picture of one writer and her writing—we can traverse different routes to new understanding (Pink 2012a, 6–7) through some of the artifacts collected in an ethnographic study. This aim is admittedly and unapologetically epistemist. By visualizing a portion of Valerie's writing, we do more than merely illustrate how writing mediated her experience; we're making something—a visceral argument about the consequentiality of her writing practices, a "picture" of everyday thinking and planning made material, a visualization of qualitative data that helps us imagine just *how much writing* shapes and coordinates everyday activities.

Figure 1.3, then, is not some objective record of Valerie's experience but an arranged composition of its own. It uses artifacts collected during fieldwork and makes a new argument about the role and impact of writing. Figure 1.3 is not a tautological repetition of a written argument but an entirely different way of imagining and understanding one writer and her work. It is a different way of *doing* visual rhetoric—a *doing* predicated on a bringing forth and a making visible. It makes something new from Valerie's writing work—a doubled *poiesis*: the "creative and generative practice" of Valerie's planning and thinking and a "creative and generative practice" of rearranging and reshaping the materials of her labor and invention (Ryan 2018, 92).

## *TECHNE:* **PRODUCTIVE TENSION**

Donna Haraway (2016, 12) argued that "it matters what matters we use to think other matters with" and that "it matters what stories we tell to tell other stories with." The tools and methods we use to explore and tell the stories of our research participants are inseparable from the ontological enactments immanent to any research site.

Stephanie Springgay and Sarah E. Truman (2017, 91–93), for example, describe the use of pinhole photography as a way of evoking movement, timescales, and affective intensities in their experiments with walking methodologies and methods. A pinhole camera is photography's simplest device: a tiny hole on the outside of a sealed box that contains a light-sensitive material (film or a digital sensor). Pinhole cameras have no lens and no shutter; since only a very small amount of light enters the box, pinhole cameras need longer exposure times than the fraction of a second required in most photography (pinhole exposures on film can last for weeks or months).

Springgay and Truman (2017) used pinhole mounts on digital cameras to prolong exposure times; they were able to wear or hold their pinhole cameras while they conducted walking research. The resulting images "undulate and animate assemblages of human and nonhuman encounters"; they are images that "do not represent the walks but incite new modes of thought and different practices of relating" (91). The resulting images, in other words, were not epistemist but rather anti-epistemist. Although they do not include any of their images, it is safe to assume (from their descriptions and the mechanisms of pinhole photography) that the images are ethereal and abstract—blurs and smudges of movement, place, light, and color that evoke enactments obliquely and creatively.

Methods, Springgay and Truman (2017, 91) argued, should give researchers "a way to pose problems differently." "How do you work with a method that is infused with movement and affect," they asked (91). Pinhole photography, as one potential answer, was "a way to think about how to wrestle with methods as affective ecologies" (91). Pinhole cameras allowed them to think movement while moving (91). They were tools for intra-acting in their environment while making affect and movement visible and felt. But their discussion of pinhole photography comes in a pivotal section of their book where they argue that studying immanence requires researchers to work from the "speculative middle," to work *without* predetermined, procedural methods (95). They encouraged researchers to focus on ways that methods "tune into" phenomena rather than "capture" or "document" phenomena (92).

Springgay and Truman (2017) engage ambience rather than salience. As I suggested in the introduction, the lines with which we attempt to bound any systematic study of phenomena must be drawn loosely so they can accommodate the flux inherent in any "speculative middle" (95). "If methods are not pre-determined in advance, and arise in the speculative middle," Springgay and Truman argue, "then they become ways of thinking about problems" while we encounter them (90). But methods, by definition, are always already ways of thinking about problems; methods are as much a part of our ambient environment during the planning stages of a research project as they are in the speculative middle.

To effectively think with and deploy any method during a research project, we must first have a sense of what is possible. We need to know something of its potential before we can use it to "pose problems differently" (Springgay and Truman 2017, 91) in the speculative middle of fieldwork. This creates something of a paradox: if, as Springgay and Truman argue, methods "cannot be pre-determined and known in advance of the event of research" (95), and if our methods "should not be procedural, but rather emerge and proliferate from within the speculative middle" (95), how do we design studies, obtain IRB approval, and know what kinds of methods might be useful or creatively deployed in any given context? We have an ethical responsibility to our participants to give them a clear sense of the methods we *might* employ during fieldwork. I do not disagree with Springgay and Truman; instead, I'm pointing out another persistent tension by asking how we might balance the need for procedural knowledge of many potential methods against the creative deployment and alignment of methods with the demands of any ongoing study.

It is unlikely, for example, that a walking researcher without a strong background in photography would envision pinhole imaging as a viable method for tuning in to affective ecologies. That researcher would first need procedural and technical knowledge of pinhole photography and its ways of intra-acting with phenomena. That researcher would need an understanding of exposure times and motion blur, of pinhole mounts for digital cameras, of a pinhole camera's affordances for producing abstract, non-representational images. It is true that we need not (and should not) enumerate and adhere *only* to a specific set of research methods before a given study, for doing so may unintentionally circumscribe and limit our ability to productively and creatively explore what happens in the speculative middle of any project.

But we *do* need familiarity with a robust set of methods beforehand to adapt to whatever unfolds during fieldwork; our participants need familiarity with those potential methods as well, as part of our ethical responsibilities. Ultimately, I cannot deploy pinhole photography without first understanding something of visual methods in qualitative research and pinhole photography's affordances for abstract imaging. To be creative in the speculative middle, I need to plan and consider the potential of various methods, procedures, and technologies. I need some background with the matter I might use to think other matters with.

This tension between requisite procedural knowledge and creative, immanent deployment has a long and storied history in the field of rhetoric, in theories of *techne*. For Aristotle, *techne* was largely procedural—"a systematic guide to performing an act, formed through experience and through observation" (quoted in Carter 1988, 108). But as Kelly Pender (2008) has demonstrated, *techne* cannot be reduced to its procedural characteristics—she noted that even Aristotle presents conflicting views of *techne* in his oeuvre.

*Techne*, Pender argues, opens up even as it closes down—it is instrumental and procedural, and at the same time it is creative and generative. As Pender (2008, 2011) shows, *techne* is creative and generative *because* it is instrumental and procedural—another productive tension. "Our ability to use language in any capacity depends, paradoxically, on our inability to turn it into an instrument," Pender argues (5). *Techne* cannot be limited to its procedural and instrumental characteristics—it is *always* a form of *poiesis*, a bringing forth that may unfold procedurally *and* creatively. It is often creative *because* it is procedural.

In the remainder of this chapter, I make a threefold argument about the role of *techne* in empirical studies of rhetoric. First, I argue that field methods are *technes* of empirical research—they are procedural and instrumental, and in their instrumentality they help researchers creatively design and adapt to the speculative middles of empirical research projects. Second, I argue that *techne* is itself a powerful practice of visibility. Third, I argue that *techne* is a form of *poiesis* and that practices of visibility, practices of empirical research, and practices of theorizing are inseparable from praxiographies of ambient rhetorics.

We need more and different kinds of procedural knowledges and methods to be in the best position to creatively respond to and theorize within the speculative middle of any research project. We need to plan *and* question our plans along the way; we need to envision possible methods before fieldwork *and* be ready to adapt to and invent new configurations in the field; we need deep procedural knowledge *and* an open comportment to the immanence and ambience of our field sites. Epistemist research designs can foster anti-epistemist imaginings.

## VISIBILITY, *TECHNE, POIESIS*

*Visual* is a ubiquitous term in rhetoric and writing scholarship. We have a variety of approaches to visuality, from visual rhetorics and visual communication, to visual perception, design, and arrangement, to visual grammar and visual literacy (see, for example, Arola 2010; Barrios 2004; Bernhardt 1986; Bezemer and Kress 2008; Finnegan 2001; Fleckenstein 2009; Gallagher and Zagacki 2007; George 2002; George and Salvatori 2008; Handa 2001; Hariman and Lucaites 2001; Haskins and Zappen 2010; Hawisher, Selfe, Moraski, and Pearson 2004; Hocks 2003; Kostelnick 1988; Kress 2005; Markel 1995, 1998; Micciche 2004; Olson 2009; Sorapure 2006, 2010; Wysocki 2005; Yancey 2004).

We have written less about the notion of *visibility*, however. Visibility, Andrea Mubi Brighenti (2010, 42) argues, "exists in the tension between seeing and noticing." Visibility is a phenomenon related to, yet distinct from, visuality. Notions of visuality are, first and foremost, related to sight and perception. Visuality concerns biological facticity—rods and cones, the negotiated practice of perceiving. But *visibility*, as Brighenti suggests, always already assumes ambient environs, "a field of action and affection that lies in the flesh of the world" (44).

Visibility involves embodied encounters that extend beyond sight—socially constituted and affective apprehensions of phenomena in our material environs that often emerge from typified, socially conditioned, normative ways of seeing (Brighenti 2010, 44–45). Scholars in visual rhetoric, of course, are very much interested in these aspects of seeing. Indeed, when scholars speak of *visuality* in rhetoric and writing, it seems that they are often interested in *visibility*.

For Brighenti (2010, 3), visibility is "a form of 'visuality at large,' making it clear that the visible entails more than the visual, more than the sensorially perceptible" because "the visual itself needs to be visibilised." Visibility is *more than* because it always unfolds in complex and shifting permutations—the *fact of visuality* needs a *regime of visibility* to flourish. Visibility cannot be reduced to its parts—to visual perception, affective intensity, or historical significance alone.

As relational and intra-active phenomena, visibilities evince a wide spectrum of possibility, from basic intersubjective recognition (as in Hegel or Goffman), to architectures of surveillance and control (Foucault, Rancière), to spectacle (Debord, the Frankfurt School), or to media, networks, politics, and publics. Brighenti (2010, 109) argues that "reciprocal visibility creates the public realm by facilitating both social rituals and action coordination." Visibility is also characterized by its practical affordances: though its permutations are complex and its enactments irreducible, visibility is a powerful concept for rhetorical scholars because many of its relations and effects can be identified, traced, and studied.

Roland Barthes (1981) and Jacques Derrida (2010) have each explored the inseparable terrain of visibility and relationality—the ways apprehension of "the meaning and enigma of visibility" (Berger 1980, 45) is an immanent unfolding of visual perception, sensation, affect, sociality, memory, and time. Seeing is culturally and historically situated, and visibility is an enactment that emerges in the confluence of everyday and historical trajectories of lived experience, in and as relationality. Take, for example, Barthes's (1981, 6) discussion of photographs as objects: "Whatever it grants to vision and whatever its manner, a photograph is always invisible: it is not it that we see." When I teach Barthes to undergraduates, I read this quote, then ask them to flip a few pages forward to the iconic Stieglitz photograph of the horse-car terminal in wintertime New York, 1893 (17); "what do you see," I ask. Their answers are usually some combination of "horse, snow, condensation, people, broom, trolley car, building, street, hat." I have yet to hear a student respond with "a photograph of . . . ," although what they visually perceive is, first and foremost, *photograph*.

We're back at Heidegger's lectern. Visibility at a single stroke.

Visibility is a function of complex relationalities—of the individual to phenomena; of the individual to their own histories of learning, knowing, and being; of the individual to others; of the individual to their own affects and embodied responses. The tendency to *see through* the materiality of photographs has nothing to do with *visuality* and much to do with acculturated *visibility*—the ways we have been situated as seeing bodies and subjects and the things we have come to expect from the myriad visual phenomena that participate in everyday life. The ways "we see what we elect to see" (Emig 1982, 65).

Visibility, then, necessarily presupposes production, disclosure and revelation. To *be* visible or to *make* visible is a special kind of bringing forth. As Derrida (2010, xxiii) has argued, the photograph, in its materiality, "announces its presence" to others. Its visuality, the fact of its existence, emerges from enactments of visibility—ontological disclosures or revelations that are predicated on complex trajectories of relationality: of camera, lens, and sensor or film to light and objects reflecting that light; of photographer to scene and all the many valences that entails, from technical training and aesthetic values to specific purposes and intents; and, above all, of relations of present and future visibilities by those both close to and far removed from whatever the photograph depicts. In its visibility, any given photograph "resist[s] definition" and represents a "complex play of presence and absence" (xxiii). This is why, for Derrida, the visibility of photography "can be seen as an operational network and metalanguage through which larger philosophical, historical, aesthetic, and political questions can be brought into focus" (quoted in Richter 2010, xxiii).

For Brighenti (2010, 186), to study visibility is to study relational ontologies. Visibility's relations stem from visual facticity, but they quickly move beyond ocular perception to manifold permutations of what visible disclosures mean, do, and are in any given instance. Visibility is a disclosive enactment, and disclosures are by definition relational (even when they seemingly go unnoticed; even when they are circumvented or ignored). Moreover, intentional *visible* disclosures, such as those fostered in photography and videography, are both technical interventions and acts of invention.

We often conceptualize photographs as representations of things as they appear, as objects "seared with reality" (Pinney 2011, 89); but all photographs are "immediately contaminated by invention in the sense of production, creation, productive imagination" (Derrida 2010, 43). The visibility of photographs not only discloses, it makes appeals, as Victoria J. Gallagher and Kenneth S. Zagacki (2007, 129) note, by "making things recognizable and by prompting future behavior." Most important, photography and videography may draw attention to visibilities without relying on representationalism, as Springgay and Truman's pinhole method demonstrates.

The contexts in which I explore visibilities in this book are admittedly narrow—the methodologies and methods detailed herein attempt to make rhetoric and writing practices more visible in a handful of empirical research projects. I use visual and multisensory approaches to fieldwork that help draw attention to visibilities in specific research sites—to the ways members of a media research firm, for example, make their writing visible to colleagues in processes of knowledge creation (chapter 3). But engaging visibility as a concept and framework may allow us to build from and strengthen what we mean by visual rhetoric.

Sarah Pink (2006, 36), in a concise distillation of the difference between visuality and visibility, notes that "things become visible because of how we see them rather than simply because they are observable." And many projects explore *in*visibility through methods of "making the hidden visible" (99). Others have focused on the complex politics of in/visibility, especially among marginalized and oppressed communities. Maggie Nelson (2015) describes her trans partner's testosterone injections as a matrix of in/visibilities. Testosterone was "a wager for visibility" that, in its enactment, enjoins new possibilities even as it disciplines: "disciplines gender, disciplines genre" (86). Serkan Gorkemli (2011) argues that critical studies of media should focus on the politics of queer visibility. Visibility is also an important concept in critical race studies (Orelus 2013), in disability studies (Caldwell 2010; https://disabilityvisibilityproject.com/), and in many other fields.

John Berger (1980, 32) quotes Goethe, who wrote that "there is a delicate form of the empirical which identifies itself so intimately with its object that it thereby becomes theory." Walter Benjamin (2011) also invokes Goethe's sense of the empirical-theoretical; August Sander's environmental portraits evoked an *aura*—an entire field of visibility—that encompasses and evokes the individual and the broader nexus of space and time in which that individual is situated. Similarly, in his essay on Paul Strand, Berger (1980, 45) argues that Strand's best photographs of people present "the visible evidence, not just of their presence, but of their life." The photographs are, in other words, evidence of their *totality*, an evocation (not a summation or essentialization) of their lived experience that "forces us to reflect on the significance of seeing itself" (45). The photograph, inextricable from a regime of visibility, is one form of matter with which to think—and theorize—other matters, other stories, Others' stories.

Jon Wagner (2011, 72) suggests that "propositions about the relationship of culture, materiality, and visibility implicate ideas about how people live, what they care about, who they are, what they see, and how they look." Attempts to make such relations visible, to attend deeply to visibility, evince the kinds of "delicate" and intimate empiricism that fosters theory and that changes how we see and feel and understand the world. For Wagner, photography and videography are important praxiographic methods that can help us tune into what is in/visible, thereby establishing "a visibility baseline against which to plot and highlight what subjects and researcher actually notice" in a field site (80).

A delicate empiricism is enriched with visual methods, particularly photography and videography, for both are sublime *technes* of visibility. Channeling Heidegger, Derrida (2010, 28) claims that "it is necessary to think photography on the basis of *Erschlossenheit*"—on the basis of *disclosure*, or as a *techne* of disclosedness. The camera's frame closes down and circumscribes reality; in doing so, it opens up and out—its visual artifacts multiply and expand fields of visibility.

### *Techne* and Visibility

Chad Wickman (2012) has argued that *techne* offers a useful framework for empirical researchers in rhetoric because it directs attention to in situ disclosures of discursive and material enactments. In his study of a chemical physics and materials science research institute, a focus on *techne* helped him conceptualize everyday enactments of scientific research as manifestations of technical arts—a finding that positions "rhetoric in the actual production of artifacts, including visual inscriptions and texts, as they emerge out of scientists' complex interactions with a range of material, technical, and symbolic resources" (23). By exploring *techne* in these practices, he showed how the scientists he studied used technical means of intervention to generate new findings about the world.

Wickman notes that for the ancient Greeks there was little distinction between the concepts of *episteme* and *techne*; as Heidegger (1977, 13) has argued, "both words are names for knowing in the widest sense." Both words, Heidegger adds, indicate a familiarity with a subject matter that is so intimate that one is entirely at home there; to know something so thoroughly, he suggests, presents opportunities for an opening up and out, for revelation, for disclosure (13). Wickman notes that in scientific practice, *techne* also functions as a means for fostering invention and transformation (25). He adds that *techne* "involves more than an instrumental capacity to simply reveal" and instead involves the "capacity to design and produce" (26). In and through *techne*, as instrumental and inventive, "the theoretical and productive enter into a dialectical relationship" where "inquiry itself becomes a productive art" (26).

Wickman's perspective illustrates some of the contradictory facets of *techne* that Kelly Pender (2008) explores in detail. For Aristotle, she argues, "*techne* is identical with a reasoned state of capacity to make, and, as such, it is always a means to some other end" (4). But Pender makes an important distinction between *making* and *creating*: when rhetoric is conceived as a *techne* in the sense of *making*—"as it so commonly is"—language itself is instrumentalized and language's creative potential is diminished (4). But "*techne* is not reducible to instrumentality" (4). For Wickman, *techne* is at once instrumental and inventional; for Pender, *techne* is at once instrumental and *creative.*

When we focus on *techne*'s affordances for *making*, Pender (2008, 21) suggests, we focus on what language (and rhetoric) can *do*; but when we focus on *techne*'s affordances for *creating*, we turn toward the very materiality of language itself. Indeed, *techne*'s instrumentality might well force us to attend, paradoxically, to language's materiality and thus its capacities for *creativity*. For both Wickman and Pender, these facets of *techne* are never either/or: *techne* is powerful because it is always all of this—instrumental and creative, a means of making and inventing, a knowledge and procedure and skill that closes down to open up.

Pender (2011, 4) argues that any focus on one part of *techne*'s many affordances yields "only a small, usually misleading piece of the puzzle." Any baseline understanding of *techne* must include its contraries—its instrumentality and its non-instrumentality, its capacity to both *make* and *create*, its symbolicity and its materiality. Even the most mundane and instrumental forms of *techne*—Valerie's lists, for example (figure 1.3)—have the potential to open up and out, to invent social possibilities even as they accomplish mundane acts, to bring forth creatively while also producing banal, coordinative resources for everyday work. Any instrumental approach to *techne* is inherently contradictory because any such approach can be *both* procedural and generative at the same time. In its most banal enactments, *techne* encompasses the *experience* of language doing what it does—rhetoric is always *more than*, by nature (121). "Actual writing"—the kinds of writing that mediated Valerie's graphic design work—closes down and opens up *because* its instrumentality is always *more*.

The poet Inger Christensen (2018, loc. 748), in tracing the etymology of *lernen* ("to learn" in German), finds interesting root meanings: to "make known by searching"; to "know, have traveled through, have experienced"; and "to follow a trail/track." Language, "merely by existing," she argues, "offers poets (among others) myriad tracks, tracks that become reality by being followed" (loc. 748). To know and learn and experience, we must often follow trails or tracks laid down by others. Well-worn trails, mundane procedures, musty foundational knowledges, epistemist field methods. Rather than stifling creativity, well-worn trails may provide opportunities for invention and imagination. To interpolate Heidegger, *technes* of writing, of research methods, of photography, or of any other skillful practice present openings and disclosures—knowing the trail intimately allows us to look up, to attend to sounds and movements and smells, to engage our ambient environs and open toward the ways it constantly engages us. Heidegger's *techne*, Pender (2011, 35) argues, is "a kind of knowledge that, contrary to modern interpretations of the term, has nothing to do with technique or skill."

Instead, *techne* "provides an opening through which the being of a work can come into appearance in the world" (Pender 2011, 35). *Techne* is the work of disclosure, of presencing and un-concealment. Pender (37) notes that Byron Hawk (2007, original emphases) also posits a non-instrumental view of *techne*, where rhetors are "embedded elements of complex [ambient] situations who work through the power of that embeddedness to act *with* nature." Ultimately, Pender (2011, 105, original emphasis) argues, non-instrumental views of *techne* leverage its inherent instrumentality for any rhetor "to locate herself in [a given] situation in order to help enact *its* possibilities for invention, not a generic strategy for imposing her own pre-conceived plans." *Techne* evinces a fundamental entanglement of rhetor and world, where instrumental or procedural characteristics foster creative practices.

Field methods are *technes* of empirical research that tune into, open up toward, and think with the ambient environs of any given site. Procedural knowledge of a wide variety of methods is essential to creative practices in the speculative middles of fieldwork. Methods are also, crucially, *technes* of visibility. Heidegger (1993, 361), in one of his most common moves, reminds us of the Greek root that *techne* shares with another term: *tiktō*, a verb that means "to bring forth or to produce." *Techne*, as a noun, belongs to the root of the verb *tiktō, tec*. "To the Greeks," Heidegger explains, *techne* "means neither art nor handicraft but, rather, to make something appear, within what is present, as this or that, in this way or that way" (361). The Greeks "conceive of *techne*, producing, in terms of letting appear" (361). In this framing, two arguments stand out: first, the notion that *techne* is a practice of *visibility*, of making, producing, or letting something *appear* in a relational and differential sense; and second, the notion that in bringing forth by making visible, *techne* is a practice of working with what is present.

It is through these twin facets of presencing and letting something (new) appear that the notion of visibility, in contrast to visuality, is brought into relief, particularly for scholars of rhetoric and writing. It is in and through these facets, in other words, that we can, following Brighenti (2010, 51), value visibility "as an achievement that goes well beyond the merely visual," wherein visibility, as fundamental to *techne*, is cast as fundamental to myriad rhetorics as well. Visibilities and the events, practices, techniques, and affects that shape and are shaped by them are "embodied and material," woven from "layers of the material and the immaterial into a single [visible] force" (56).

*Techne* is a practice of visibility, of illumination, because it brings forth, discloses, and draws attention to relations that are material, immaterial, and differential. As a practice of visibility, *techne* works with and reimagines what is present, in an ambient sense. In other words, *techne* is grounded in material and affective relations and in the bringing forth or making visible some of the permutations of those relations in specific contexts. By making visible, *techne* fosters not merely a shift in mental states but something both world transforming and world forming. In this sense, *technes* are means by which we seek out and embrace worldly disclosures, illuminate and make them visible, and see their relationality and combinatorial permutations as the very ground of rhetoric itself.

For Vilém Flusser, photographic acts of visibility constitute a *techne* of "phenomenological doubt" (quoted in Von Amelunxen 2000, 90). This is a criticism of photography, of the ascendance of images over text, and of an inherent circularity in the collective memory of photographs inundating contemporary society (90). But the notion that photography—as a *techne* of engaging ambience and working with what is present—expresses phenomenological doubt is a *productive* criticism in methodological terms, the kind of unbracketing praxiography that Mol favored. It is precisely because we can and should doubt what we observe in fieldwork—for example, in our impressionistic inscriptions from field notes and memos—that photography and videography serve as methodological ballast to traditional methods. Carefully enumerating and accounting for what is visible in any given research site does not, by fiat, create an agential cut.

Representational materials such as photographs and videos composed during fieldwork are *technes* of visibility, but visibility is always ambivalent, always haunted by *in*visibility. Writing field notes, documenting field sites with photographs and videos, interviewing participants, collecting artifacts, and immersing ourselves in the many sensual particulars of a field site—using both procedural and creative interventions—are all ways of embracing the ambivalence of visibilities. We're constantly closing down and opening up. But to embrace Heidegger's (2013, 57) sense of *techne*, "to have seen in the widest sense of seeing," involves measured attention to what happens after we've helped things appear and made them visible; *techne*, as Pender (2011) has shown, is a powerful form of *poiesis*.

### *Techne* and/as *Poiesis*

Susannah Ryan (2018, 94) argues that "*poiesis* puts to bed any expectations that a message or meaning is transmitted or even merely 'understood'; instead, language (and the other sharing in it) enjoys the loving liberty that comes from being let to be." Having a more creative (rather than an instrumental) relationship to rhetoric, she adds, "requires a radical openness," one that, in turn, "requires letting the other pull from our words whatever he or she sees in the expression without the rhetor burdening him or her with what it really means" (94). Our research participants, by allowing us into their lives, give us the gift of their being and doing. They trust that we have been transparent about our methods and procedures; they trust that we will render their experience in good faith; they trust that by sharing, others may benefit and enjoy new understanding; they trust that what we pull from *their* words and acts will reflect and shed light on their reality.

They trust us enough to let go—they know that we will pull from *our* observations and interviews and photographs and *their* stories to tell other stories. What we do as researchers—how we move from what we observed to what we saw and felt, to what we make visible in scholarship—is necessarily an abstraction, but one in which our research participants can see themselves and their practices and environments. Rüdiger Safranski (2017, 453) notes that *poiesis* means both *to make* and *to shape*. Our empirical research practices, as *technes* of visibility, bring forth "those things that cannot come into existence on their own" (Pender 2011, 31). But it is what we do next that makes all the difference, our acts of *poiesis*: how we *shape* what we observed, how we make visible what was observable, how we respond to the gifts given by our participants in their enactments.

Karl Ove Knausgaard (2018a, loc. 197) poses and answers the question "why do I write." He writes not to reveal something but instead to allow "something to reveal itself." In doing so, he shapes what already exists into *something else*: "Whatever it is that reveals itself may well be something already known, for there is hardly anything uncharted in the human psyche or in the world anymore, but it has to show itself unguardedly, with a kind of trust" (loc. 197–98). Knausgaard plumbs the inadvertent; sitting still and waiting for things to become visible and accessible is "the novel's way of thinking," he argues (loc. 204). Sometimes, as we move about, we stumble into something and knock it clear, into the light.

In both the novel's way of revealing and in stumbling and knocking things loose, something shows itself inadvertently—this is the goal: "Thoughts are the enemy of the inadvertent, for if one thinks about how something will seem to others, if one thinks about whether something is important or good enough, if one begins to calculate and to pretend, then it is no longer inadvertent and accessible as itself, but only as what we have made it into" (2018a, loc. 206–209). Knausgaard's writing allows something to reveal itself, something inadvertent, uncalculated, unguarded, perhaps hidden in plain sight. In research, we plan and think and deploy procedures; we follow well-worn trails and tracks; but where we end up is often inadvertent. Our *technes* guide us, but *poiesis* is the shaping of "the generative modalities of impulses, daydreams, ways of relating, distractions, strategies, failures, encounters, and worldings of all kinds" (Stewart 2008, 73). "Disparate things come together differently in each instance," Kathleen Stewart argues, "and yet the repetition itself leaves a residue like a track or a habit" (73). *Poiesis*, she notes, "is a mode of production in an unfinished world" (77).

To study writing and rhetoric is to study and enact *poiesis*. Thomas Rickert (2013, 91) argues that seeing human subjects as materially "emplaced and dispersed" rather than as autonomous and cognitively masterful agents "suggests . . . invention attuned less to seeking advantage over or success against an audience than to working with what an audience and a material situation bring forth." This is congruent with Heidegger's perspective on *techne* as a bringing forth and making visible by working with what is present. And this is the basis of Rickert's argument for *poiesis* (236–39). In his discussion of Heidegger's fourfold (*das Geviert*), Rickert notes that *poiesis* is a gathering and tracing of disclosures that also apprehends the *conditions* of such disclosures (236).

Stewart (2008, 71), also drawing from Heidegger, argues that the objects of study in a cultural *poiesis* of the everyday are "textures and rhythms, trajectories, and modes of attainment, attachment, and composition." We should attend to where these trajectories "might go and what potential modes of knowing, relating, and attending to things are already present in them" (71). *Poiesis* is world building, world shaping, a bringing forth accomplished by attunement to and composing from everyday disclosures—material and immaterial, here and now, there and then, what is, what was, and what is possible. Disclosures and visibilities, for Heidegger, Rickert, and Stewart, emerge from both humans and non-humans. Attunement, and what Rickert (2013, 122) describes as one's "affective comportment," establishes the grounds of rhetorical action, which often manifests as *poiesis*—the world-building, world-shaping work of bringing forth and making visible.

Picturing writing and rhetorics is methodological *poiesis*. I have argued that mundane acts of writing and rhetorical practice are forms of *poiesis*—contingent, malleable, epistemically and ontologically small and uncertain (McNely 2016, 2018). Stratigraphies of such practices accumulate, intermix, and through their accreted layers assume the weight of elemental, seemingly unchanging, epistemically and ontologically sanguine perspectives that stabilize and shape realities. On a continuum, everyday rhetorical acts vacillate between known contingency—a to-do list, a draft memo, a hallway conversation—and experienced permanence: textbooks, organizational lore, keynote speeches delivered by experts. The moments of known contingency are, for many actors, moments of uncertain *poiesis*. By bringing forth and making visible forms of knowing and being in everyday rhetorical practices, we add to the layers of sedimented knowing and being, uncertain of the weight of such contributions.

Picturing writing brings out the textures of everyday rhetorical practices, enumerates and thickens—by suspending and by layering—moments of *poiesis*, makes them visible and articulable, and places them within the broader context of experienced permanence. Visual methodologies and methods, as *technes* and as forms of *poiesis*, thus bring forth and make visible the conditions, contours, topographies, and practices through which people attune to, comport themselves toward, and create worlds. In moments of known contingency, we make visible small acts of *poiesis*, for ourselves and others. Engaging ambience means tracing these small acts of *poiesis*, demonstrating how they accrete into more stable forms of experienced permanence.

### THIS-NOW-HERE-NESS

Heidegger (2013, 57) argues that *techne* denotes "a mode of knowing," and "to know means to have seen, in the widest sense of seeing, which means to apprehend what is present, as such." The Greeks, according to Heidegger, saw knowing as "the uncovering of beings" (57). *Techne*, in Heidegger's interpretation, is thus "a bringing forth of beings" (57). To know is to uncover and see; to know—through *techne*, the procedural *and* creative act—is a simultaneous epistemological and ontological enactment that brings forth "beings *out of* concealedness and specifically *into* the unconcealedness of their appearance" (57, original emphases). *Techne*, for Heidegger, is not an act of *making*, although, as Pender (2008) notes, it is often glossed as such. It is, instead, attunement and apprehension—moving nearer to what is already present (though perhaps latent, concealed, or obfuscated); in this movement, *techne* causes "something to emerge as a thing that has been brought forth" (Heidegger 2013, 58).

*Techne* allows "something to reveal itself" (Knausgaard 2018a, loc. 197). This is, admittedly, a swirl of abstract verbs: attuning, apprehending, bringing forth, un-concealing, moving toward and moving near. The verbs are abstract because the longing—the desire for unconcealment and apprehension—is often directed to that which is nearest to us, to that which, Heidegger argues, is therefore most difficult to apprehend: what is right here, now, and what is always with us, as part of us, inextricable from what and how we know, who and what we are. These verbs belie a longing for *techne* as *poiesis*—forms of apprehension that bring into relief that which is near us and already present and that more effectively embraces, un-conceals, and presences that nearness.

*Techne* is adaptive, diffractive, and intra-active. It is a means for tuning to moments, waves and resonances, and disclosures in an environment and developing—in concert with such attunements—responses that acknowledge, accept, un-conceal, and bring forth some of the myriad ambient intensities and trajectories of a given world. It is, in in other words, a *techne* of light, of lightening, of illumination—not in any metaphysical sense but in the literal sense of bringing phenomena into the light. What surrounds us and participates with us in everyday life—desks, lab notebooks, sticky notes, whiteboards, coffee cups—is nearest, not only mediating but *conditioning* and *participating in* what we do and who we are. "Yet the near," Heidegger argues, "remains farthest" from us (1993, 234). That which is nearest must be illuminated, uncovered, brought into the light.

Heidegger's *techne* is not something *made* by "an ontologically secured subject" (Trapani and Maldonado 2018, 280) but rather a result of intra-action, immersion, attunement, un-concealment, illumination. For Heidegger, it is a movement of phenomena "*into* the unconcealedness of their appearance" (2013, 57, original emphasis). We need *technes* of visibility to know, to see in the "widest sense of seeing" what is here, now.

*Techne* and *poiesis* are modes of illumination, apprehension, and invention. They focus on everything that shows up, everything that thickens and vividly renders an ambience that is constantly in flux. They offer practical means for inculcating "the widest sense of seeing, which means to apprehend what is present, as such" (Heidegger 2013, 57). Visual and multisensory methodologies and methods, articulated to new materialist and ambient theories of rhetoric, are *technes* of *poiesis* that can help us bring forth and vividly render *this-now-here-ness*.

\* \* \*

Safranski (1998) traces Heidegger's fascination with *nearness* to the philosopher's early work on Duns Scotus, where he identifies "the hairline crack between thought and Being" (62). In Duns Scotus, Heidegger discovers the relationship between oneness and otherness as seen from a metaphysical and categorical perspective. "This is a discovery of far-reaching importance," Safranski argues, because "it states, in Heidegger's formulation, 'what really exists is individual' " (62). Safranski adds that we could clarify Heidegger's formulation by way of Duns Scotus and the "'this-now-here-ness' of things," the idea that "what each time occurs is something unique at its point in space and time" (62).

Heidegger "seems to be mesmerized" by the concept of this-now-here-ness and the fact that things are heterogeneous, individual, and, by necessity, intra-active (Safranski 1998, 66): "The metaphysical vertical" of traditional philosophy "begins to tilt toward a historical-phenomenological horizontal" (67). This notion of a "historical-phenomenological horizontal" turn in Heidegger's thought is similar in principle to rhetoric's recent turn toward renewed understandings of historical-material ambience and the role of rhetoricity (Davis 2017) in situating both human and non-human forms of addressivity and responsivity. Ambient rhetoric, in other words, is inescapably wedded to the this-now-here-ness of everyday life and its environs—we are but one intra-active component among many others, real and virtual, right here, right now, in absolute particularity.

In *Autumn*, Knausgaard (2017a) writes about the world's coterminous and intra-active heterogeneity and particularity. One afternoon, as he is washing up and preparing supper, he looks out his kitchen window to the sky above rural southern Sweden, arrested by the sight of migrating birds. "It's drizzling, the sky is grey and the air perfectly still," he writes, and "somewhere above me there is a honk, then another" (143). He sees a wedge of geese. Then he attunes to this-now-here-ness. The geese are seen and felt and apprehended in concert with the washing up, the autumn sky, the smell of supper cooking:

> In the kitchen the slices of sausage have developed a brownish-black crust from the heat, especially at the edges, and they've swollen a little and are bulging. The macaroni, which is swirling around on the eddies of seething water, is done. I pour it into a colander in the sink, toss it. Within me the migrating birds are living a life of their own. I'm not thinking of them, but they are there, in the stream of sensations and feelings which at times freeze into images. Not clear and distinct images, as with photographs, for that isn't how the external gets depicted within us, but as if in rifts: a few black triangles, a sky, and then that sound, of several pairs of wings beating up in the air. That sound awakens feelings. What kind of feelings? I ask myself now, as I write this. I know them so well, but only as feelings, not as thoughts or concepts. The sound of birds' wings beating maybe fifteen metres up in the air, heard twice or thrice every autumn for forty years. (143–44)

It is tempting to assume that Knausgaard is simply internalizing the external, subjectifying the objective externalities of everyday life, applying human understanding to the many heterogeneous non-human elements of his ambient this-now-here-ness.

But that is not what he apprehends in this episode—that is not, ultimately, his full sense of knowing. Slowly, he understands the migration of birds *as such*. "They flew all that way under their own power," he writes, realizing that the world is not "boundless but limited, and that neither the place they left nor the place they arrived at were abstract but concrete and local" (Knausgaard 2017a, 144). He concludes as the early Heidegger might have if considering a similar moment, mesmerized by particularity: "Yes, that is what I sensed as I wedged the spatula under the slices of sausage and placed them on the green serving dish, then poured the macaroni into a glass bowl. The world is material. We are always in a certain place. Now I am here" (144). Knausgaard's realization of a heterogeneous and ambient this-now-here-ness evinces his response to sensory addressivity—he is hailed by any number of others in this moment (the green serving dish, the honk of geese, the smell of curling sausage frying in the pan), and he responds by feeling, thinking, writing. He responds with *poiesis*.

In Knausgaard's (2017a, 144) recollection, engagements are impressionistic, "not clear and distinct images, as with photographs." Yet photography is a sublime tool for rendering what is here, now, in any given place—representationally or impressionistically (as in Springgay and Truman's [2017] pinhole photography). For empirical researchers, both perspectives may be engaged—our phenomenal intra-actions may be simultaneously impressionistic and precise, internally directed and externally documented.

Indeed, photography may be *ontographic*. For Ian Bogost (2012, 38), *ontography* is "a name for a general inscriptive strategy, one that uncovers the repleteness of its units and their interobjectivity." Ontography is a "compendium, a record of things juxtaposed to demonstrate their overlap and imply interaction through collocation" (38). In his discussion of Gary Winogrand's photographs, Bogost (2011) encourages us to look at any given image and ask "what's in it? what else" as a process of "cataloguing being in a context." Photography lends *durability* to processes of cataloging being—documenting, fixing, and noting ambient this-now-here-ness in its remarkable particularity. Ontography, Bogost argues, "pulls inanimate things up to the level of human surfaces." It is a way to "see the world of things as things in a world rather than *our* world with things in it" (emphasis added). It fosters distance and strangeness and in doing so brings us closer to that which is nearest.

Ontography surfaces what is present. It is a *techne* of visibility and *wonder*. To wonder, Bogost (2012, 124) argues, "is to suspend all trust in one's own logics . . . and to become subsumed entirely in the uniqueness of an object's native logics." This is Knausgaard's wonder: in recognizing this-now-here-ness, he bends toward the logics of seething water, crackling sausage, honking geese—each pursues its own course and is recognized, in Knausgaard's slowly dawning responsivity, for what it is. Wonder, Jason Kalin (2017, 134) writes, "is a way to orient to objects as objects, to respect objects as objects in themselves." Visual methodologies and methods, "seared with reality" (Pinney 2011, 89), are *technes* of wonder that revel in ambient this-now-here-ness.

# 2
## REALIST VISIBILITIES, IMAGINATIVE PRAXIOGRAPHIES

This-now-here-ness assumes that things in the world are *real*—that crackling sausage, birds' wings, seething water, novels, lecterns, desks, and feelings accumulated and layered over decades have their own logics, disclosures, and potentials. All these things *really* affect us in extraordinarily complex permutations that are enacted within the ambient environs of where we have been, where we are, and where we will be. These things *really* live in us, move with us, stay with us, and we with them. "The integrity and intensity of the place," Tom Sparrow (2015, 209) notes, "gets reflected in the body." As a result, "The range of sensations and affects the body is capable of gets determined by the range of sensations and affects it receives from its environment' (209). As I argued in the introduction, praxiographic approaches to empirical research are grounded in realisms; this need not signify, as Karen Barad (2007, 37) notes, veridical representations of an independent reality but rather "the real consequences, interventions, creative possibilities, and responsibilities of intra-acting within and as part of the world."

Barad's realism assumes a subject is *somewhere*, inseparable from the environment, inseparable from everyday enactments, response-able, an intra-acting component of a given *something* as it "throws itself together" (Stewart 2008, 73). It is a realism that assumes "direct engagement with the ontology of our world is possible" (Barad 2007, 44). Visual and sensory methods are *technes* for direct engagement with the ontology of our world; using them fosters *poiesis* by attending to, seeing, and making visible the "specific material configurations of the world" (206). Crackling sausage, desks, bicycle parking, and coffee cups matter because they are here, now—not on some transcendent plane and not solely as a figuration of human intention and discourse.

Graham Harman (2018, loc. 126) argues that object-oriented ontology (OOO) is a "bluntly realist philosophy." This means that OOO takes a commonsensical perspective on the world and its myriad phenomena: it exists whether we do or not, whether we are aware of its existence or not. However, this perspective "cuts against the grain of the past century of continental philosophy, and leads in directions surprisingly alien to common sense" (loc. 126).

Harman describes in detail the ways OOO differs from other contemporary philosophical movements that share a bluntly realist perspective—most notably actor-network theory, speculative realism, and the looser collective of work often described as new materialism. There are important differences, but there are also important resonances—beginning with the simple yet radical idea that the world *really* exists without us and our intentions, and it affects us and conditions our comportments. Phenomena in the world can *really* be observed, followed, traced, and understood to some degree, so long as we grant that our observations and tracings affect and intra-act with that self-same phenomena. Meaning is not transcendent, locked in our heads, or separate from the real and strange world in which we are inescapably embedded.

Literal language or literal depictions, however, are anathema to OOO's realism. The literal is always an oversimplification—the idea that any object or phenomena could be described in terms of its literal and observable properties even though "objects are never just bundles of literal properties" (Harman 2018, loc. 437). For Harman, literalism is a pitfall for any bluntly realist philosophy because "any literal description, literal perception, or literal causal interaction with [any] thing does not give us that thing directly, but only a translation of it" (loc. 477). Even though we can feel, see, touch, trace, and understand a phenomenon at some level, we cannot *literally* paraphrase it, "as if it were truly equivalent to a sum total of qualities or effects and nothing more" (loc. 3121). Harman has many fellow travelers here, from Roy Wagner (1975), who argued that literalism was tantamount to cultural appropriation and ethical reduction, to Sara Ahmed (2010), who encourages us to resist literalist interpretations of affect and happiness that align with moral economies of the good life.

For Susan Sontag (2004, 47), "Everyone is a literalist when it comes to photographs." But Robert Hariman and John Lucaites (2016) echo OOO's distinction between realism and literalism with respect to photography. "Every photograph," they argue, "consists of both a referential and an imaginative orientation" (57). Photography thus always balances verisimilitude with aesthetic and affective imagination and interpretation. Every photograph "is both more or less a record of what happened and more or less an artistically enhanced experience; both more or less empirical and more or less interpretive; both more or less accurate and more or less suggestive" (57). Photography is ambivalent. And the realist and imaginative aspects of photography need not conflict (58).

Realism, Hariman and Lucaites (2016, 58, original emphasis) argue, "*has to be the first principle of photographic meaning, but it cannot be achieved completely without imaginative presentation and response.*" "The camera," they add, "records the surface of the world like no other instrument, but the truth of what is shown can be realized only through an act of imagination" (58). A photograph is, thus, always already a "heterogeneous object" (58). What is visual does not equal what is visible; photography's *techne* is a form but not the entire shape of *poiesis*; what is observable is not the same as what is seen.

Sontag's influence led to a *literalist*—rather than a *realist*—view of photography. A literalist view often leads to reductio ad absurdum. Hariman and Lucaites (2016, 69) invoke Errol Morris (2011), noting that "the epistemological questions" raised by a literalist perspective "can never be answered in full, and they displace other substantive questions." For example: "The literalist asks whether the photo is accurate but not what other statements it might be making" (Hariman and Lucaites 2016, 69). It boils photography down to binaries: fake or real, staged or not, manipulated in or out of the camera; "an insistence on literal accuracy alone can sever the most vital connections between the photograph and the world" (69). From a realist perspective, however, "photography is a medium of social interaction: photographs depict people in relationship with one another, they are used to make sense of the social world, and they create and inflect relationships among those who use them" (69).

Photography is *both* representative and imaginative. It evokes material and affective aspects of everyday life—our relationship to, comportments toward, and everyday enactments with people and things and non-human organisms. "The shift from literalism to realism," Hariman and Lucaites (2016, 70) argue, is "a shift to an imagined community, that is, to a relational understanding of the photographic event and of everything depicted in the photo." Literalism is suspicious of both aesthetics and rhetoric (70); but the imaginative aspects inherent in a realist perspective toward photography constitute a "mode of extraordinary seeing," an achievement of *visibility* that "brings the viewer closer to reality . . . not further away from it" (71).

Imagination, Hariman and Lucaites (2016, 72) contend, "is necessary for reality to be apprehended at all." Any given photograph "is always both image and optic: a picture of some part of reality and a way of seeing that reality more expansively; a recording of specific facts and an act of imagining a world" (72). Any photo can present multiple facts, engender multiple interpretations, offer multiple optics. This is a flaw for literalists but a boon to realists. What is instrumental is also creative. Any photographed enactment is "simultaneously grounded in the particular event being depicted and extended beyond that moment to other actual or potential events that are part of some larger pattern" (72).

A commitment to realist photography, Hariman and Lucaites (2016) argue, ultimately rests on several assumptions: first, the camera can intra-act with, suspend, and thicken ("document," "record," or "capture") the material conditions of everyday life (76); second, realism posits that the photograph, in regimes of visibility, may be potentially democratic—"every image of the contradictions defining ordinary life," they argue, "is also an image of what could be changed for the better" (77); and third, realist photography presumes imaginative, collective, critical spectatorship (77). Above all, "the realist photograph," for Hariman and Lucaites, "takes the spectator inside another world, asks how it is also the viewer's own world" (78). The camera does not accomplish this work on its own: what is optic must also be made visible; what is representative must also be imagined; what is brought forth in *techne* must be shaped in acts of *poiesis*.

Visual and sensory fieldwork methods afford us *technes* that we rarely deploy: methodological complementarity to our emerging theories and a means for exploring and extending those theories. As with any empirical research in writing and rhetorics, documenting what shows up is a crucial but incomplete practice. As researchers, we bear the responsibility of shaping and making visible the matter we explore.

By using visual and sensory methodologies and methods, we engage ambience through an interplay of representational and impressionistic means—through sequential textual data: field notes, memos, and interviews—and the more sharply defined, simultaneous presencing of rhetoric's remarkable materiality: in short, everything that is seared into the camera's digital sensor or film emulsion. This interplay—of the textual and the visual, of the sequential and the simultaneous, of the impressionistic and the sharply defined—can foster an intriguing *poiesis* that offers something new and different to visual rhetoric.

## REALIST RHETORICS

In Jack Selzer and Sharon Crowley's *Rhetorical Bodies* (1999), Carole Blair (1999) questions the idea that rhetorical effectiveness is yoked to a given rhetor's aims. "Rhetoric has material force beyond the goals, intentions, and motivations of its producers," she argues, "and it is our responsibility as rhetoricians not to just acknowledge that, but to try to understand it" (22). Rhetorical scholarship has demonstrated an excessive reliance on rhetoric's symbolic properties, a reliance, she argues, that cannot account for its material force and consequentiality (20). Blair wants us to rethink rhetoric itself, not just its effects, *as material*; rhetoric is "just as substantial and consequential"—just as *real*—"as any element of its setting" (16). Her claims for rhetoric's materiality are tied to her claims about our overreliance on symbolicity: rhetoric's materiality cannot be reduced to symbolicity. Its materiality hails us, implicates us, makes claims on us in concert with—and in excess of—its symbolic meanings.

To theorize rhetoric's materiality—including the fact of its visibility—we must ask different questions, make different methodological moves. We must explore not just what a text or image or artifact *means* but also what it *does* (Blair 1999, 23). As Kathleen Stewart (2007, 128) has argued, "Every scene I can spy has tendrils stretching into things I can barely, or not quite, imagine." How, then, do we follow the tendrils, account for material force, and consider what seeps in, whether intended by a rhetor or not? By practicing "a speculative and concrete attunement" (128) to the actual, real somewheres (Mol 2002) where things affect us.

Richard Marback's (2008) work presents an illustrative case in point. His aim is to present a "non-reductive account of the embodiment of rhetoric" (46). Like Stewart, Marback is interested in the tendrils stretching beyond a communicative event, an image, an object; like Blair, he is interested in rhetoric's material force; like Annemarie Mol, he studies these facets of an embodied, material rhetoric in a specific place (Detroit, Michigan), at a specific time (February 2004), during a specific enactment (an act of racist vandalism). His approach gives objects their due, makes sense of the sensations we feel when seeing, touching, and interacting with them.

Marback's (2008, 47) perspective explores "the interconnectedness of actions, objects, and words." His argument is grounded in acknowledging and following "the resources and ambitions in rhetorical studies available for making sense of our sensations of rhetoric as embodied" (49). And to make sense of sensations, we need to practice a notion of mutual vulnerability (a concept I explore in more detail in chapter 6). Marback's approach to seeing and feeling suasion is radically open to the potential of visual, material, and sensory entanglements—to the "availability and vulnerability of spaces, bodies, and objects to each other" (50). Mutual vulnerability and openness are speculative and concrete, real and imagined, seen and felt. "Just looking" is not enough (50).

The objects with and through which we live our everyday lives are "more than featureless repositories of consequential responses" (Marback 2008, 52). Any object is "more than a mirror reflecting some idea that precedes it, shines through it"; any object thus "exists despite our best efforts to change it" (52). Meaning and significance—like visibilities—are moment-bound: located in a specific place and time, in the midst of specific practices and actions, in engagements with and through specific objects, and framed by specific historical perspectives (52). The meaning found in a civic monument in downtown Detroit "is made and made to endure in an ongoing series of actions in the perpetual present" (53).

To trace and explore actions in the perpetual present, we need to attend carefully to the visual, material, and sensual force of rhetoric as an entanglement of mutually vulnerable suasive actors. Marback (2008, 54), prefiguring the work of other scholars in material rhetorics, thus makes an argument for tracing practices in *enactments*: "Attending to what gets done involves attention to physical actions, attention to the things that get done with discourse as well as attention to things with which and through which discourse works." Drawing on Blair, he argues that attention to materiality and to things is "attention to the concreteness of embodied activity in its richest sense" (54).

Marback (2008) sees enactments as more than just symbolic interactions. Mutual vulnerability in the perpetual present involves human and non-human suasion in, through, and with one another. The Detroit memorial—the Monument to Joe Lewis—and the vandals "each reached out toward the other to meet in an undetermined movement forward into embodying expression" (57). Rhetoric—as an embodied, material, and symbolic enactment—requires that we "forego the claim to agency we make when we project our sovereignty over objects" (59). Echoing Barad, Marback illustrates the futility of trying to locate agency, for agency has no discrete origin but rather "lives in the event as the availability, the responsiveness, of ourselves and objects to each other" (61; see also Gries 2015). "Our theories of rhetoric must give the objects in the world their due," he argues, and we must likewise "give up assertions of agency for the contingencies of vulnerability" (Marback 2008, 64). The reality that objects are vulnerable to human machinations is a commonplace; that humans are vulnerable to suasive objects is a radical departure from traditional perspectives on rhetoric.

Both Blair and Marback chose public memorial sites and sculptures, and it is no stretch to say that most people experience and apprehend these memorials *visually*—the fact of their public visibility and the ways the memorials make history and culture *visible* are foregrounded in the public imagination and in everyday experience and spectatorship. The Vietnam Veterans Memorial in Washington, DC, studied by Blair, and the Monument to Joe Lewis in Detroit, Michigan, studied by Marback, could each be productively considered from the perspective of rhetorical criticism, in a search for symbolic salience (many studies in visual rhetoric do exactly this; see, for example, Lucaites and Hariman 2001). How astonishing, then, that the questions asked of these memorial sites and the rhetorical theories developed from studying them differ so markedly from the typical analyses of visual rhetoricians. Scholars of material rhetorics have emphasized the importance of *being there*, of experiencing and feeling what these memorials communicate to a particular body at a particular time.

These scholars asked expansive questions about visual phenomena by taking on issues of sensation, material force, agency, and non-discursive suasion. Although their methodologies are not typically empirical, they often relied on actual, material engagements with the phenomena under scrutiny. For example, Greg Dickinson, Carole Blair, and Brian L. Ott, in their collection *Places of Public Memory* (2010), fostered a series of engagements with public memorials and the broader spatial contexts in which they were erected. They acknowledge that public memory, in the highly calcified visual-material forms of memorials, is "animated by affect" (7).

Public memory is partial, always evolving; statues are not static in the public imagination, yet they promote stasis in the rhetorical sense—we see, sometimes we touch and feel, and in finding stasis we might encounter rhetorically generative reconceptualizations of public memory. But we must *be there*, perhaps making several visits, to foster this kind of affective stasis. Material rhetorics evolved alongside visual rhetorics; yet despite frequent cross-pollination, material rhetorics scholars were often asking very different questions of ostensibly visual phenomena, with different assumptions about how to engage such phenomena. Scholars in material rhetorics were interested in what shows up, the remarkable materiality of enactments.

## ONTOLOGICAL CONSTITUTION

What shows up in empirical studies of writing and rhetorics may be identified with systematic attention to *mediated actions*. Jody Shipka (2011, 10) called for a focus on forms of ephemeral and interstitial writing that support multimodal composition: non-digital inscriptions such as doodles, marginal notes, and to-do lists. These are *mediated actions*, the "varied and various places *in which*, times *at which*, and resources *with which* literate activity is typically accomplished" (15, original emphases). In praxiographic methodologies, attention to mediated actions is crucial; many of the actors that matter show up in and through these actions.

Systematic attention might lead us to the marginal notes and annotations that contribute to "writing as the exposed edge of thought" (Freedman and Smart 1997, 239); the ways a coffee mug is used to aid map readings and transformations (Spinuzzi 2003); how a failure to make a seemingly inconsequential database note has far-reaching, unintended repercussions (Spinuzzi 2008); or how a missing office door encouraged substantive informal discussions that might not otherwise have occurred (McNely, Gestwicki, Gelms, and Burke 2013). Attention to mediated actions can show us the material force of rhetorics as they are enacted.

Martin Packer (2011) sees mediated action as ontologically commensurate with everyday life. Such activities help *constitute* both how people know and who they are in any given context. Everyday realities are constituted in "practical know-how, concrete and tacit knowledge" (65). Such activities are not abstractions or solely cognitive constructions but specific and situated forms of mediation and communication that substantially constitute the work of—and identification with—a particular profession, pursuit, or way of life.

Packer (2011, 203) thus advocated an ontological constitution, where "objects and subjects, not just ways of knowing, are formed in practical activity." More important: "Constitution itself is *visible*. Embodied, practical, and concerted activity in the material world can be seen; it is not hidden away on some transcendental level of the mind. And if it can be seen, it can be studied" (206, original emphasis). The visual research methods used by Chad Wickman (2010), for example, helped him trace writing processes through the laboratory, but they also helped him illuminate an *ontology*: the circumstances, material contexts, and mediated actions that help *constitute* the lived experience of one chemical physics researcher.

Ontological constitution is visible, and it is also *sense-able*. It is formed in part through mediated actions, to be certain, but Packer has little to say about other facets of rhetoric's sensorium (Hawhee 2015) that are inescapably entangled in who we are or who we will be. Some of these relations will be visible and readily identifiable in the typical domains of rhetoric and writing research—as doodles, marginal notes, and lists. Some of these relations will be audible—the sounds of a colleague in a nearby cubicle yawning and sighing each afternoon; the sounds of the office air conditioner starting up. Some of these relations will be haptic—the feel of a favorite writing chair; the subtle, tactile feedback of a ballpoint pen in the firm middle pages of a journal. Some of these relations will be olfactory—the cedar incense burning in the home office of a history professor—an essential component of a daily writing ritual. Some of these relations are aesthetic and non-correlational (Shaviro 2014), layered in one's past and current affective comportments toward the practical activity of writing. Most often and most important, as Barad (2007, 33) argues, these various sensory relations are cumulative and intra-active, forming an ontological inseparability within phenomena.

How we show up and how our engagements are ontologically constituted begins with what we can see but by no means ends there. How we show up always concerns how we feel, what we hear, what we remember and project, where and when and why we *are*. The practical activity of rhetoric and writing is conditioned by a host of agentially intra-acting sensory, material, spatial, and virtual actors.

Thomas Rickert's (2013) theory of ambient rhetoric provides a framework for understanding the many actors and situational variables (Faigley and Witte 1981) of rhetoric and writing that "more or less virtually, more or less actually" condition, move, and constitute rhetorical practice and being. Rhetoric, he argues, "must be grounded in the material relations from which it springs, not simply as the situation giving it its shape and exigence, but as part of what we mean by rhetoric. Rhetoric in this sense is ambient" (Rickert 2013, x). This perspective attunes to the agentive capacities of non-human objects, their "relationality, conditionality, [and] withdrawal" (204). Not everything is rhetoric, and not everything matters; rather, the "dynamic relationality" of human and non-human actors "brings to presence vectored forms of affectivity galvanized by [their] interactions" (208).

There are many ways we can explore what shows up. We can begin by *picturing writing*, by using *technes* of visibility to explore, document, archive, and analyze the things that matter in rhetorical enactments. In their introduction to data displays, Matthew A. Miles, A. Michael Huberman, and Johnny Saldaña (2013, 108) argued that most qualitative data—particularly interview transcripts and field notes—are dense, voluminous, and sequential rather than simultaneous. Although much of a participant's practice is experienced simultaneously, it is rendered by typical fieldwork practices in sequential recordings and texts. This makes it difficult for a researcher (and a reader of qualitative research) to examine the multiple, intra-acting variables that *constitute* an ontology (108).

Many situational variables are, in fact, lost altogether in sequential approaches. But visual research subverts sequentiality. Photographs, videos, drawings, and diagrams of mediated actions allow researchers to examine situational variables holistically. And readers can see—to a much greater extent than in traditional, sequential fieldwork methods—what researchers themselves saw, an important glimpse into the data record. Audiences can analyze visual data alongside researchers: equipped with an understanding of the researcher's theoretical frame, methods, and practices, they can also dive into the research site, even drawing discrepant or new conclusions from those data.

## "EXCESSIVE INCLUSION"

In his history of photography and anthropology, Christopher Pinney (2011, 15) notes that for anthropologists, photography was quickly recognized and embraced "as a vital tool in the transmission of data, and what was thought to be reliable data at that." Photography was viewed as a viable way of documenting the scenes and contexts of anthropological research. Pinney thus positions "photography as a kind of writing" (14), a technology that was recognized as a "crucial mediator" in social scientific understandings of cultures (15).

But photography offered something that writing could not: an alluring sense of certainty in data collection. For Pinney (2011, 25), this seeming certainty "would generate further anxieties particular to itself"; among those anxieties, questions of ethical representation would be paramount. These anxieties led to a decades-long theoretical and practical divide over the use of photography in fieldwork, vacillating between "culture as a lived practice caught up in the rhythms and idioms of speech" and "culture as objectified in visual and material representation, culture in other words as a form of 'writing'" (25). Some early anthropologists, such as Everard im Thurn, advocated fieldwork photographs that helped "write" the lived experience of everyday practices and positioned research subjects as complex subjects (36). Im Thurn saw the potential for photography to evoke the humanity of cultures and groups through visual fieldwork techniques that were "sensitive to intersubjective relations" (Griffiths 2002, 101).

Despite these aims, anthropological uses of photography often supported imperialist perspectives through essentialist and racist photographic documentation of non-white bodies. In anthropometric photography, for example, research subjects were made to assume standardized poses, often in front of grids that were designed to measure and classify the physiological characteristics of "native" cultures. For anthropologists such as im Thurn, such methods were dehumanizing, "merely pictures of lifeless bodies" (Griffiths 2002, 99). Early approaches to photography in anthropology thus varied widely, from "the use of photographs as vehicles of conviviality and a means for eroding barriers between anthropologists and locals" to its use "as a theatre for the staging and reinforcement of colonial asymmetry" (Pinney 2011, 48).

Anthropology matured in tandem with photographic technologies, and many of the most influential studies included photographs from field sites; some anthropologists even experimented with videography. Bronislaw Malinowski's *Argonauts of the Western Pacific* (2015) included fieldwork photographs that helped popularize his work (and exoticize his locations and subjects). Franz Boas used anthropometric photography in the 1890s to document physical characteristics of Indigenous North Americans; but as Anne Maxwell (2013) argued, Boas later used these visual data to create counterarguments against discriminatory racial theories, foregrounding the epistemic ambivalence inherent in all photographic representation. Boas sometimes partnered with professional photographers, and images from his fieldwork in British Columbia are among the most visually compelling (and poignant) anthropological photographs ever produced.

Gregory Bateson and Margaret Mead were especially innovative, using both still photography and videography during their fieldwork in Bali in the mid- to late 1930s. Their work was so different from established ethnographic practice that it led Ira Jacknis (1988, 160) to argue that Bateson and Mead essentially "began the field of visual anthropology." Their visual fieldwork was prodigious: they generated about 25,000 still photographs and over 22,000 feet of film (162). Bateson and Mead distilled and shared their work in *Balinese Character: A Photographic Analysis* (1942). Mead returned to the data in the 1950s, publishing *Growth and Culture: A Photographic Study of Balinese Childhood* (1951, with Francis Cooke Macgregor) and a series of six films (Jacknis 1988, 160).

But a central problem in visual anthropology was objectivity. Bateson and Mead (1942, 53) argued that "each single photograph may be regarded as almost purely objective, but juxtaposition of two different or contrasting photographs is already a step toward scientific generalization." Early visual anthropologists found photography useful as "a potential solution to the *problem* of observation" (Pinney 2011, 79, original emphasis). "Photography was a technical procedure," Pinney explained, "and one that ideally facilitated a distance between the photographer and what was photographed" (79). Yet Pinney noted that rather than solving problems in data collection and representation, visual fieldwork often simply created new problems. Photographs "are usually taken to tell a story: their 'difficulty' stems from their insistence on always telling their own story" (80).

In anthropology's debates about objectivity, comparisons between written and visual fieldwork methods were inescapable. Observational field notes tell one story, and fieldwork photographs potentially tell others. Both modes might engender a more comprehensive story in concert, but as Pinney demonstrates, the collective, multifaceted story is never simply a given. *More* does not equal *more accurate*. Drawing on Rudolf Wittkower, Pinney (2011, 80) noted "the visual's tendency to solidify presences and claims which in their linguistic form are always more uncertain." "The camera," therefore, "records what is placed in front of it and on its own is incapable of making distinctions about the relationship of its visual trace to psychic, social or historical normativity" (81).

A camera, in other words, "never knows and can never judge whether what it records is 'typical,' 'normal' or 'true.' This would make photography very useful, but also very troublesome, to anthropology" (Pinney 2011, 81). As Pinney (2003, 7, original emphases) has argued elsewhere, no matter how "hard the photographer tries to *exclude*, the camera lens always *includes*." "Photographs, necessarily seared with reality, always have to contend with this excessive inclusion," he argued (2011, 89).

Yet because of photography's inherent ambivalence, the "excessive inclusion" of the camera's lens and sensor is a powerful *techne*. A realist (rather than a literalist) approach sees photography as "not simply a mechanism for capturing the world as it is, but rather a capacious public art that participates with all other media in making reality meaningful" (Hariman and Lucaites 2016, 78). Can fieldwork photos be mentioned in the same breath as photographs classified as "public art"? Certainly, as the examples of Boas and Bateson and Mead demonstrate. At the least, realist conceptions of fieldwork photographs and videos broaden our agora, where cultural conceptions of writers and rhetors participate in collective pictures of writing and rhetoric.

In fieldwork, there are times when the "excessive inclusion" of representational photography and videography serves important ends, working ontographically to trace and make visible the remarkable materiality of a given research site. Photography cannot be limited to literalist or representationalist paradigms; like all *technes*, it opens up even as it seemingly closes down.

## AMBIENCE AND AMBIVALENCE

In the 2018 novel *Asymmetry*, the narrator confronts one's incredible talent for filtering and unseeing the ambience of everyday life: "What do I remember? What do you remember of last year? Of 2002? Of 1994? I don't mean the headlines. We all remember milestones, jobs. The name of your freshman English teacher. Your first kiss. But what did you think, from day to day? What were you conscious of? What did you say? Whom did you run into, on the street or in the gym, and how did these encounters reinforce or interfere with the idea of yourself that you carry around" (Halliday 2018, loc. 1796–1800). The narrator quickly switches perspective, from the first person to the second—what do *I* remember? what do *you* remember? what did *you* think? how did *your* encounters shape who you were and who you would become? This shift fits the context of the scene, but it's also a common distancing move, a way of unseeing. Instead of confronting what *I* saw and felt during an accident or trauma, I displace my *self*: "you just don't know how to react in that situation, so you ignore the warning signs." It's a discursive move we use to filter out and mollify what we know about ourselves. Does all that ambience matter anyway if we so easily unsee it, displace it, and forget it?

We remember signal events—the *salience* of the first kiss or the consequential job—and forget the ambient. What *did* you think on April 12, 2014? What *were* you conscious of that day? What things *did* you pick up and use and discard? We've developed *technes* to document ambience; journaling, for example, can help us re-create what we might have been thinking or doing or interacting with on a given day. Photos of everyday life may also be powerful in an ontographic sense, bringing *everything* that's pictured to the surface—a thick slice of place and time and things. Both inscriptive strategies—both *technes*—are tricky. Documenting ambience invites ambivalence. Lisa Halliday's (2018, loc. 2041–2043) narrator says: "Sometimes I think I remember the pomegranate. Its tannic sweetness, the sucky juice running down my chin. But to this day there is an instant Polaroid of the moment taped to our refrigerator in Bay Ridge and again I cannot be certain whether if there were no photograph there would be no memory." What do we remember without our *aides-mémoire*? More to the point, what do our *technes* do to our memories? For Barad, our *aides-mémoire* are inter-agentive—as much a part of what and how we remember as they are part of what and how we enact.

In the 1995 film *Smoke* (Wang 1995), Auggie (played by Harvey Keitel) is a Brooklyn tobacconist whose corner storefront faces Sixteenth Street and Prospect Park West. Early in the film the recently widowed writer Paul (played by William Hurt)—a solitary man who writes alone in anguish in his nearby apartment—shows up as Auggie is closing for the evening. Auggie welcomes him inside, and Paul sees Auggie's film camera sitting on the counter. The next scene moves to Auggie's kitchen, where Paul flips through photo albums of a startling project: Auggie sets his camera on a tripod across the street from his shop and shoots an image every day at 8:00 a.m. He doesn't take vacations. He needs to be there, to show up, to create a record of what shows up. He hasn't missed a shot in over 4,000 days—eleven years of ontographic documentation of one Brooklyn street corner. "It's just one little part of the world, but things take place there too," Auggie says.

Paul speeds through the albums, flipping page after page. "They're all the same," he says to Auggie. "You'll never get it if you don't slow down," Auggie says, putting another album in front of Paul. "They're all the same," he adds, "but each one is different from every other one." Each image, indeed, is inescapably different; each image depicts a scene of manifold variables that will never again coalesce in just that way; each image records a unique enactment of space and time, of light and heat, of movement and stillness; each image fixes everything that shows up and moves it forward, this-now-here-ness as an ongoing moment (Dyer 2007). Auggie tells Paul that people show up and disappear, that the same people become different, that weekends and weekdays trace rhythms and nuances over the years. "Every day the light from the sun hits the earth at a different angle," Auggie says, pointing out the kind of obvious ambience we so often ignore. The photographer directs the writer to ambience, until the writer directs the photographer to salience: Paul flips a page and is stunned to see a photograph of his wife, the year she died.

The ambivalent relations of memory and meaning, salience and ambience, and writing and photography are inextricable from visual methodologies and methods. *Both* writing and photography yield partial truths. In the next section, I briefly trace foundational work from visual anthropology, visual sociology, visual cultures research, and material cultures research—work that informs the case studies in later chapters. Rhetoric and composition has a long history of judicious borrowing and adapting from other fields (Lauer 1984); I describe and adapt approaches from these fields to delineate my own judicious borrowing. I join new materialist and ambient theories of rhetoric to rich traditions of visual research that inform the praxiographies in part 2 of this book.

## DOING VISUAL RESEARCH
### Visual Anthropology and Sociology

Howard S. Becker (2004, 193) argued that "anthropologists and sociologists have been using photographs ever since the beginnings of both disciplines, but have never been able to agree on just how these images should be used or to what ends." Historically, both anthropology and sociology are disciplines of *words*, and both have been uneasy with visual material in empirical inquiry. But both fields are home to robust implementations of visual methodologies and methods. Beginning in the 1960s, researchers used visual fieldwork to document and analyze culture and social life (194).

Sarah Pink's *Doing Visual Ethnography* (2007) spurred the growth of visual anthropology in the 2000s. She argued that technologies of visual representation matter in ethnographic fieldwork because all manner of material artifacts are interwoven with and participate in human cultures, and the camera is especially well-suited to document such artifacts (7). The relationship of visual data to "other sensory, material and discursive elements" involved in ethnographic fieldwork, she argued, can help co-constitute ethnographic knowledge (6).

This understanding stems from the reflexive turn in anthropology precipitated by James Clifford and George E. Marcus (1986). A scientific-objective approach to photography was seen as incompatible with disciplinary trends because it "did not account for the possibility that any attempt to represent a 'whole view' itself constitutes a 'partial truth'" (Pink 2007, 10). By the late 1990s, scholars began to critically examine what visual fieldwork methods *do*. As David MacDougall (1997, 292) argued, this involved "putting in temporary suspension anthropology's dominant orientation as a discipline of words and rethinking certain categories of anthropological knowledge in the light of understandings that may be accessible only by non-verbal means." Visual ethnographers reimagined what "counts" as viable methods of anthropological research and representation (see, for example, Banks 2001; El Guindi 2004; Pink, Kürti, and Alfonso 2004).

As the reflexive use of visual phenomena became more accepted, the sophistication with which researchers deployed such approaches increased. Still images were used to do more than simply render a scene or catalog phenomena. Marcus Banks (2001) and Sarah Pink (2007) developed approaches that have had lasting impacts on visual anthropology. They argued that visual research enables wider frames of analysis that may help account for the complex entanglements of social relations and the spaces and artifacts that mediate them. They used visual methods to document field sites, but they also used photographs as artifacts of interaction and discussion through which they could come to a better understanding of how participants valued visual material, how they viewed their own ambient environs, and how they interacted with visual phenomena in everyday life.

Pink (2007, 12–13) has argued that visual sociology was late to the reflexive party, however, and that it was "slow to engage with the visual beyond using it as a recording method and [as] support for a word-based discipline." Clarice Stazs (1979), Elizabeth Chaplin (1994), and Douglas Harper (2012) have each written histories of visual sociology, and more recent work is clearly reflexive of and attentive to problems of visual representations (see, for example, Knowles and Sweetman 2004a; Mitchell 2011). The major difference between visual anthropology and visual sociology seems to be methodological: ethnography originated in anthropology, and despite rich traditions and innovations of ethnographic practice in sociology, anthropology seems to have tolerated more methodological experimentation with visual methods earlier in its history than did sociology.

But visual sociology had its own reflexive turn, and contemporary visual researchers in any discipline commonly cite sources from visual anthropology, visual sociology, documentary photography, and visual cultures research. Harper (1998, 140) argues that a reflexive approach to documentary photography "begins with the idea that the meaning of the photograph is constructed by the maker and the viewer, both of whom carry their social positions and interests to the photographic act." Chaplin (1994) argues that visual phenomena collected in fieldwork have their own sociological and ontological value, that they are something more, in other words, than merely data points subject to verbal analysis. Pink (2007, 13) draws from these and other visual sociologists to argue for "engaging with the visual not simply as a mode of recording data or illustrating text, but as a medium through which new knowledge and critiques may be created."

Contemporary work thus complicates the ontological properties of photographs, videos, and drawings, offering nuanced perspectives on visual phenomena in both fieldwork and scholarship (see Harper 2004; Pink 2006, 2007, 2012a; Ruby 1995). Visual sociologists such as Caroline Knowles and Paul Sweetman (2004a, 5, original emphases) argued that visual methods "include ways of *doing* research that generate and employ visual material as an integral part of the research *process*."

Stephen Spencer (2011) argued that visual materials collected as part of such fieldwork processes may provide additional, qualitatively different forms of thick description in studies of social life.

Roger Brown (2011) suggests that fieldwork photography is a form of *discourse*, an "intentional sociological action" (203) that "links together tacit knowledge, observational, and empirical content to the sensory aesthetic poetics of their performance" (201). Brown positions documentary photography as a kind of fugue: "a marriage of precision and passion and a technique rather than a fixed form where the sequence of images can state a theme, a response, a theme, another response and so on with photographs working together as variation succeeds variation" (201). Visual fieldwork asks researchers to consider written, spoken, and visual modes in concert (202).

Visual methods thus foster ontological complexity. Different routes to understanding can give researchers a rounded perspective of complex social lives and practices. Any given fieldwork photograph, in other words, may raise ontological questions about "the perception and interpretation of what we believe to be social reality" (Spencer 2011, 37). Spencer favors a phenomenological approach to fieldwork photography because it can help researchers "understand phenomena as they are perceived by social actors in context" (44). Using multiple methods in fieldwork—for example, observation, interviews, and photographs of material phenomena used by participants—does not, Spencer argues, "hammer home the 'truth'" but seeks instead to "explore the complex interwoven, historical, social and cultural associations by which the ways of life in question are delineated" (140).

Ultimately, visual methods in anthropology and sociology have three primary aims: (a) they de-center and displace an overreliance on textual and verbal data; (b) they add complementary contextual details—the ability to capture rich, granular, and non-sequential information about the material phenomena with which participants live their lives; and (c) they attend to and enliven researcher understandings of how participants themselves perceive and interact with their phenomena, often by creating feedback opportunities in which visual data captured in situ are discussed with participants.

### Visual and Material Cultures Research

Cultural studies scholars have contributed much to our understandings of visual phenomena in social life. But the primary focus, Pink (2007, 14) argued, is "interpreting existing images and objects and the social and cultural conditions within which they are produced." An additional focus explores how images *produce* social and cultural conditions. The methodology is typically *critique*—of visual phenomena, their circulation, and their reception. In visual cultures research, then, a focus on symbolism, representation, and salience takes precedence, as does a preoccupation with interdependencies between word and image and the relationships between verbal and visual modes of symbolizing (see, for example, Evans and Hall 2005). But visual cultures researchers explore visual phenomena from diverse disciplinary perspectives, modes, and media. It is therefore not possible or fruitful to classify the work of visual cultures scholars as performing a coherent disciplinary approach other than to say, as Pink (2007, 14) does, that in cultural studies, the *production* of visual phenomena is uncommon.

Visual cultures research differs from visual anthropology and sociology most clearly in the role of the researcher as a *producer* of visual phenomena, or the use by the researcher of visual phenomena produced or procured during fieldwork *in collaboration with* research participants. Visual cultures research tends to explore broader societal and cultural manifestations of, and responses to, visual phenomena. A brief example illustrates these differences.

Pink, an anthropologist, explored some of the sensory experiences of contemporary Western life—the mise-en-scène of kitchens in ordinary United Kingdom homes. She used videography to conduct walking interviews with participants who showed her their homes, offering insights about the objects they valued, the pictures they hung, the smells and sights they cultivated, and the artifacts they used in everyday life (Pink 2012b). Her methods allowed her to better understand participants' "tactile ways of knowing"—finding the right water temperature for doing dishes, knowing the amount of soap to add, feeling the clean smoothness of flatware under a sponge, or understanding the correct pressure to apply when drying dishes (60). By making videos of participants, Pink was able to revisit practices as they happened and also to analyze the footage alongside participants' discussion of their practices, discerning sensory details she might have missed (or misunderstood) in situ.

A visual cultures approach to similar subject matter might focus on the tendential forces in society that circulate through visual phenomena both within and outside the home but that significantly shape understandings of home. One might analyze advertising campaigns for dish soaps, exploring the ways gendered, racialized, and class-oriented themes are reinforced, appropriated, or resisted by consumers. Roland Barthes (1977) notably conducted such critiques—of detergents, of plastics, of margarine. The visual phenomena of advertising campaigns—in print ads, billboards, television commercials, and interstitials on platforms such as Facebook—might be analyzed for the ways they reinforce or subvert hegemonic themes about what Western homes should look like, about who performs the labor of kitchen chores, or about class assumptions that underscore the vision of home life produced by the ads.

The methods and assumptions of visual ethnographers and visual cultures researchers may thus complement each other by approaching research questions orthogonally. On the one hand, Pink's study is defined by granular attention to the lived experience of her participants, and visual phenomena aid in situ understanding of both practice and influence across cases (that is, with multiple participants in multiple homes). On the other hand, the cultural studies approach analyzes visuals that circulate in society and performs a more general assessment of trends that impact lived practices.

Pink's approach to visual phenomena is *heuristic*, whereas a visual cultures approach is more *hermeneutic*. This distinction admittedly paints with a broad brush—a visual ethnographer will often use some of their photographs and videos in hermeneutic ways, just as a visual cultures researcher will see heuristic value in some of the visuals central to any given study. The distinction holds, however, in the following sense: empirical visual researchers *produce* and *use* visuals as one method, among several, to understand participant experience and practice. Visual phenomena thus constitute an inventional and productive method for exploring social life. For visual cultures researchers, who rarely *produce* visual phenomena, the interpretation of visuals takes precedence, affording a predominantly hermeneutic methodological and theoretical orientation. Whereas visuals are produced in Pink's study as one heuristic method among several for understanding lived experience, the visuals examined by Barthes are interpreted in broader cultural and societal critiques.

Material cultures research offers yet another approach. Such scholars are often aligned with anthropology or sociology, but influences from visual cultures research are also prominent. Scholarship on material cultures, therefore, often combines the orthogonal perspectives provided by visual ethnography's heuristics and the hermeneutic emphases of cultural studies. Inge Daniels (2010), for example, takes an ethnographic approach to everyday material cultures in Japanese homes. She used still photography in both her fieldwork and her published work. Her goal was to present Japanese homes holistically. "Images," she argued, "are said not only to bridge subjective and objective understanding but also to stimulate new ways of thinking about social life across cultures" (22). Visual methods move beyond the textual dominance of ethnography and enhance studies of material cultures, since it is extremely difficult to "adequately capture or express the power of things in texts" (23).

Her project included images selected by participants, images composed by participants, images she composed, and images composed by a professional photographer during fieldwork. This helped Daniels triangulate her visual fieldwork, but it also provided multiple perspectives on the artifacts, spaces, and arrangements of participants' homes. The combination of insider and outsider views helped foster local truths and helped participants see their everyday artifacts in a new light (Daniels 2010, 24). A key mode of inquiry in material cultures research involves acceptance of—and systematic investigation into—the ways repeated behaviors are accomplished in concert with things, the ways "artifacts participate in everyday life" (Arnold, Graesch, Ragazzini, and Ochs 2012, 124).

Jeanne E. Arnold and her colleagues (Arnold, Graesch, Ragazzini, and Ochs 2012) also explored the materiality of contemporary everyday life. The possessions in our homes "define who we are and reveal much about our social identities, family histories, aesthetic preferences, behavioral patterns, affiliations, and economic standing" (3). They systematically documented how people live and interact with their objects and spaces: generating 20,000 images and 1,500 hours of videotaped daily activities, making scan sampling observations, mapping home spaces, and indexing and categorizing visible material artifacts inside thirty-two Southern California homes (3).

Their fieldwork demonstrates how material cultures research combines methods from both ethnography and cultural studies; they argued that in North America, "in as few as three generations, mass media broadcast . . . has all but replaced oral history and become the primary conveyor of culturally shared ideas" (Arnold, Graesch, Ragazzini, and Ochs 2012, 199). Televisions inside private home spaces have become "witness to . . . intimate and emotionally bonding experiences" shared by American families (119). Arnold and her colleagues thus derived insights from in situ empirical fieldwork as well as from the broader tendential forces of visual cultures and their impact on home life.

Similarly, Elizabeth Shove and her colleagues (Shove, Watson, Hand, and Ingram 2007, 3) demonstrated how "things are implicated in the development, persistence and disappearance of patterns and practices of everyday life." Like Daniels and Arnold and her colleagues, their work crosses disciplinary boundaries to de-emphasize semiotic and hermeneutic readings of material cultures. Instead, they suggest "the simple but radical move of arguing that agency is distributed in, and emergent from, interactions between humans and nonhumans"; this perspective, they add, "opens the way for new lines of enquiry regarding the role of artefacts in social life" (7). Many material cultures researchers explore how humans and non-humans co-create and inhabit everyday environments. And visual methods are used to present and enliven discussions of *things*, the practices we repeatedly engage with those things, and the ways our artifacts, in turn, live around and with us, as ambient and active participants in everyday life.

**Engaging Ambience with Visual Research**

Many of the approaches developed by scholars in visual anthropology, visual sociology, and visual and material cultures research may be productively articulated to studies of writing and rhetorics from ambient or new materialist perspectives. Whether the focus is on the agency of non-humans—that is, what objects *do* to and with humans and other objects (Bennett 2010; Latour 2007); the existential significance of objects *as objects* (Bogost 2012; Bryant 2011, 2014; Harman 2011); the constant flux, contingency, and multiplicity of materiality in everyday life (Barad 2007; Coole and Frost 2010; Mol 2002); or a return to Kant's things-in-themselves as a radical example of how objects are neither transcendent nor immanent *but all we have* (Harman 2018; Shaviro 2014)—all such perspectives value and interrogate materiality for its own sake. Ambient and new materialist perspectives flatten and democratize (Bryant 2011) relations between humans and non-humans and between non-humans and other non-humans. The idea that non-human, often non-sentient objects have agency seems de rigueur in the wake of actor-network theory (see, for example, Latour 2007; Spinuzzi 2008). The idea that non-human, often non-sentient objects merit a profound existential reconsideration, however, fuels much of the debate for scholars exploring new materialisms.

Ambient and new materialist perspectives may both inform and be supported by visual methods and methodologies. Across the theoretical perspectives often grouped under new materialisms we can discern at least three broad foci: (a) a focus on non-human objects as objects, (b) a focus on the relationships of objects to other objects and of objects to humans and non-human organisms, and (c) a focus on flattened ontological relationships between humans and non-humans. Empirical investigations of these three foci are aided by visual and multisensory methodologies and methods because the excessive inclusion of still photography and videography in fieldwork means that objects of all kinds can be documented and imagined, ad infinitum, at little cost. Visual methods can play an important role in studies of materiality, practice, and the ontology of non-humans.

As Christopher Pinney argued, the camera includes what is in front of it; unless it malfunctions or the operator makes errors, the camera registers objects nearly as we see them, where they are. Unlike the divided attentions of a researcher writing observational field notes, the camera does not sift and winnow what exists; instead, it includes everything that is illuminated. In Pinney's terms, "The camera lens always *includes*" (2003, 7, original emphasis), and photographs are "seared with reality" (2011, 89), including and especially the material realities of field sites. In this way, visual methods make hyaline the emplacements and relationships among participants—humans and non-humans alike.

The camera's excessive inclusion means that many more of the relationships among participants in each field site may be registered, mapped, and analyzed than with traditional methods of observation alone. The significance of this fact, for studies informed by new materialist theories, simply cannot be understated. In using such practices, visual methods help researchers flatten—literally and figuratively—relationships between humans and the places and things that co-constitute practice and being.

## EMPIRICAL RHETORICS: THREE PRAXIOGRAPHIES

To conclude part 1 of this book, I briefly describe the methodologies, methods, field sites, and participants explored in part 2. I also preview some of the key findings that cut across and connect these studies. I flesh out the particulars of praxiographic studies of writers and rhetors guided by new materialist and ambient theories of rhetoric. These studies explore inter-agentive practices in specific spaces and places and demonstrate a methodological ethos of showing up, systematically, to see how worlds are "thrown together" (Stewart 2013, 660). As Mol (2002, 152) argues, praxiography "follows objects where they are being enacted in practice"; visual and multisensory methodologies and methods help us follow objects and enactments as they are realized—they are methods that work as *technes* of *poiesis* to bring intricate practices to light and help make everyday ambient environments visible, sense-able, and imaginable.

Chapter 3 follows the work of three media researchers over a nine-month period in which they conducted focus group studies about digital privacy with demographically diverse users of web and mobile applications. My participants developed a series of public deliverables for colleagues and potential clients in the media research industry. The study traced enactments by focusing on the role of writing and interpersonal communication in collaborative knowledge construction and the circulation of ideas across documents and presentations in professional genres.

A praxiographic approach fostered key questions about the media researchers and their work, to wit: how does writing circulate in their organization, and what does it *do* by circulating? How did media researchers make writing *visible* in their organization, and what effects did the persistent visibility of writing have on collaboration and knowledge development? What did writing *look like* in this organization? Does making it visible tell us about how participants conceived of their own processes of knowledge construction? What these researchers consistently *made visible* was inextricable from how they stabilized knowledge and understandings of professional identity.

Guided by writing, activity, and genre research (WAGR), chapter 3 models visual ethnography. This approach allowed me to comprehensively document and trace the material contexts of writing and communication and to share nuanced aspects of the field site that would be difficult to demonstrate in writing alone. I used several methods to study my participants' everyday practices, including formal and informal observations aided by still photography and videography and accompanied by in situ field notes and analytic memos; a series of semi-structured interviews with each participant and informal discussions with them, alone and together; and photo-elicitation interviews that explored how participants understood their own writing practices and the systemic material contexts in which they worked.

Findings from this study centered on participants' understanding of the materiality of their writing and the ways spatial affordances facilitated collaboration and knowledge construction. I introduce and explore the notion of factorial rhetorics—a way of theorizing rhetorical enactments that emerge in complex ways from many intra-acting factors—to demonstrate how a given ontology is always much more than the simple sum of its parts. By obsessively tracing writing in all its forms, this study also demonstrates how media researchers built from and stabilized contingent forms of knowledge by frequently writing in interstitial genres—something between sticky notes and published reports—that helped them collaborate, refine, and solidify ideas they would eventually make public.

Chapter 4 details an eighteen-month study of Eucharistic Adoration practices among parishioners and priests at three different Catholic churches in one midwestern city. Eucharistic Adoration is a form of worship wherein Catholics spend time with the consecrated host—the Eucharist—typically in an adoration chapel but occasionally in public services in which the host is displayed in a monstrance on the altar or carried in a procession. The project explored extra- and non-discursive rhetorics and affects—I systematically attended to how practitioners of Eucharistic Adoration understood sounds, smells, visible artifacts, and haptic feedback (for example, the feeling of kneeling on a kneeler while praying) during periods of adoration.

I explored how feeling and knowing murmur to one another, how sensation and mood condition religious understanding, how practitioners understand and intra-act with non-human artifacts, and how rhetorics are realized in extra-discursive ways. I focused on the role of material artifacts and spaces in framing and conditioning participants' experience of adoration, their devotion to and practice of their faith, and their sense of the ineffable. The study was guided by new materialist and ambient theories of rhetoric, with attention to mood and affect.

Using visual ethnography, I studied the sensory experience of participants: observations and interviews focused on sounds, smells, visible (and invisible) artifacts and concepts, and, especially, haptic interactions (such as kneelers, the feeling of rosary beads in one's hands, tight lower-back muscles from sitting for prolonged periods). I studied adoration practices in three different locations among demographically diverse parishioners. My methods included observations of each form of Eucharistic Adoration (from the relative privacy of the adoration chapel to public services and processions) accompanied by written field notes, still photography, and short videos. I wrote analytic memos that focused on my own sensory observations and impressions, and in them I tried to synthesize and make connections between my sensory experience and the observed practices of participants. Photographs and videos documented material contexts, artifacts, and the bodily comportments of parishioners. I conducted both semi-structured interviews and photo-elicitation interviews with parishioners and with two priests. And I collected written artifacts from formal services and journal excerpts from participants.

Chapter 4 theorizes the role of *sensory artifacts* in adoration practices—objects purpose-built to engage the sensory faculties and affects of parishioners. Drawing from both Heidegger and Rickert, I describe how such artifacts are designed to appeal to sensory modes of seeing, feeling, and understanding the ineffable—the Eucharist exemplifies Heidegger's notions of presence and withdrawal. Although my protocol was designed to trace and explore non-discursive rhetorics, observations and interviews revealed the importance of reading and writing in parishioners' experience. Several participants connected reading—the Bible, a devotional, a saint's autobiography—to the experience of being with Christ in the Eucharist. Participants also used adoration to reflect and meditate in writing. Chapter 4 details a confluence of rhetorics and affects that conditioned and enacted participant understandings of faith.

Chapter 5 attempts to bound ambient boundlessness. Using visual and multisensory autoethnography, I designed a protocol for engaging ambience: I studied this-now-here-ness in an ordinary pedestrian commute. The project engaged some of the myriad sounds, sights, smells, and rhythms of an ordinary neighborhood over a month-long period, tracing as much of the ambient environment as possible during daily thirty-minute walks to and from my office.

In *Plastic Bodies*, Tom Sparrow (2015) reexamines phenomenology from a new materialist perspective by making a distinction between perception, which is intentional and subject-directed, and sensation, which is embodied, affective, and object-directed. "Perception is personal while sensation is not," he argues (64). "Our identity is constituted," he adds "by the sensations we receive as well as the sensations we give off," and "these sensations do not belong to us, but rather we belong to them" (64). We are our environs; chapter 5 explores what this might mean, how it might work in practice, and what it looks, sounds, and feels like in one concrete example. The study was an attempt to explore nearness and distance by making the familiar strange. Autoethnography is especially well-suited to studies of ambient rhetorics and vibrant matter; indeed, it is a central means through which researchers in the field may operationalize those theories, empirically.

I used analytic autoethnography and made regular, meticulous observations of my commute, writing field notes immediately after each walk. I also wrote weekly analytic memos, shot at least two still photographs during each walk, and made sound walks, wherein I used an audio recorder and a directional microphone to capture rhythms—of footfalls in snow and ice, of car tires on wet pavement, of morning birdsong. Several long-exposure photographs evoke the movement and rhythms of my neighborhood, and I used documentary photography as a method not merely of data collection but rather as a way of being there—realist photographs that can stand alone as arguments and artifacts of particularity. I attempted meditative walks wherein I focused on one sensory experience—smells, for example—and attended to the wanderings of my mind as I moved through tree-lined streets.

I shot brief videos evoking non-human embodiment and movement—squirrels in trash cans, plastic bags filling like lungs suddenly taking in breath when the doors to my building opened, steam rising from the bowels of the physical plant, water rushing through sewer pipes beneath the pavement—out of sight yet lucid and full of rushing fury. My study demonstrates mutual vulnerability—we belong to our sensations and our environs, and we are vulnerable to the rhythms of our ambient worlds. Heidegger's notion of *Gelassenheit*, usually translated into English as "releasement," is an apt term for evoking our vulnerability to the things, spaces, moods, and affects that surround us.

These studies—though conducted in varied sites, with varied aims and participants—share much methodologically, and they play off of one another theoretically. All three studies were guided by theories focused on materiality, everyday practices, and ambient environs; all three are praxiographic in that they attend, above all, to *enactments*—to worlds thrown together. These chapters attend, as well, to sensory and affective forms of suasion—the tactile and haptic topographies of writing (chapter 3), the smells and sights of sensory artifacts (chapter 4), the sounds and rhythms of an ordinary neighborhood (chapter 5). All three chapters use visual methods as means for engaging *more*—more of what is there, in a given somewhere; more than what can be said or written or remembered by a fieldworker; more of what can be felt and intuited. And all three chapters demonstrate empirical rhetorics—they are predicated on the idea that we can study ambience systematically, that showing up to see what shows up can help us tune into the *more* that elusively conditions rhetorical enactments.

Mutual vulnerability is discussed in detail in chapter 5, but the concept is essential to chapters 3 and 4. I encourage readers to think about, for example, how the office arrangement of the media researchers in chapter 3 made them vulnerable to one another, or how the sensory artifacts discussed in chapter 4 assume a fundamental vulnerability of parishioners to the moods and affects endemic to faith. The notion of factorial rhetorics, discussed in chapter 3, can be easily discerned in the complex web of concepts, artifacts, and affects central to chapters 4 and 5. And the sensory artifacts at the heart of chapter 4 have fellow travelers in some of the artifacts discussed in chapters 3 and 5. In short, the findings from these chapters are reflected in and diffracted by the varying emphases and varied sites and participants discussed therein.

# PART II

*Lightening and Clearing*

# 3
## TOPOGRAPHIES AND TRAJECTORIES OF WRITING

After you've pulled up a chair, gotten comfortable, and made a few notes in longhand, what does your writing *look like*? What is the unique topography of the page—the contours, slopes, and confluences of your written letterforms, words, paragraphs, and paratexts? How does your writing show up to you, to the page, to the world?

During an observation with Mike, Michelle, and Jenn, media researchers who were brainstorming findings after recently completed focus group sessions, I learned the importance of such questions. I learned to pay attention to what we make visible to ourselves and others and to what the things we make visible actually *look like*. As John Berger (1980, 45) has argued, so much popular interest in visual phenomena is subdivided and atomized—we treat painting, photography, film, and everyday appearances as special interests within circumscribed domains. In the meantime, we forget (or willingly evade) "the meaning and enigma of visibility itself" (45).

The question of how we picture and enact our writing is one that breaks open assumptions about how we materialize our own thoughts and feelings, how some of those thoughts and feelings are made tangible, and how we present those thoughts and feelings to others in forms that are semi-permanently fixed—forms that travel across space and time. Writing has textures, valences, spacings, distributions, and arrangements whose full significance may only make sense *to us*. These topographies are stratigraphic; written words evince layers and years of learned and disciplined movements made tangible through our muscles, bones, and tendons—in the contours of which are embedded historical inflection points, arguments won and lost, and punctuated equilibriums in our development as writers and thinkers. The fact that these layers are both rhetorically saturated and visible for inspection is significant—perhaps even a little breathtaking if one focuses on what is, itself, *visible* when we write.

\*\*\*

On a warm, late September day, after two months of fieldwork, I arrived at the offices of Investigation and Foresight to observe a debrief—Mike, Michelle, and Jenn were meeting to discuss reactions to the series of four focus group sessions about online privacy they had recently conducted with almost ninety participants. After some deliberation and grumbling stomachs, they decided to debrief over a late lunch at Scotty's, a burger place three blocks from their office. I said I'd meet them there, then rushed to my office to return my camera equipment (tripod, digital camera, lenses). I felt self-conscious about lugging my gear into the restaurant and did not want Mike, Michelle, and Jenn to feel uncomfortable with a camera looming over their lunch.

But leaving the camera behind was a tactical blunder. Shortly after settling into a booth and ordering drinks, Jenn passed paper-clipped sheaves of focus group field notes to Mike and Michelle. Mike suggested that they should jump in with impressions about the focus group sessions. Michelle, though, argued that they each should first write down their thoughts to better organize and theme their impressions. After doing so, Michelle said, they could share what they found most arresting, giving them a means for noting where their individual ideas converged or drew apart.

Sitting in the booth next to Michelle, across from Mike, and diagonally from Jenn, I observed them as they wrote silently for several minutes. I was struck by *how* they wrote, by *where* they wrote on their respective pages of loose ruled paper, and by what their writing *looked like*. I would love to say that I had approached the visibility of their respective writing practices heuristically, that I began this observation with the methodological intention of attending to, comparing, and contrasting the topographies of my participants' varied writing practices.

The reality, however, is the opposite. The topographies of Mike's, Michelle's, and Jenn's writing were so arresting, so varied, and so tied to their own situated histories of argument, practice, and bodily comportments that my participants changed the way I approached such observations. The textures of their writing reflected their thinking and argument in crucial ways, and my attention to their individual topographies became important to my understanding of their work practices.

Mike is left-handed, and he began his notes on the right-hand side of the page, perhaps an inch from the edge, working down the page in a right-hand column. Once he neared the bottom of the page, he moved back to the top, writing in the white space remaining on the left-hand side of the page, creating a middle column. His paper filled with large and commanding print to the right, and after a few minutes, he began to draw rectangles around chunks of text. After creating a few rectangles, he continued to jot new ideas in the remaining white space until he filled most of the page, working his way down a third column to the left. After brainstorming, the only white space remaining was along the left-hand margin and in the lower-left corner of the page.

Jenn began writing at the left-hand margin and then stashed ideas in the center of the page. Eventually, she nested other items to the far right, underneath the centered notes. She wrote in a large and loopy cursive, often taking several lines of white space between items. After a few minutes she had filled her first page and moved to the back, continuing in the same fashion.

Michelle began with what seemed to be headings, justified to the left margin, with notes nested beneath each heading, which she underlined. She used less space and less spacing than Jenn, and she filled about ⅔ of her page by the time Jenn turned over her first page.

As the silent writing slowed, Jenn returned to previously untouched white space on her first page to add to the ideas she had already noted. In total, they spent eleven minutes in silent writing before Jenn suggested that they wind down to discuss their findings.

In my field notes and a subsequent analytic memo, I noted two strong impressions: first, I wondered whether each participant's unique writing practices were typical for them and whether those practices might tell me something about their respective thinking processes; second, I was fascinated by the workflow, the fact that these three media researchers sat in silence, writing both for themselves and for colleagues in the vague intimacy of a restaurant booth, as a way of preparing for a discussion about research findings from a major initiative. Even though I was at a tactical disadvantage on at least two accounts—I left my camera behind, and I was not prepared for the writing practices that emerged during this observation—my methodology, visual ethnography, and one of my methods, photo-elicitation, gave me a solid foundation for later exploring and understanding these written topographies. Although I didn't have my camera, I used my smartphone to snap photos of the handwritten pages so I could later discuss my participants' writing practices, using the photos as pivots for questions about how they write and how their writing reflects their organizational and argumentative thinking.

*\*\**

This chapter explores two crucial aspects of picturing writing and rhetorics: (a) the "meaning and enigma of visibility itself" in any discursive act and the concomitant methodological challenges of rigorously exploring and understanding rhetoric's visibility, and (b) the attendant material and haptic affordances and environs that shape complex, collaborative rhetorical work—the particularities and conditions of ambient this-now-here-ness in any given research site. To rigorously picture writing and, more important, to develop theoretical insights about how and why the visibility and tactility of writing matter in professional environments, I describe findings from a visual ethnography that deployed the participatory method of photo-elicitation as a means for better describing and presenting the rich materiality of writing and rhetorical work.

I begin by detailing the work environment at Investigation and Foresight, the media research firm that employed Mike, Michelle, and Jenn. I then discuss my methodology, my framing theory, and the practical methods of conducting a praxiography of writing in the organization. I return to Mike, Michelle, and Jenn to demonstrate the utility of photo-elicitation for exploring and theorizing both individual and collaborative writing work. Photo-elicitation helped me understand the topographies of participants' writing, the ways their material environments and rhetorical histories conditioned their communication practices, and the rationale motivating what they chose to make (and keep) visible to one another. Visibility itself was inescapably yoked to argumentative stability at Investigation and Foresight. What they consistently made visible—to themselves and to others—was inextricable from how they stabilized professional knowledge and understandings of their own organizational identity.

## VISUAL ETHNOGRAPHY AT INVESTIGATION AND FORESIGHT

The fact that Mike, Michelle, and Jenn chose a casual restaurant booth for one of their most formative project development sessions was no accident. To be sure, they'd missed lunch and were hungry, but by removing themselves from their office environment, they intentionally stripped away the distractions of colleagues, of other projects, and of the office itself. In the booth at Scotty's, their tools of rhetorical invention were self-consciously spare: they brought only their affective comportments, their memories of the focus group sessions, their professional experience, a few field notes, and the writing implements—pens and ruled paper. Each had a mobile phone, but none were used during the brainstorming session and subsequent discussion. Mike, Michelle, and Jenn understood that this was an important meeting in the trajectory of what would become, for them, an eight-month-long user privacy research project. This was, after all, the first official debrief session that followed two weeks of intensive focus group sessions.

But the acts of *poiesis*—the items brought forth and made visible to one another—were, at this point, unsettled, nascent, and processual. What they determined in this meeting, however, disproportionately shaped the scope and reach of the more formal written, visual, and oral deliverables that communicated their work to clients and colleagues—the work that represented their firm publicly. Connecting these contingent and early forms of *poiesis* to the later sedimentation and dissemination of ideas required a sufficiently long methodological view.

The significance of this inventional moment, in other words, can be understood only when viewed in the context of the full project. In the remainder of this section, I describe Investigation and Foresight in more detail, and I likewise describe my methodological long view—the theories, methodologies, and methods that helped me articulate daily acts of *poiesis* across the course of Mike, Michelle, and Jenn's research on consumer privacy.

**Inside Investigation and Foresight**

At the time of my study, Investigation and Foresight (I&F; this is a pseudonym) was an independent media research firm with offices and financial support provided by a large research university located in the midwestern United States. In this unique arrangement, professional media researchers and project managers such as Mike, Michelle, and Jenn worked alongside faculty and graduate students from the university. Often, the firm's projects emerged as joint efforts between faculty members and non-faculty researchers. Just as often, non-faculty researchers developed and disseminated work from projects that were not affiliated with the university (this was the case with the privacy research discussed here). Investigation and Foresight employed several professional staff members and interns—three different graduate student interns were involved at various points with the privacy research project, adding expertise in graphic design, videography, and audiovisual editing. Investigation and Foresight was uniquely situated within the broader campus community but was viewed as an independent hub of creativity and industry influence.

Investigation and Foresight's energy and public profile led me to see the firm as a site of potential research. As a faculty fellow in emerging media at the university, I had several informal conversations with members of I&F; these conversations were invigorating—we shared similar interests, I found, in social media, in media ecologies more broadly, and in the firm's role as a university-industry mediator. After getting to know several of the firm's principals, I approached Mike with nothing more than a request to study what they do. In other words, I had no set agenda other than to explore the writing and rhetorics that mediate work at Investigation and Foresight.

I was invited to create a formal proposal and protocol that would be reviewed by both Mike, the firm's director, and Michael, the firm's faculty liaison. Through this process, my study was shaped as much by Investigation and Foresight as it was by my own scholarly inquiry. My contribution to the discussion was largely methodological: I suggested visual ethnography as a possible approach; I indicated my interests in tracing *all* the writing that potentially mediated work at I&F, in tracing oral discussions to the extent possible given my methods, and in their spaces and tools of interaction. In turn, Mike and Michael, in consultation with Michelle and Jenn, suggested that I study a nascent project investigating user privacy in online spaces. This project, they reasoned, would allow me to trace their research from the first stages of ideation to the dissemination of their work in a variety of industry-focused deliverables.

I was grateful for their direction. What was planned as a relatively brief project—two to three months, maximum—grew and evolved over almost nine months, from the first ideation session to my final interviews. I was able to trace most of the communicative interactions shaping and mediating an entire I&F project, from start to finish.

Mike, Michelle, and Jenn were determined to study user privacy in online applications for three primary reasons. First, they recognized the need for systematic research investigating what kinds of information users were willing to share and with whom; second, such a project was timely, given recent public backlash over changes to Facebook's default privacy settings; and third, the project came during a moment when I&F was interested in expanding the kinds of consulting projects it offered to clients, so the privacy research was viewed as a building block of future firm expertise.

The timing of my own involvement was fortuitous. I was able to see how I&F generated and developed protocols for a specific project. I was able to follow along as Mike, Michelle, and Jenn shaped and executed the privacy research and, more important, how they discussed the role of such research as contributing to the firm's portfolio of services. I was able to trace their work in a variety of professional genres that shaped their organizational image and identity.

## A Praxiography of Writing

I used visual ethnography at Investigation and Foresight to address three primary aims: (a) to trace, as comprehensively as possible, the material environs of Mike, Michelle, and Jenn as they developed and executed a major research project; (b) to document, as comprehensively as possible, the practices of media research—from brainstorming to focus group sessions to the collaborative writing of summative reports; and (c) to provide, in my scholarship, both visual and written presentations of media research in all of its remarkable materiality (Mol 2002).

I used both still photography and videography alongside traditional ethnographic methods. Still photography was my primary mode of visual documentation, but I also used videography to document and analyze positioning, gestures, turn taking in verbal discourse, and other aspects of everyday talk and writing that cannot be fully accounted for in field notes alone. Still photographs provided a record of artifacts and material environs and provided presentations of the research site that could be both analyzed and used in published scholarship.

Visual ethnography thus shaped the entire research project—the ways in which I would observe Mike, Michelle, and Jenn; the period in which I would be embedded as an observer; and the fieldwork practices I would deploy during my time with I&F. But, as Clay Spinuzzi (2003) notes, methodologies reflect and direct theoretical perspectives. My visual ethnography of I&F was guided, theoretically, by writing, activity, and genre research (WAGR).

In WAGR approaches, socio-cultural theories of communication and rhetorical approaches to the study of genre are brought together to explore everyday practices and contexts of communication (Russell 2009; Spinuzzi 2010). As I have argued previously (McNely 2017), WAGR provides theoretical and methodological lenses for studying what Jody Shipka (2011, 15, original emphases) describes as mediated action: the "varied and various places *in which*, times *at which*, and resources *with which* literate activity is typically accomplished." Attention is thus given to the specific places, times, and resources that support communication. WAGR is well-suited to studies of complex collaborative writing projects because analyses are grounded in the documentation and tracing of mediated actions and the broader activities they support. It is, in short, an epistemist approach to fieldwork.

But analysis of my project was informed by ambient rhetorical theory (Rickert 2013) and object-oriented philosophy (Harman 2016). Rather than representing different schools of research practice, these approaches may be held in productive tension with a WAGR-oriented methodology. WAGR's emphasis on everyday practices, organizational and societal norms, and the material environs of composing and communicating are complemented by new materialist and object-oriented theories that account for non-human agency and suasion. The variables that shape the practices of professionals such as Mike, Michelle, and Jenn may be unaccounted for in many methodologies, but they are central to a WAGR study informed by ambient and object-oriented rhetorics.

Mediated actions matter, but so too do the tools, technologies, and material spaces that both facilitate and condition those actions. The practices of participants were a key area of focus, but those practices were never divorced from the non-human actors and spaces that facilitated and conditioned them. Indeed, those practices are inseparable from non-human and environmental participation. To interpolate Bruno Latour (1994), a human with a pen and paper is different than any of those actors alone. When combined with visual ethnography, tracing, accounting for, and interrogating the roles played by non-human actors and material environs become more feasible than relying on traditional (non-visual) methods alone.

I used several different methods to support triangulation and iterative reflexivity (Ashmore 1989). To facilitate observations and document the general practices of participants, I wrote field notes during or immediately after every observation I conducted, whether the observation was planned or informal. Because of my physical proximity to the I&F offices (a five- to six-minute walk) and my strong working relationship with participants, I was able to conduct regular formal observations when Mike, Michelle, and Jenn met to discuss aspects of the privacy research project, as well as informal observations wherein I simply stopped by the office when time and space allowed.

During data collection and analysis, I wrote analytic memos that helped me compare and contrast observed practices, synthesize ideas, and identify discrepant data. In almost every observation I also composed still photographs that documented (a) the scene overall (for example, Michelle at her desk, with a wide-angle view of her office and various items ready to hand), (b) the specific tools or technologies in use during the observation, and (c) the positionality of participants to both their material environs and colleagues. During major work sessions (these were identified as such by participants and were always planned observations), I also composed brief videos of participant discussions and the tools mediating them. These videos helped me document and analyze turn taking, concurrent talk, gestural communication, and tools in use.

I also used collaborative methods to explore how participants accomplished their work and how they viewed that work as part of a team. My protocol included a series of three semi-structured interviews with each of the main participants, as well as one interview each—near the beginning of the project—with four other members of the firm who provided support and research to Mike, Michelle, and Jenn. These semi-structured interviews focused on the scope and plan for research, the roles performed by each participant, and the tools, spaces, and practices that mediated their work.

As the privacy project developed, interviews became more open-ended and focused on the ways writing and communication mediated work for each participant. In the second and third interviews with Mike, Michelle, and Jenn, I used photo-elicitation to explore the tools, technologies, and material environs that shaped the privacy research project. One strength of photo-elicitation is that it helped me make visible to my participants many of the taken-for-granted forms of writing that mediated their work. By making these forms of writing visible *to them*, I was better able to interrogate how and why such writing mediated the practices and artifacts they identified as the product of their work (their "actual writing").

I followed I&F's privacy research project over nearly nine months of fieldwork—using a variety of methods in concert—across many instances of observation, from the initial stages of planning through dissemination of public-facing deliverables. Because of my friendly relationship with the I&F principals, I had unique access to their everyday practices—in the office, outside the office, in the circulation of draft documents through email and file-sharing applications, and on social media. I collected almost 200 participant-produced written artifacts, made and transcribed over 60 hours of audio recordings of meetings and interviews (both informal and formal), conducted more than 20 semi-structured and open-ended interviews, composed over 400 photographs, and traced my participants' communication practices through 2 different social networks—collecting and archiving over 2,400 tweets while simultaneously monitoring several hundred Facebook status updates.

My approach to analyzing this data was twofold.

First, visual data were analyzed iteratively and progressively. As I conducted fieldwork, I also reviewed, annotated, and wrote analytic memos about observed phenomena and practices that were documented visually. This iterative analysis is a key way in which visual ethnography can be adapted to studies of writing and rhetoric. It is important for the researcher of writing and communication practices—and even more to the point, for the researcher interested in ambient environs and non-human mediation—to consistently and frequently triangulate visual data against both observational field notes and participant feedback. By consistently exploring the visual data against my ongoing impressions and reactions in field notes, I was able to engage the ambient communicative contexts and material environs of I&F. I was also able to develop and iterate interview questions grounded in the data record, using photo-elicitation to prompt such interviews.

Second, transcripts, field notes, analytic memos, and participant-produced written artifacts were analyzed using process and descriptive first-cycle coding techniques, then themed using second-cycle pattern coding (see Miles, Huberman, and Saldaña 2013; Saldaña 2009). With these coding techniques, I was able to focus on participant processes and the tools and environments that mediated them. In the remainder of this chapter, I focus on the significance of the visibility—and stability—of written communication in media research and the material environs and tools that mediate these visibilities.

## FACTORIAL RHETORICS

The idea that material artifacts and environs are potentially suasive is one of the most consequential arguments in Thomas Rickert's *Ambient Rhetoric* (2013). Suasion is ambient and "therefore prior to rhetoric," forming the "condition of possibility for rhetoric's emergence" (159). To acknowledge these ideas is to acknowledge what seems to be a rhetorical doubling—material suasion and discursive attunement, *together*, constitute rhetorical becoming. But attunement to material suasion and openness toward the conditions of rhetoric's emergence are more than merely doubled. The relationship is instead *factorial*.

Ambient rhetoric helps us understand rhetorical events that emerge in complex ways from many intra-acting factors. In any act or moment of *poiesis*, the factors or variables are multiple, combinatorial, historically laden, individually situated, and idiosyncratic; the products of such variables are factorial in the sense that they proliferate quickly and produce potentially dizzying follow-on effects. Doubling 5 yields 10, but a factorial of 5 yields 120. The effects of 120 variables may be many orders of magnitude more complex than the effects of 5; ambient rhetoric, I argue, is factorial—suasive variables proliferate, multiply, and diffract kaleidoscopically. Such variables are suasive before and beyond our intentions, any impressions we can grasp, and any understandings we can articulate.

Empirically studying factorial rhetorics is very different than studying rhetorics with a traditional perspective—as the product of human agency and intent in some circumscribed "rhetorical situation." Suasion is in things and places and sensations, but *how*? And how do suasive material environments inculcate factorial rhetorics, wherein humans—entangled and immersed in remarkable materiality—respond, appropriate, and extend suasion in *poiesis*? Rickert (2013, 164) notes that "persuasion is prior to rhetoric. Worldly affect, modulated in persuasion, itself hollowed out the space for rhetoric's emergence." Rhetoric, he argues, is a mode of attunement to the world. We work from originary entanglements to bring forth or make visible something different or new. Attunement to ambient suasion is the very ground of rhetoric, and rhetoric is the ground of *poiesis*.

We can investigate factorial rhetorics empirically with methodologies and methods that facilitate the kinds of attunement Rickert describes. Picturing writing and rhetorics, for example, may foster methodological *poiesis*. At Investigation and Foresight, visual methodologies and methods not only helped make visible and bring forth the everyday acts of writing and communication central to media research, but they also brought into relief the central role of material and spatial suasion. Visual methods helped participants interrogate their own practices of attunement—their own ways of working with what is available to them in their everyday work environments, the disclosures made and appropriated in those environments, and the acts of *poiesis* fostered by their rhetorical becoming in those environments.

To explore factorial rhetorics, I focus first on perhaps the most mundane feature of any contemporary built environment: walls.

### The I&F Conference Room

Mike was proud of the I&F conference room. With four tall café-style tables, several adjustable chairs, and a few low-slung armchairs, it was the kind of space that afforded comfort and configurability. During the privacy project, the conference room changed several times to suit the needs of I&F staff and focus group participants.

Mike was especially proud of the wall on one long side of the rectangular space: gleaming and bright, covered in whiteboard paint, the wall was a key location of rhetorical invention and *poiesis*. It was a space where I&F colleagues frequently made rhetorical attunements visible to one another. This environment—a long and prominent wall, the special paint that transformed its surface into a tool for writing, with ample space for inventional starts and stops—was a suasive factor in the work of I&F. Differential attunements to the wall by I&F colleagues—to its affordances and to the inventional space of the conference room more broadly—served as the ground for the more identifiable forms of rhetoric that writing researchers are accustomed to tracing: note making, brainstorming, outlining, and drafting.

In this section, I detail two scenarios in which the material environments of I&F fostered and supported factorial rhetorics: the material suasion of the space itself and ad hoc attunements to that suasion by participants, and the collaborative suasion made visible and carried out by those same participants.

Most of the planning for the privacy research took place—in the conference room—during the summer, in anticipation of focus group sessions the researchers would hold early in the fall semester. The proximity of I&F to the university campus meant there was, nearby, a wealth of potential participants from several demographics important to the firm. Michelle and Jenn were able to recruit from undergraduate, graduate, and faculty populations so that each focus group session included a cross-section of participants in terms of age, gender identity, ethnic background, and familiarity with popular social media platforms and mobile/web-based services (such as internet or mobile banking). I&F planned four focus group sessions: each would have twenty to twenty-five participants who would provide insights on privacy concerns during 150-minute sessions. In September, Michelle and Jenn, with occasional oversight from Mike, conducted these sessions in the I&F conference room.

The conference room was transformed. The four café tables—often grouped together during I&F meetings—were separated, and each was surrounded by four or five chairs. The tables were covered with white butcher paper and a variety of artifacts—what Michelle described as "thinking tools" (figure 3.1). Crayons, colored pencils and pens, stress balls, bouncy balls, loose scratch paper, and sticky notes were ready for focus group participants. The butcher paper was a surface on which participants could doodle, jot ideas, draw, or make notes.

During each session, Michelle and Jenn led participants through exercises designed to elicit opinions about online privacy. According to Michelle and Jenn, one of the most useful was the "privacy stoplight." Participants were asked to jot a variety of online activities on sticky notes—everything from "posting a tweet" to "transferring money" to "online dating." They were then directed to place each note on a stoplight Michelle and Jenn had created: an easel with large paper circles of red, yellow, and green. Online activities were thus clustered according to the level of comfort felt by each participant while completing

*Figure 3.1. Focus group table with "thinking tools" and participant jottings. Author photo.*

them—where green indicated little to no trepidation, yellow indicated some caution or worry, and red indicated clear discomfort (figure 3.2).

The stoplight exercise eventually moved from the easel to the wall-length whiteboard. After participants had clustered activities on the stoplight and categorized their levels of comfort, the whiteboard became a space of deeper reflection.

Focus group activities had their genesis in the discussions and planning notes made by Mike, Michelle, and Jenn several weeks before the sessions. From those first acts of speaking—and making visible—the techniques to be used, a written protocol was developed and various artifacts were gathered and enrolled. Unstated, though, was the significance of the conference room wall; the whiteboard's affordances were assumed, and those assumptions shaped the activities carried out by participants. Before the final draft of the protocol was complete, conversations in the office, email exchanges, and notes on the conference-room whiteboard were mediated actions that helped shape and refine the eventual focus group sessions.

During the sessions themselves, many more mediated actions and acts of visibility—many of which were ad hoc—shaped enactments. Jenn and Michelle talked with participants and with each other to manage the activities planned in the protocol. Participants talked with one another and made visible the ideas that seemed significant. They jotted notes on butcher paper, they doodled and drew, they wrote on sticky notes and

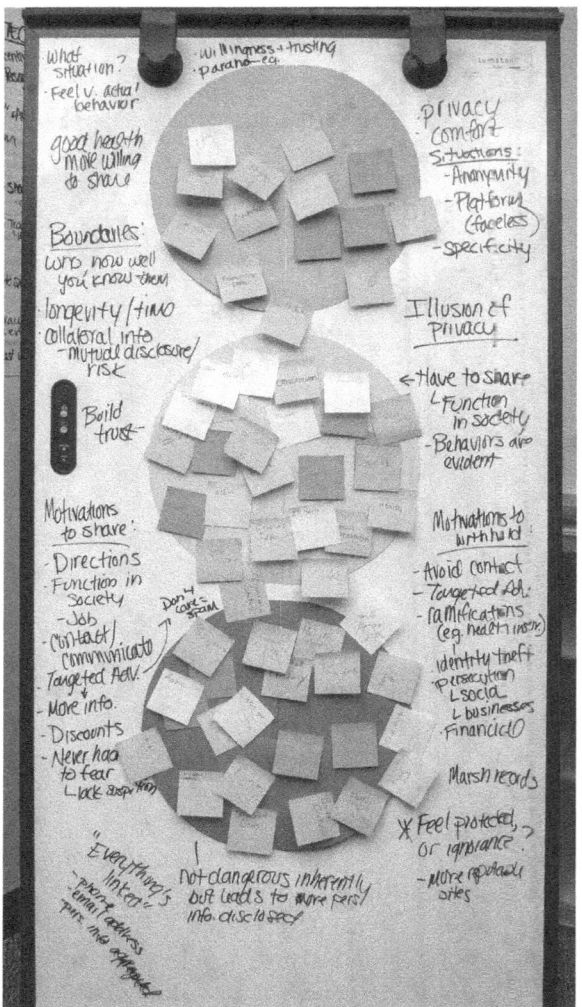

Figure 3.2. Privacy stoplight exercise from focus group session. Author photo.

on the whiteboard; they made their ideas visible across a shifting topography of surfaces and spaces. In collaborative acts of *poiesis*, Michelle, Jenn, and focus group participants worked with—and were influenced by—an array of material resources whose use was, in turn, circumscribed by spatial affordances: an easel, the covered space of a café table, the wall-length whiteboard, the marginal space of sticky notes.

The work of focus group research at I&F was a continual process of making ideas visible—first to oneself and then to others—and then sifting and winnowing those visibilities through acts of nuanced understanding and refinement (such as the clarifications written by Michelle and Jenn and visible on the margins of the "privacy stoplight" in figure 3.2). These visibilities were foundational to the *poiesis* of both focus group participants and I&F researchers. But they were forms of visibility that would be largely *in*visible in the firm's eventual public deliverables. Like the contributions of Lauren detailed in chapter 1, they were moments and artifacts of *known contingency* that would be folded into more stable genres—in this case, whitepapers and conference talks—genres that would be experienced both internally and publicly as *permanent* forms of knowledge and work.

### From Sticky Notes to Whitepapers

A trope of professional and technical writing research suggests that most of the work that mediates and supports written documentation in stable, professional genres is invisibilized by those self-same genres. Dorothy Winsor (1990), in a now canonical example, demonstrated this idea in the context of engineering communication. For the engineers she studied, writing was seen as a part of the job but not as part of *engineering* (58). Despite the many different forms of writing that mediate daily engineering practice—from instrumental inscriptions to lab notebooks to outlines—engineers themselves saw writing as an appendage to their work, as the final step in "writing up" and sharing the results of their "actual" work.

One of the key reasons for this view, which persists in many fields, is that the definition of writing itself is insufficient. Writing, for Winsor's engineers and many other professionals, is defined as the final, official documentation that circulates among colleagues. Note making, outlining, brainstorming, emailing, and any number of other contingent, mediated actions carried out in writing are simply not considered writing—not "actual writing," as Valerie, the graphic design major on the *Transmedia Indiana* project, had suggested (see figure 1.3). But as I have demonstrated previously (McNely 2010, 2011a, 2011b, 2013b, 2017), these forms of everyday writing may be (a) made visible, (b) traced through the course of projects, and (c) shown to significantly shape the more recognizable forms of writing sanctioned by professionals in official genres. Although public audiences see only what ends up in the final report, my own work (and the work of many others—see, for example, Latour 1988; Rule 2018; Wickman 2010) has shown that it's often writing all the way down.

A pivotal moment of collaboration and invention during I&F's privacy research demonstrates this dynamic. I have previously described

102  TOPOGRAPHIES AND TRAJECTORIES OF WRITING

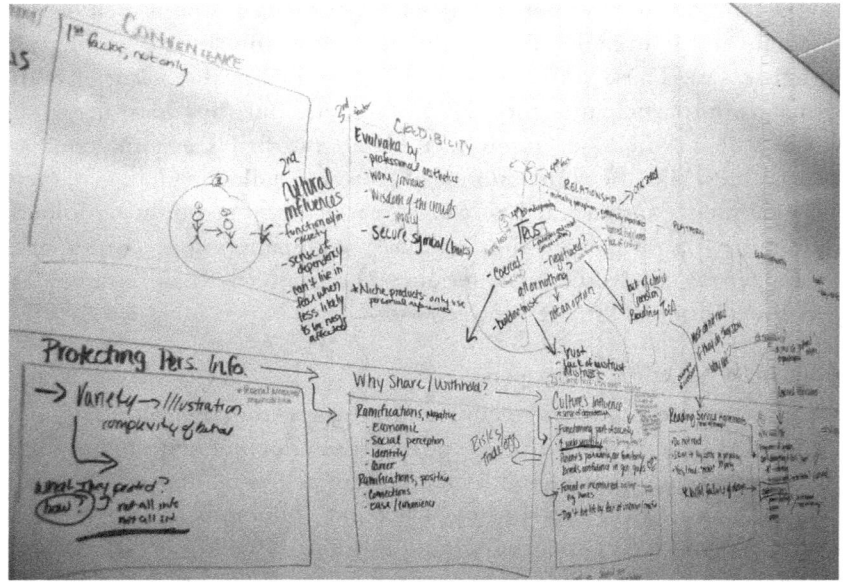

*Figure 3.3. The conference room whiteboard with a key interstitial genre: the project outline. Author photo.*

this work as "interstitial writing" (McNely 2011a)—the kinds of writing and rhetorical work that mediate the movement from early ideas on ephemeral materials such as sticky notes to finalized documentation in official genres. Interstitial writing is rarely, if ever, visible in official genres, yet its visibility is crucial to organizational knowledge work. And such writing is often invisible *as writing* to the people who produce it. By tracing some of this writing at I&F, I was able to demonstrate how everyday mediated actions, accomplished in writing and in verbal and gestural rhetorics, significantly shaped both epistemological and ontological organizational outcomes.

Sticky notes, whiteboard jottings, one-off ad hoc conversations in the office, outlines, and collaborative writing sessions comprised a through-line in I&F's professional work. It was in and through such collective mediated actions and interstitial genres that foundations were built: what Mike, Michelle, and Jenn would eventually recognize and sanction as "findings" and organizational knowledge and how such knowledge positioned the organization—what it *was*, as a firm, in the media research industry, and what it *could be* for new or existing clients. Propping up this activity was the wall-length whiteboard in the I&F conference room.

Small bits of writing in unofficial genres circulated among participants and eventually collected like sediment in a riverbed, creating the foundation for I&F's findings about consumer privacy concerns. What Mike, Michelle, and Jenn did with those bits of writing after the focus group sessions unfolded across several meetings, including the debrief meeting with which this chapter began (and to which we will soon return) and, more important, across many hours of individual and collaborative analysis by Michelle and Jenn. These moments of analysis and interpretation—these many hours of difficult and sometimes tedious work—culminated in a key interstitial genre, a project outline, which relied on the affordances of the wall-length whiteboard (figure 3.3).

After the initial debrief session, Michelle and Jenn coded and analyzed video from focus group sessions, returned to the results from exercises such as the privacy stoplight (figure 3.2), and triangulated their analysis by discussing with one another the insights they were developing as analysis progressed. They also held both ad hoc and planned meetings with Mike to discuss their findings. I am not doing justice to the many hours of work Mike, Michelle, and Jenn devoted to analysis between the focus group sessions and the creation and refinement of the outline in figure 3.3. I'm zooming past hours and hours of work to arrive at a brief, pivotal period in the development of I&F's privacy research program.

The outline, which remained relatively stable and visible for several weeks, was a crucial written genre in the eventual privacy research project. It was never to be seen outside I&F, yet its visibility *within* the organization made the more recognizable and public fruits of the researchers' efforts possible. It was the epistemological foundation on which all of I&F's public-facing genres were built—a series of industry talks, an interactive, web-based infographic, a series of videos, a number of tweets and Facebook posts, a whitepaper promoting similar research, and a technical report detailing insights from the study for other media research professionals. This outline—developed, iterated, and stabilized on the I&F whiteboard—thus represented an important interstitial locus of writing within the privacy project, with its own specific topography shaped by the material and haptic affordances of the space itself and by the contributions of the different people who had continual access to it and who added to it, refined it, and discussed it. It emerged factorially from bits of writing and talk over several weeks of research, and it functioned factorially and centrifugally in the development and dissemination of subsequent deliverables in several different public- and industry-facing genres.

During a meeting about six weeks after their focus group research and amid Michelle and Jenn's ongoing analysis of the data, Mike,

*Figure 3.4. Open-plan office space at Investigation and Foresight. Author photo.*

Michelle, and Jenn met in the conference room to theme their findings. In this session, they itemized, juxtaposed, and built from many of the smaller, ongoing forms of analysis they had conducted—alone and together—since the final focus group session. These included the initial debrief session (described at the beginning of this chapter), coding of some of the video data composed during focus groups, coding of participant responses to the major exercises (such as the privacy stoplight), and, significantly, ad hoc discussions afforded by the open-plan office space (figure 3.4). In their meeting they began to formulate, refine, and make visible and stable the ideas that would be central to their research. Although this process is not groundbreaking—qualitative researchers in academe and industry take similar approaches to analysis—it is nonetheless fruitful to trace the factorial rhetorics involved in such work: the material circulation and concrescence of many smaller written and verbal acts afforded by the working environment.

Ideas constantly circulated verbally and through small bits of writing: Mike, Michelle, and Jenn shared space next to one another on a mezzanine overlooking much of the activity among the other members of the firm. It was not unusual for any member of I&F to exploit the affordances of this arrangement, providing verbal feedback and ideas to one another in a free-flowing manner. Mike had a small whiteboard in his cubicle, and I observed him jot ideas on it and then, in a louder than normal speaking voice, encourage Jenn or Michelle to come over so he could briefly discuss ideas with them. Similar exchanges occurred between Michelle and Jenn, especially as they analyzed data from the focus group sessions. Either might say to the other, without leaving her own desk, something of consequence about the coding process or about a particular participant response. In turn, the other would jot a note or offer feedback.

In much the same manner that the material affordances of the conference room whiteboard shaped the activities and ideas generated in the focus group sessions, so too did the open-plan office facilitate the relatively free circulation of ideas during analysis and theming of focus group data. Walls are suasive, but so are half-walls. The ambient environs contributed in no small measure to participants' ability to ideate, provide feedback, and refine analyses. The three media researchers also often shared and responded to ideas in writing—semi-publicly or publicly, in services such as Facebook and Twitter (where ideas might be further refined through feedback from other industry professionals), and privately, through text messaging and collaborative writing in Google Docs.

Ideas must eventually be stabilized and refined. Moments of everyday *poiesis* moved Mike, Michelle, and Jenn toward a more stable and durable form of visibility, knowledge production, and ontological realization. The stabilization of these ideas is grounded by the *literal visibility* of writing; the whiteboard wall in the I&F conference room became the space where a roadmap or blueprint was generated from the smaller, everyday acts of contingent *poiesis* made along the way. The very best ideas were brought forth, but not all were made visible and stable on the whiteboard. The topography of the whiteboard outline represents the fruits of collaborative sedimentation and concrescence over the course of the project. Many new layers were laid down, some were subsumed by others, some were erased. What remained was visible to all, open to scrutiny and refinement but also stabilized in a way that promoted next steps: moving from the outline to formal deliverables in recognizable professional genres.

The importance of the wall, the whiteboard, and the outline in the eventual public-facing work of I&F cannot be understated. It certainly was not understated by Michelle and Jenn, whose admonition, in bold, underlined capital letters—"DO NOT ERASE"—helped stabilize and keep visible the central insights of their research and the plans for making that research public. The outline's visibility initially took shape over the course of one meeting among Mike, Michelle, and Jenn, but it was

106   TOPOGRAPHIES AND TRAJECTORIES OF WRITING

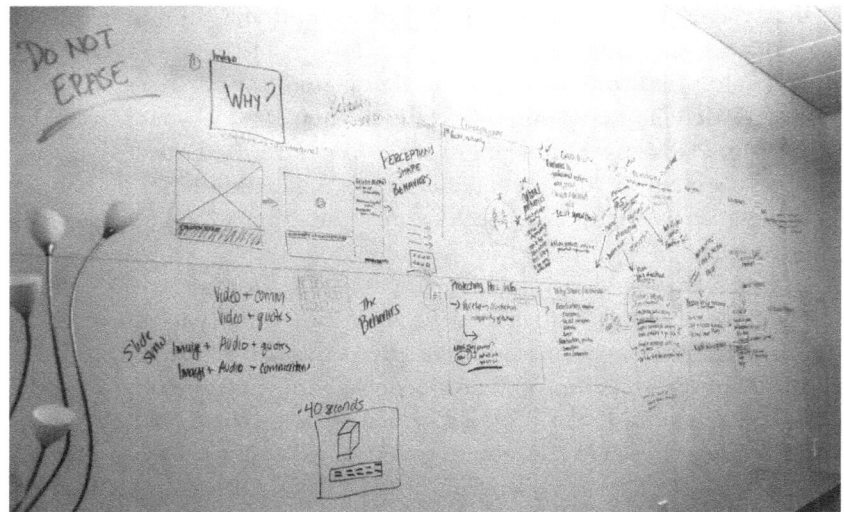

*Figure 3.5. "DO NOT ERASE": conference room whiteboard with semi-stable project outline. Author photo.*

refined over several subsequent ad hoc and formal meetings. Its written topography was thus shaped by all three researchers, whose acts of individual and collaborative *poiesis* in the conference room were informed by additional input from myriad other sources and interactions. The fact that it was visible—and that its visibility was stable—enabled inventional iterations and refinements. The outline remained on the board in essentially the same basic form over eight weeks, with refinements added as the team developed work in formal genres.

In both the focus group sessions and the subsequent planning and analysis sessions, walls were materially suasive and formed the ground of rhetorical possibility and *poiesis*. Half-walls enabled fluid exchange; the conference wall visibilized and stabilized the most consequential exchanges. These mediated actions substantively shaped professional forms of *poiesis*. Interstitial visibilities—drawings on butcher paper, sticky notes in the stoplight exercise, the whiteboard outline—eventually assumed new and more durable forms of visibility in professional, public-facing genres.

### THE MEANING AND ENIGMA OF VISIBILITY

In the booth at Scotty's restaurant, I watched three different topographies of writing take shape. Later, I used photo-elicitation to explore how and why those topographies emerged. Photo-elicitation uses visual phenomena as pivots in semi-structured or open-ended interviews. The visual phenomena may be made by participants, they may be part of a participant's everyday life, or they may be selected by a researcher. My methodology—visual ethnography—generated many photographs of participant enactments: the mediated actions I observed during fieldwork. Together, fieldwork photographs and photo-elicitation interviews helped make my participants' familiar, everyday environments temporarily strange, opening new routes to understanding about their *poietic* practices.

Everyday work often becomes so routinized that we may not even be aware of our actions, tools, and sensory environments. But visual ethnography documents and suspends those practices. And photo-elicitation interviews, drawn from fieldwork images, can encourage participants to step outside their routinized practices—helping them consider how those practices became routinized, why they became routinized, and what those entrenched practices mean. Photo-elicitation is a way of engaging the meaning and enigma of visibility *with* participants. We can learn about which material artifacts are necessary to work and why; the ways the positions, structures, and adaptations of spatial and environmental surroundings condition work; the things made visible and the things hidden; the means through which ideas circulate—on paper, on digital screens, on sticky notes, on whiteboards, on the backs of hands. Visual ethnography and photo-elicitation can help writing researchers better understand topographies of writing.

Michelle began writing what appeared to be headings—short phrases that were justified left and written in a bold and strong script. She wrote several such headings and underlined them before returning to the first and then to each in turn, nesting ideas underneath them. Although there may be nothing particularly unusual about the development of Michelle's page, it seemed clear to me that she had a very specific process that she had used before and with which she was comfortable. The eventual topography of her page differed dramatically from both Mike's and Jenn's. Indeed, each person's page was strikingly different from the others.

This may seem trivial—*of course* three different media researchers of different ages and backgrounds and hometowns produced writing that looked different from one another. But this leads to more meaningful questions: How did these writing practices develop? Why, in other words, does each person write the way they do? Why do their respective pages look the way they do? And how cognizant were they of their own histories and idiosyncrasies of writing?

During my second interview with Michelle, I showed her two of the photographs I had taken (with my mobile phone) of her notes during the debrief session at Scotty's. I asked her to tell me more about the practice of first creating headings and then adding nested, related items, point by point. I showed her the page and then asked her, in essence, why it looks the way it does and how it came to look that way. I wanted her to think about and talk through how her writing takes shape and becomes visible, for her own use and for her colleagues.

She said: "I like to conserve space on the page to leave lots of room for notes. . . . And I'm a former debater, so I'm, I mean I've stopped writing without vowels, and I don't always write everything in a flow chart, but you know . . . there's only a limited amount of space on the page, and it's very important to get every point there. So, I think my note taking is driven by the fact that I used to debate." Debate experience had deeply conditioned her thinking and writing processes. Although she was cognizant of how debate influenced her thinking, this is something I was not likely to intuit from fieldwork alone. It was not something I would have even considered asking about. Instead, it was something I came to understand only because I was attuned to her writing processes and, more important, because I was able to *make visible to her* what I had observed.

To be sure, I could have relied on my field notes and asked her questions about her writing process. But *showing* her what I observed was essential to understanding her experience. Fieldwork photos of the topography of Michelle's writing helped me elicit these insights. Although she was cognizant of the ways debate informed her thinking, she was not fully aware of how that experience influenced her *composing processes*; during our photo-elicitation interview, she began to see her own writing anew and to connect the topography of her writing to her understanding of her debate-trained thinking.

> BRIAN: It seems to me that you have a very, kind of, orderly style of debrief. Like, here are the things not only that were important, but here's how they relate to each other, maybe. . . . You're figuring it out as you write, maybe?
>
> MICHELLE: Mmhmmm. Yeah. Building an argument while I write.
>
> BRIAN: Okay. So you feel yourself doing that? Is it something that you're cognizant of?
>
> MICHELLE: Yeah, it is actually. Everything is structured as an argument.
>
> BRIAN: And that's because of your debate background, do you think?
>
> MICHELLE: Yeah. Speech and debate, oh definitely.

Michelle reflected on how the structure of the debrief session was different than usual. In a typical debrief, Mike, Michelle, and Jenn would not write beforehand; instead, each would take turns verbalizing insights and impressions while Jenn wrote them down. The debrief session at Scotty's, however, gave each researcher room to map all their impressions on paper before interacting with one another. Michelle was the last to speak up, and several minutes elapsed between the end of the silent writing session and her first verbal contribution. The fact that she had already written her impressions in an orderly way afforded Mike and Jenn more time to elaborate their own ideas—Michelle didn't feel the need to jump in because her impressions were organized, visible, and stable.

I asked Michelle about the value of the process they used at Scotty's: "It gave us a chance to all think about what we got out of it, and I think that maybe . . . I don't know if more unique ideas came out of it, but everybody got a chance to think about their perspective or their take . . . without being influenced by what everyone else was saying." She added: "Maybe the orderly process of discussing was part of my debate influence too because you've got . . . one person goes through their flow and then you go up and point by point go through it." It was Michelle's idea to engage the silent writing practices at the start of the debrief meeting. As she reflected on the connections between debate and her writing, Michelle began to see her processes in a new light. "A lot of my notes," she said, "include [a] thought . . . arrow . . . more about the thought, which is totally linked to debate." "It's a really geeky way of processing things," she added.

In Mike's photo-elicitation interview, he told me that boxing items and beginning from the right-hand side of the page reflected the ways he liked to sift and winnow ideas. He used the page as he would a whiteboard—"I'm just as likely to start [from] left to right as I am right [to] left," he said. But Mike did not have Michelle's debate background; instead, he told me about his history of poor penmanship and the desire "to quickly capture key thoughts" to provide "enough detail so they're self-explanatory when you look at them two weeks later, or somebody else looks at them and says, 'I think I get that.' " Mike thinks quickly and writes quickly, but writing with too much urgency produces unreadable topographies that are impossible to traverse.

His solution is rooted in past failures—he said his handwriting was not "user friendly" or "teacher friendly," so he generates groups of standalone ideas, rendered quickly and legibly. His practice of boxing snippets did not connect ideas but rather demonstrated that ideas *weren't connected*. "If I wanted to do that [make explicit connections], I would have had adjoining lines or some signifier to say they're linked," he said. "They were really standalone things," he added, impressions "we'd link up appropriately when writing up the outputs [i.e., in formal genres]. So that was really the exercise: I was just covering a page."

Mike's note-making practices were useful in brainstorming and data analysis, but he wouldn't use this process, he said, when working in professional genres. He was cognizant, therefore, of when the strategy of filling and boxing served him and when it did not. Like Michelle, he also noted that this was not a typical debrief session, as the usual process involved verbalizations with a designated scribe (usually Jenn). "Somebody else will be catching it on the whiteboard so it'll be legible," he said. I asked how the experience of reflective writing at the beginning of the debrief session related to the in-process findings they had developed to that point.

Writing first "allowed for a natural consistency for what was top of mind for each of us to emerge when we went back to the paper and started to share. But it also meant that we were sort of not inhibited by each other in terms of the kind of, the less obvious thoughts we'd have—that one of us might think of an idea, well, it was gonna get expressed because we were writing it down." "And that's [taking time to write first] not something that you've done here all the time?" I asked. "I haven't done it here before," Mike said, adding, "I've done it a few times in my past life and it worked well." "I don't want to make too much of this," I said, "but I do want to be clear: Did the experience at Scotty's kind of reignite the value of doing that kind of thing?" Mike replied: "Yeah, yeah. No question."

For Mike, making ideas visible and stable was a crucial aspect of media research. But his normal process for doing so at I&F had always been to verbalize ideas, usually in a group, while relying on a designated scribe. The debrief session at Scotty's, however, promoted a more factorial understanding and development of focus group impressions and eventual findings. The session, in other words, more than doubled the instances of written impressions by combining individually written insights with the collective insights and refinements on the conference room whiteboard.

The subsequent rhetorical effects of these written topographies were also factorial. Individual impressions from all three researchers coalesced in the project outline (figures 3.3 and 3.5) and achieved stability and visibility that fostered additional adjustments, insights, and refinements that eventually became the basis for complex organizational knowledge delivered across a variety of technical and professional genres.

In Jenn's photo-elicitation interview, she noted the importance of the whiteboard and hinted at its factorial effects. I asked, "Why is this such an important piece of your thinking for projects like this? What does it do?" "Yeah," she replied, "it's magic":

> I don't have to be limited to trying to fit everything in and I can be really sporadic and just get the thoughts that are in my head on the board and not worry about how they fit yet. And once they start coming out and especially when there's other people in the room to start adding to it, I feel very . . . not that I'm anywhere on this level, but I feel very *Beautiful Mind*, where it's just like I see numbers and things and I don't know how they fit together, then I can step back, so long as it's all up there. . . . It's easier for me because it's just so large, and I can draw arrows to connect and just see it all. And then they're all out there. And then when I take my [individual] notes later [from] the whiteboard, then I can make more sense of it. So it's kind of that constant process of making sense.

Once the ideas are on the whiteboard in a stable and visible form from which she can make connections, Jenn comes back and takes notes, "almost like minutes for a meeting," she says. She linearizes the key insights, creates lists, moves from the whiteboard to presentation slides, to tweets and text messages, to drafts of white papers and technical reports. She *factors* the visible, stable, collective insights of her research team and moves them forward into other genres and other forms of visibility.

## FROM KNOWN CONTINGENCY TO EXPERIENCED PERMANENCE

For the most part, we experience both walls and writing as permanent. We assume, from both, stability and strength. They are ever visible (at least potentially) yet often function as background elements. Their visibility makes itself conspicuous in non-typical circumstances: when we run into the wall, when a fresh coat of paint is applied, when a new piece of artwork is hung, when a smudge appears, when the digital file is lost, or when handwritten notes, left on a patio table, curl and smudge and pull apart in a summer afternoon thundershower.

We take for granted the relative permanence, stability, and visibility of walls—and writing. This makes sense—we cannot see and know and appreciate every wall or every instance of writing. Both are infrastructural, surrounding us, supporting our work and ideas, conditioning our comportments and cares and understandings of what may be possible in any given moment. But walls and writing are just as often places where contingent moments of *poiesis* emerge—infrastructures for testing ideas, for making them visible to us and others, for bringing insights to light. They are surfaces of invention, sites of immanence and potential, locations laden with factorial possibilities. Walls and writing even support the relative permanence of known contingencies; this may be one reason why Jenn described them, together—in the form of a whiteboard's topography—as "magic."

About four months into my study of I&F's privacy research, I scheduled a group interview with Mike, Michelle, and Jenn. I quickly learned that there was a problem with the execution of one of their methods. In each focus group session, their protocol called for one or more I&F graduate assistants to film the proceedings. However, as Jenn noted, with obvious understatement, "we have a big obstacle with our video.' Mike, Michelle, and Jenn did not realize that the videographers were not shooting continuously; further, they were not shooting, from one session to the next, with identical equipment and video encoding formats. What Mike, Michelle, and Jenn expected was seamless raw footage of each 150-minute focus group session; what they had instead were snippets from each session in different video formats, some of which had sound and some of which did not.

In short, they were not able to easily bring their video footage into a qualitative data analysis program and could not, therefore, work with the data in systematic ways. Jenn, who led analysis of the video footage, was dealing with what Mike described as "shredded outputs." All three researchers were visibly and audibly frustrated. "For whatever reason," Jenn added, not pointing the finger at anyone in particular, "something was shredding the video into different pieces." The mood in the room turned, however, when Jenn mentioned the debrief session discussed throughout this chapter. "Thank God we did that," she said.

What they *did* was contingent—a moment of brainstorming at the brewpub. But what they *had* from that debrief session, several weeks later, was something stable and visible: impressions, generated by each researcher immediately after the last of the focus group sessions, written as contingent insights on ruled paper yet enduring as permanent organizational knowledge. They had, on the wall behind them, an outline or blueprint—"DO NOT ERASE"—which provided a visible and stable distillation of insights from the debrief session and subsequent analysis. They had, too, the whiteboard in Mike's office, the tweets and texts shared between them and other colleagues, sketches for infographics, a few snippets of useful videos, scripts and slides for impending public talks, and work from other ongoing projects that buttressed the privacy research.

Small acts of known contingency—little bits of written *poiesis*, moments where ideas were realized and made visible—had factorial effects on the experienced permanence of Mike, Michelle, and Jenn. Little bits of writing at I&F acted like the proverbial swirls of butterfly wings in chaos theory—small changes to initial conditions that had massive effects in later work. It may seem that I'm making too much of the debrief meeting, of the subtle change in protocol that day, of the change in work environment, and of the importance of making ideas visible across three very different topographies that were later layered within a new topography on the I&F whiteboard. But here is how Mike and Jenn described that meeting and its subsequent factorial impact, considering the troubles with their videographers:

> MIKE: Jenn was also finding she'd get so bogged down in the crap that was being foisted on us by the breakdown of the video and all the rest of it. You know, she was getting . . . losing interest in the project. Like "oh God, this is becoming such a burden." That the original interest in the project was being beaten out of her, understandably. So we said, "Well, step back and just write what you think we concluded out of that brainstorming session," which goes to your [Michelle's] point earlier about the value of doing that cold turkey detox straight after the project. Get together. Get a beer. Informal. [Ask ourselves] What did we think?
>
> [Jenn "mmhmmm"s a great deal through these statements.]
>
> BRIAN: I was actually gonna follow up on that earlier because you mentioned how valuable it was to have some [written] artifacts, basically, that were produced in the immediate aftermath of the [focus group] sessions. So all of the stuff on the whiteboard, the stuff that you all did individually, you know, on blank pieces of paper at Scotty's . . . those things are now supporting your recall of the most important aspects . . .
>
> JENN: Oh, they're the foundation of it now, yes.
>
> BRIAN: Okay.
>
> JENN: Without that, we would have been . . . trying to do that now. Trying to remember and construct all of those little nuances that we had, so yeah, it's the foundation of where we're going.

An ordinary *techne*, individual moments of *poiesis* leading to collective moments of *poiesis*; moments of known contingency in mundane and temporary forms and places that were experienced as permanent: these became the foundation of I&F's privacy research program.

Visual ethnography and photo-elicitation framed both how I understood media research and how Mike, Michelle, and Jenn understood the role of writing and their material environs in their work. It is certainly true that they had a practical understanding of some of the ways their tools, spaces, and writing practices contributed to their work. But what photo-elicitation added were insights, "seared with reality" (Pinney 2011, 89), about how so many of these factors played into that work. By making their familiar workspaces and practices strange, photo-elicitation helped us reflect together on the ambient this-now-here-ness shaping *poiesis* at I&F.

For example, I composed several photos of each researcher's workspace and asked them, in photo-elicitation interviews, to tell me about how those spaces were structured. I showed Jenn a picture of her conference room arrangement and asked her about how a workflow diagram jotted on a sticky note—discarded soon after the meeting—helped frame her work in that session. I showed Mike two images of his cubicle and pointed out the drawings from his son on the whiteboard. These moments, he noted, were cherished for a time but then lost. In photo-elicitation, he was able to reflect on how those traces of his family, even momentarily present in his office, changed his perception of the workspace. On the smaller whiteboard next to his desk hung conference badges, a holiday card made by his son, and lots of writing in dry erase pen: an inspirational quote, notes about media "platform promiscuity," a pithy placeholder for a developing project—all of which, echoing the topography of Mike's handwriting in other environments, were written to the right of the board, nearest his desk chair. These notes took shape around a drawing by his son (figure 3.6).

The fieldwork photos composed over the course of my research thus served four important functions in my study of the writing and communication practices at Investigation and Foresight: (a) they helped me document and trace the topographies, tools, and practices of writing; (b) they helped me make visible much of the writing work that is only temporarily visible in media research; (c) they helped me elicit more thoughtful and nuanced responses from participants when their routinized practices and environments became momentarily strange, helping them see their work anew; and (d) they helped me evoke the rich material environments of media research.

Figure 3.6 visualizes fieldwork data, but not in the way we typically use the term *data visualization* in studies of writing or rhetoric. Rather than providing tabular or graphical representations of statistical or ordinal data, figure 3.6 offers up hyaline particularity. From figure 3.6 we cannot and should not generalize; indeed, that is the point. The particularity of this work environment—with Jenn just barely visible in the foreground, Mike in the background, and the various personal and professional artifacts with which they have surrounded themselves—enriches the sense of what it means to be media researchers at I&F. The particularity

*Figure 3.6. Mike and Jenn's office space, with Mike's personal whiteboard in the background. Author photo.*

is simultaneously a form of data and an empathic glimpse into the lived experience of Mike and Jenn and of Michelle, too, for she often spent time here, on the small couch to the left of the frame in figure 3.6. This is not big data—it doesn't carry the generalizing imprimatur of statistical inference and significance—but it is not *small* data either. It is rich, layered, textured, and nuanced—just like everyday work in a media research firm.

Factorial rhetorics emerge, coalesce, develop, and circulate in such environments. Material affordances form the "condition of possibility for rhetoric's emergence" (Rickert 2013, 159). Attunement to variable and differential forms of suasion in the material environs of Mike's workspace—by Mike, Michelle, Jenn, and their focus group participants—forms the ground of rhetorical possibility and development. In and through such attunements and through *technes* that make ideas visible and stable, Mike, Michelle, and Jenn enacted collective *poiesis*, bringing forth organizational and professional knowledge. Their writing in professional genres—further enactments of *poiesis*—charted new ontological directions and possibilities for who I&F *is* in its industry and who it *will be*. Picturing their writing is a methodological *poiesis*, bringing forth rhetorical enactments central to media research.

Visual ethnography, when paired with photo-elicitation, can help scholars of writing and rhetoric understand the meaning and enigma of visibility itself from a participant's perspective. We can explore how participants make ideas visible in the unique topographies of their writing. We can explore how participants make use of the material affordances for writing and thinking available to them. And we can explore *why* participants use the tools and spaces they do, in the ways they do. We can make the familiar strange for participants, gaining insights into how altered perspectives of looking at their own environments and practices can foster reflection on such work. Finally, we can offer visualizations of writing and rhetoric's rich particularity—hyaline presentations of lived experience.

# 4
## THE INEFFABLE IN THE TANGIBLE

The rituals of Roman Catholic liturgies and sacraments are carefully structured sensory engagements. During the mass, many of the following sensations are experienced at some point by most participants: burning incense permeates the air, engaging one's sense of sight, smell, and even hearing in subtle ways; bells, liturgical chants, cantors leading hymns, and calls and responses are all auditory engagements; kneelers, holy water, making the sign of the cross, and making peace offerings to those nearby engage one's sense of touch; in the sacrament of Holy Communion, the sense of taste is engaged, as Catholics consume by mouth what they believe are the body and blood of Christ; and the worship space itself, with all its artifacts and architectural features, is designed to engage one's sense of sight—from stained glass and statues to the flickering lone flame of the sanctuary candle, which burns perpetually to signal the presence of Christ in the Eucharist.

The mass engages lesser-known senses too. One's equilibrioception may be challenged when moving from sitting to standing to kneeling positions (and back again), and one's sense of proprioception is engaged: when reaching out to shake the hand of someone nearby, when grabbing the back of the pew to aid one's movement to a kneeling posture, or when holding one's arms away from the body, one hand cupped on top of the other in supplication and preparation for receiving the Eucharist—one's eyes held fast, focused on the body of Christ held aloft by the priest.

The idea that these movements and sensory engagements are suasive and have a rhetorical character is a commonplace. Scholars of rhetoric and religion have demonstrated how religious rituals have evolved and how they were carefully developed and refined over centuries to evoke the power and mystery of the ineffable (see, for example, Burke 1961; Enos and Thompson 2008; Graves 2009; Houck and Dixon 2006; Lewis 2007; Pollini 2012; Ridolfo 2015). In the Roman Catholic mass, an everyday practice for many devout Catholics, sensory engagements are myriad—harmonized and strategically paced acts and artifacts help participants engage the ineffable in both cognitive and affective ways. Rhetorical scholars are well practiced at exploring the cognitive, epistemic, and discursive aspects of religious practice.

But identifying methodologies and methods for engaging the affective and sensory experience so crucial to religious rituals is more challenging. Our typical approaches are well-suited to addressing epistemological questions in religious belief and practice—how rhetorics shape knowledge construction and circulation in specific faith traditions. Our theories are well-suited to questions of discourse, agency, appeals and ethos, deliberation and debate. But despite a growing body of scholarship exploring and extending theories of affect (Barnett and Boyle 2016; Davis 2010, 2017; Gries 2015; Ingraham 2017; Pruchnic and Lacey 2011; Rice 2012; Rickert 2013; Walsh et al. 2017), rhetoric as a field has been slower to take on *empirical questions* of feeling, affect, mood, and sensation.

Deborah Hawhee (2015, 13) argued that "finding the places where rhetoric and sensation converge is less challenging than knowing what to do from there." In her survey of rhetorical scholarship on sensation, she describes one troubling consequence of the field's strong epistemic turn in the 1980s and 1990s: studies of sensation, affect, and emotion—prevalent in work from the early twentieth century—were superseded and eventually obviated by work that focused on rhetoric's role in knowledge making and circulation. Hawhee's research begs the question: how can we explore the "constitutive roles of sensation in participatory, rhetorical acts" (13). She answers by suggesting some potential methodologies, leading, in fact, with ethnography (13).

This chapter—following Hawhee and other contemporary rhetorical scholars of affect and sensation (particularly Rickert and Rice)—applies visual ethnography and photo-elicitation to the study of extra-discursive rhetorics. Hawhee (2015, 13) argued that "the epistemic approach to rhetoric has run its course; rhetoric is not, or not only, a means of knowing and needn't be so attached to meaning." I explore sensation and affect in Roman Catholic practices of Eucharistic Adoration, wherein participants focus on simply *being with* the ineffable—sharing space and time with the Eucharist, what they believe to be the true body, blood, and presence of Christ. In adoration practices, rhetoric is a kind of energy (13), an embedded charge or an immanent potential engaged and illuminated by sensory experience and ritual practice, the feeling of *being* rather than (only) knowing. As I will demonstrate, feeling and knowing may often murmur to one another, intertwine like incense tendrils around a priest's vestments, each lingering with the other, moving with the other, remaining with the other.

*Figure 4.1. Incenser used during a Eucharistic Procession. Author photo.*

I used visual ethnography and photo-elicitation to trace and analyze the sensory engagements, effects, and affects of contemplative practices designed to engage the ineffable. These approaches can, as Hawhee (2015, 12) suggests, help us "exploit the intensity of feeling, or at least dwell there for a while." By dwelling with sensation, methodologically, we can learn much about how sensory artifacts and acts are built, how they gather and condition us, how they shape bodily and affective comportments in both presence and withdrawal, and how, through things, we are our *there*, wherever we may be.

## EUCHARISTIC ADORATION AND MULTISENSORY RESEARCH

For devout Catholics, Eucharistic Adoration assumes three main forms.

Most common is the everyday practice that takes place in adoration chapels or, in some parishes, in the sanctuary itself, outside of mass or other events. In adoration chapels, the Eucharist is held in a tabernacle (figure 4.2). A candle burns nearby, signaling for parishioners Christ's presence—his true body and blood. Parishioners spend time—as much or as little as moves them—in Christ's presence, simply by entering the chapel and sitting, kneeling, or, as is often the case, assuming both postures at different points. Adoration chapels are often small, holding no more than fifteen or twenty parishioners. They are hushed, reverent spaces where practitioners meditate on Christ's presence, read scripture or devotional literature, and write in journals. In some communities,

*Figure 4.2. Adoration chapel, with a tabernacle in the foreground. Author photo.*

adoration chapels are continuously accessible to parishioners—sites of *perpetual adoration* wherein parishioners volunteer to spend anywhere from fifteen to sixty minutes in the chapel over the course of a given twenty-four-hour period, ensuring that at least one parishioner is *always* in Christ's presence, sharing time and space with him.

Eucharistic Exposition and Benediction is the form of adoration with which most Catholics would likely identify. This is perhaps because of the visual interest generated by the monstrance—an intricate, ornate vessel, often made of gold or plated in gold, designed to display the Eucharist (figure 4.3). In Exposition, the monstrance is placed on the altar in the sanctuary; unlike the Eucharistic hosts shrouded inside the tabernacle within an adoration chapel, the Eucharist itself is displayed. During Benediction of the Blessed Sacrament, a priest grasps the monstrance through a garment called a humeral veil, which is draped over his shoulders and extends along his arms and over his hands. Holding aloft the monstrance and the Eucharist, he blesses supplicants. This blessing is seen to originate directly from Christ, fully present in the consecrated host, untouched by human hands. Many parishes hold monthly services of Eucharistic Exposition and Benediction.

Finally, in Eucharistic Processions, the consecrated host, held aloft in the monstrance by a priest wearing a humeral veil, is carried outside of the sanctuary, sometimes through public spaces. Processions are

*Figure 4.3. Eucharistic Exposition: a monstrance on the altar in the sanctuary. Author photo.*

typically held on the feast of the Blessed Sacrament, which is celebrated in June, although some parishes hold additional processions at other times of the year. A procession includes many members of a parish community: the priest, typically one or more altar servers with incensers (figure 4.1), a cantor to lead hymns or prayers, and all parishioners willing and able to participate.

Eucharistic Adoration is a continuum of practices—from the quiet, private, everyday meditation found in a chapel or sanctuary space, to the discursive, musical, and public demonstrations of the Eucharistic Procession. Each practice involves sustained and intentional sensory engagements that are arguably more focused and intense than in the mass. Adoration is a practice of rhetorical attunement to a host of environmental and ambient sensations, affects, artifacts, and identifications. Participants are immersed in and entangled by carefully orchestrated sensory environments with rich histories of development and traditions of practice.

A central aim of my study was to explore and reflect upon—with multisensory methods—participant immersion in such environments: to observe and sit with the "intensity of feeling" and to simply "dwell there for a while" (Hawhee 2015, 12). In this chapter I demonstrate (a) methodological attunements to ambient rhetorics and (b) new theoretical perspectives that emerge from such attunements—perspectives that evince the "constitutive roles of sensation in participatory, rhetorical acts" (13). This chapter and the next directly engage sensation and explore "what we do from there" (13), as scholars and researchers of rhetoric and writing. I demonstrate how visual ethnography and photo-elicitation are methodological strategies for tracing and exploring ambience, eliciting participant perspectives on sensation and affect, and extending theories of dwelling.

\* \* \*

I conducted a multi-site visual ethnography of all three forms of Eucharistic Adoration over the course of eighteen months. My two primary sites were Roman Catholic parishes located in the same mid-sized midwestern US city, less than two miles from one another (all names are pseudonyms). St. Xavier served the campus community of a large research university and its surrounding neighborhoods. It was also home to the university's Newman Center, a branch of the worldwide Catholic ministry program found at many non-Catholic universities. The Newman Center at St. Xavier provided living space and spiritual formation to university students. St. Xavier had a dedicated adoration chapel adjacent to (and closed off from) the main sanctuary (figure 4.2).

St. Michael, in contrast, was not affiliated with the university and served a largely middle-age and elderly population. There was no adoration chapel at St. Michael, so daily adoration took place in the sanctuary, where the tabernacle was housed adjacent to the altar. I worked closely with the priests of both parishes: Mark, of St. Xavier, and Fred, of St. Michael. I had permission from both priests (and from the diocese) to visually document all forms of Eucharistic Adoration in both parishes. I also conducted observations at a third site in the same city, St. Augustine, and had diocesan permission to make photographs and videos of Eucharistic Exposition and Benediction services. St. Augustine's priests and deacons did not participate in my study, however.

The study was informed by new materialist approaches to material engagement and sensation (Barad 2007; Bennett 2010; Bryant 2011; Ingold 2008; Stewart 2007). My research question—how do extra-discursive rhetorics and sensations shape practice among participants in Eucharistic Adoration—informed the study design, the aim of which was to better understand the ways non-human phenomena shape experience and the ways extra-discursive rhetorics are suasive and meaningful for participants.

I was interested in whatever shows up: a dull and insistent pressure on one's knees and back when kneeling during Eucharistic Exposition;

the moments of interrupted quietude when a subtle, gradual drop in the air temperature of the adoration chapel triggers the thermostat and causes the blower from central heating to cycle on; the warmth and slant of sunlight, late in summer evenings, shining with a piercing intensity through the only window of the adoration chapel, illuminating the statue of Mary; the lingering smell of body soap and cologne clinging to the cloth-wrapped cushions of the chapel's chairs, a reminder of another's presence. Some of these sensations and affects may enhance adoration practices, and some may be distracting. By studying them, I hoped to understand sensation's role in suasion and the rhetorical import of such engagements to Eucharistic Adoration.

The research protocol was informed by Sarah Pink's (2011, 2012b) work with multisensory ethnography, an approach that combined methods of visual and discursive investigation across everyday experience. My primary fieldwork methods included observations of Eucharistic Adoration in all three forms (chapel or sanctuary, services of Exposition and Benediction, and Eucharistic Processions); photographic and videographic documentation of spaces, artifacts, and bodily comportments in all three forms; semi-structured interviews with priests and parishioners exploring the sensory, affective, and ontological experiences of adoration; photo-elicitation interviews with participants who had completed at least one semi-structured interview; and analytic memos that often focused on my own sensory experiences during observations.

Because this project investigated adoration at three different field sites with three different parishioner populations, I was able to compile well-rounded perspectives that fostered productive comparisons. For example, the priests of St. Xavier and St. Michael, respectively, were at different stages of their careers, giving me two different perspectives on the practice and role of adoration in the life of their respective congregations. St. Xavier had a dedicated adoration chapel, but St. Michael and St. Augustine did not; this fostered contrastive observations of the sensory engagements of adoration at each parish and the bodily comportments of parishioners in each.

Participants, too, were diverse in terms of age, gender, and religious identification. I observed and interviewed college students living away from home for the first time. I observed and interviewed parishioners in their mid-twenties who were dedicated to campus ministry and attended daily adoration. I observed and interviewed men and women in their thirties, forties, and fifties, for whom daily adoration was not possible because of work and family commitments but for whom regular evening services of Exposition and Benediction were feasible. And I observed and interviewed parishioners in their sixties and seventies about the role of adoration in a lifetime of Catholic devotion.

Findings provide insights about the role of sensation and affect in Eucharistic Adoration practices across three dimensions. First, sensory artifacts contribute to what Thomas Rickert (2013) calls ambient dwelling. I demonstrate how the sensory artifacts of Eucharistic Adoration foster both presence and gathering, even in withdrawal. Second, I explore how pain, discomfort, and unease shape participant understandings of the ineffable. Third, I detail the role of writing in ambient dwelling—how, for example, journaling or note making becomes an important means of making the ineffable tangible for some participants.

I begin with three interrelated concepts: sensory artifacts, presence, and gathering. I argue that participants' engagement of these concepts (whether tacit or explicit) brought them closer to their own ideals and aims—and thus closer to the object of their worship. Through photo-elicitation interviews, I trace sensations of pain and discomfort in adoration. I conclude with an exploration of writing in adoration practices. Writing is a key form of engagement; it is often *through writing* that parishioners intentionally dwell with God. Writing helps some parishioners encounter spiritual presence and gather sensations, affects, and understandings of the ineffable.

### BUILDING, GATHERING, DWELLING

Any artifact can engage the senses, but in this chapter I use the term *sensory artifact* to denote those that are intentionally *designed* and *built* to address and heighten one's sensory experience. As I demonstrated in chapter 3, one's material environment may be productively suasive. A long wall, with the right paint, becomes a linchpin of collaborative invention; half-walls, partitioning a group of gregarious media researchers, enable and support the free flow of ideas. Although we can assume that Investigation and Foresight's walls were intentionally designed to be suasive, at a different firm the same material environs may have inhibited the kinds of practices I observed.

But the artifacts central to Eucharistic Adoration are intentionally designed to engage the senses, to *always* exploit participants' sensory experience. Any given *sensory artifact*, then, is carefully *designed* and *built* to address and heighten the sensory experience of parishioners. Such artifacts can be found outside religious contexts too—from the ergonomics of one's couch to the touch screen display of one's smartphone.

But sensory engagements in everyday life are often by-products or epiphenomena of artifacts: the smell of diesel exhaust, the drone of commercial aircraft, or the cold splash of water from a puddle that is deeper than it appeared to be. To be clear: all these examples engage the senses, and all are potentially suasive. But *sensory artifacts* denote those that are designed and built to intentionally engage one's senses.

The idea that they are *built* is crucial. In using the word *built* (rather than constructed or crafted or fabricated), I am connecting to Martin Heidegger's discussion of building and dwelling. In 1951, Heidegger gave a lecture, "Building Dwelling Thinking," to the Darmstadt Symposium on Man and Space. In his brief introduction to the published version of this lecture (which was translated into English and collected in *Martin Heidegger: Basic Writings*), David Farrell Krell cites two lines from Rilke (quoted in Heidegger 1993, 344):

> Jetzt wär es Zeit, daß Götter träten
> aus bewohnten Dingen.

> Now it is time that gods emerge
> from things by which we dwell.

Krell argues that Heidegger's notion of *thing* (*das Ding*) suggests "the place where the truth of Being, disclosedness, happens" (344). Things are locations of being, multifaceted, disclosive; they are understood in and through dwelling and meditative (rather than calculative) thinking (on meditative thinking, see chapter 5).

The language of "Building Dwelling Thinking" is poetic and laden with mythological concepts rather than technical philosophical jargon. A thing is a "concrescence . . . of the fourfold (*das Geviert*) of earth, sky, mortals, and divinities" (Krell quoted in Heidegger 1993, 345). For Heidegger, things—*built* things—gather the elements of the fourfold; in contemplation of them, in dwelling with them, the elements of the fourfold may likewise emerge. Expanding Rilke's formulation, gods emerge from the things we *build*—the things that are purpose-built for dwelling with us and around us in everyday life. The sensory artifacts of Eucharistic Adoration are things with which parishioners dwell and from which God emerges. But I am getting ahead of myself; to explore *sensory artifacts* in action, I need to parse three Heideggerian concepts: building, dwelling, and the fourfold.

### We Build *because* We Dwell

In "Building Dwelling Thinking" Heidegger asks two questions: what does it mean to dwell, and what is the relationship of building to dwelling? He argues that building *belongs to* dwelling. The commonplace is the opposite: we build homes, offices, and worship spaces *to dwell in them*, a relationship of means (we build) and ends (so that we may dwell). But Heidegger (1993, 348) argues that building *is* dwelling and belongs to dwelling not as means or end: "to build is in itself already to dwell." The etymology of *bauen*—"to build" in contemporary German—suggests a nuanced relationship of building to dwelling: the old High German word for building, *buan*, means to dwell but also to remain, to stay in place (348). A richer meaning of *bauen*, then, is to dwell, a meaning that has been lost in contemporary usage (348)

To build is to dwell, but what does to dwell mean for Heidegger? Dwelling is an activity, something one does *here* but not there. Heidegger traces the roots of one variant of the conjugations of the irregular verb *sein*, "to be": *ich bin, du bist*. These conjugations are related to *bauen*, and they mean, literally, I dwell, you dwell (rather than I *am*, you *are*; see 1993, 349). "The way in which you are and I am," he argues, "the manner in which we humans *are* on the earth, is *buan*, dwelling" (349, original emphases). To be human is to be mortal, to abide in place, to dwell (348–49). One *is*, therefore, "insofar as [one] dwells" (349). But *bauen* also means "to cherish and protect, to preserve and care for, specifically to till the soil, to cultivate the vine" (349).

Building in this sense is not a *constructing* but rather a *preserving*—stewardship—cultivating what and where one dwells. We build—we create worlds—*in dwelling*. The fact that our commonplace understanding of dwelling has eclipsed these underlying valences points to a bigger concern: in current usage, "dwelling is not experienced as [one's] Being; dwelling is never thought of as the basic character of human being" (Heidegger 1993, 350). Moreover, when we use the term *to build* without keeping in mind its roots in dwelling, we elide the traditional meaning of building, or what the building of structures and artifacts really entails.

"We do not dwell because we have built," Heidegger (1993, 350) says, "but we build and have built because we dwell." Dwelling's etymological roots are entangled with notions of freedom, peace, and sparing (something or someone) (351). "To dwell, to be set at peace, means to remain at peace within the free, the preserve, the free sphere that safeguards each thing in its essence" (351). The fundamental character of dwelling, Heidegger argues, is sparing: "to free actually means to spare," and this notion of sparing "pervades dwelling in its whole range" (351). This is brought into relief when we acknowledge that "human being consists in dwelling and, indeed, dwelling in the sense of the stay of mortals on the earth" (351).

This leads Heidegger to the fourfold *das Geviert*. Although the concept has been productively explored by scholars whose approaches overlap my own (e.g., Harman 2009; Wrathall 2011), I follow Rickert's explicitly non-reductive perspective toward *das Geviert*. Heidegger's language is often oblique, but as Rickert has shown, we can approach the fourfold as a literal manifestation and embodiment of dwelling without reducing its components to metaphorical representation (as in Harman 2009) or as a reworking of Aristotle's causation (as in Backman 2015). The fourfold instead is a consideration of practice as open comportment toward the world's disclosures—some of which are readily present, but many more of which ebb and flow, come to presence and withdraw (see Rickert 2013, 233–39). As Heidegger (1993, 351) argues, the fourfold of earth, sky, mortals, and divinities is simultaneously a onefold: when we say or think "earth," "we are already thinking of the other three along with it." Too often, though, "we give no thought to the simple oneness of the four" (351).

We are forever bracketing, limiting, atomizing. We cannot help ourselves from extracting salience; in doing so, as Rickert (2013, 243) argues, there is a cost. The fourfold is not an abstract formulation but a practical approach to ambient disclosure and attunement. As Rickert claims, "The fourfold is not simply a description of presence, of directly revealed things and their lived relations, *but an ongoing process of disclosure* that never fully wrests being from the world and brings it into human service" (233–34, original emphasis). Heidegger's examples—weddings, songs, dances, poetry—are often dismissed, but as Rickert notes, "the fourfold is itself responsive to concrete issues of everyday life" (234). Such examples combine "philosophical principle with everyday practice" where ongoing and dynamic disclosures emerge through the affectability of organisms to things, objects, and artifacts. Rhetoric, Rickert claims, "inheres in the fourfold" (234)—rhetoric emerges in any attunement to this-now-here-ness.

If building belongs to dwelling and if dwelling is a manifestation and expression of fourfold disclosures, then the artifacts we build and with which we dwell are both a response to ambient disclosures and a dynamic bringing forth—or *poiesis*—of disclosive potential. Seen this way, the sensory artifacts of Eucharistic Adoration are rhetorical in the traditional sense, in that they are intentionally built by human hands as vessels of persuasion; they explicitly make appeals that evince epistemological structures and sanction particular worldviews. But they are also rhetorical in an ambient sense in that they are "a form of affectability made possible in how the world already worlds as affectability" (Rickert 2013, 245). They are meant to persuade but are themselves built in response to, in concert with, and as a site for gathering the fourfold.

What happens, then, when we build? In short, we dwell: we gather, abide in, steward, and propitiate the fourfold.

**Gathering and Ambient Dwelling**

Rickert (2013, 354) takes the fourfold literally in his approach to dwelling by considering a traditional Black Forest farmhouse. Heidegger's (1993) example, too, is concrete: building belongs to dwelling in the figure of a bridge, a structure that "brings stream and bank and land into each other's neighborhood," a structure that thus "*gathers* the earth as landscape around the stream" (354, original emphasis), guiding and attending to the stream "through the meadows." The bridge abides the fourfold. It "*gathers* to itself in *its own* way earth and sky, divinities and mortals" (355, original emphases). Heidegger notes that gathering, by an ancient German word, is called *thing* (355; see also Rickert 2013, 225–29). The bridge is a thing, of course—a built thing that gathers and abides the fourfold (355).

It is a built thing that, in Rickert's (2013, 222) terms, gathers and emerges from dwelling as a material-symbolic-discursive confluence. From an everyday perspective, a bridge is just a bridge, with occasional added symbolism (Heidegger 1993, 355). But for Heidegger, its meaning is far more significant because it *gathers*, even in its everyday, commonplace manifestations. In gathering, the bridge determines "the places and paths by which a space is provided for" (356). A bridge establishes locales and circumscribes boundaries. And boundaries, for Heidegger, denote "not that at which something stops, but . . . that from which something *begins its essential unfolding*" (356, original emphasis).

Any discussion of human being, Heidegger contends, is a discussion of dwelling, of one's *stay* within the fourfold. Building is dwelling and we dwell with things. We relate, too, with things not present, not in reach, withdrawn. When we relate to Heidegger's (1993, 358) bridge or to Rickert's Black Forest farmhouse, we are in fact "staying with the things themselves." The bridge and the farmhouse are not mere mental representations. There is some sense in which we *are* at the bridge in and through our thinking. Indeed, "From right here we may even be much nearer to that bridge and to what it makes room for than someone who uses it daily as an indifferent river crossing" (358–59). Spaces thus "open up by the fact that they are let into the dwelling of [humans]" (359). Our relationship to space, to locales, "inheres in [one's] dwelling.

The relationship between [humans] and space is none other than dwelling, thought essentially" (359).

That final clause is provocative. It can be read in a straightforward manner: "dwelling, the concept, as thought about in its essence." But there is another way of approach that is congruent with Heidegger's perspective on dwelling in both "Building Dwelling Thinking" and his *Discourse on Thinking*. We can read the clause in this sense, too: "dwelling is, essentially, thought." The essence of building, for Heidegger (1993), is "letting dwell," and the essence of dwelling is thought—meditative rather than calculative thought. From this perspective, his summative claims about the relationship of building to dwelling are brought into relief: "Only if we are capable of dwelling," he repeats toward the end of his lecture, "only then can we build" (362).

\* \* \*

The sensory artifacts of Eucharistic Adoration *gather* and inculcate dwelling. Heidegger and Rickert provide a way of understanding how adoration *gathers*: (a) sensory artifacts are built in and from forms of dwelling—specifically, Roman Catholic ways of conceiving and engaging the fourfold—that bring together materiality, sensory experience, and discursive and embodied ways of being; (b) building belongs to dwelling, and dwelling is, in essence, meditative thinking; (c) the ineffable—Christ in three persons for Roman Catholics, gods for Rilke, divinities for Heidegger—is embodied in and emerges from our *things*.

The reality that the typical Roman Catholic might not conceive of adoration in these terms is assured; the fact that these perspectives, however, help us better understand their relationship to the suasive power of sensory artifacts in dwelling *as* Catholics, in contemplating and meditating on their God, is likewise assured. Indeed, the foregoing helps us understand Eucharistic Adoration as an everyday practice of *ambient dwelling*. In Rickert's (2013, 240) farmhouse example, "dwelling arises with craft and the acquisition of skill"—through building, in other words—and "these in turn emerge through an attuned engagement with the surroundings"—from dwelling, in other words. Attunement—engagement of the fourfold—is central to ambient dwelling. And rhetoric is our central mode of attunement.

Rickert (2013, 243) argues that "while dwelling includes building, such activity is not the work of humans alone. Dwelling is activity conditioned by the land and the things of the world." This notion is central to Heidegger's bridge example: humans, materials, and concepts come together and in so doing *gather* and abide in the fourfold. Agency is dispersed in both Heidegger's and Rickert's notions of dwelling, and ambient environs thus "take part in the doing" (243). This is why notions of preservation, saving, gathering, and stewardship are so crucial to Heidegger's notion of dwelling and, more to the point, to any conception of dwelling with the sensory artifacts of Eucharistic Adoration.

The monstrance, for example, gathers the attentions of practitioners through sensory and spiritual engagements; gathers them quite literally in place and time; and gathers them, above all, within the presence of Christ in the Eucharist. In this way, the monstrance works with what is given: its circular shape mirrors the circular shape of the consecrated host; its visual and tangible ornaments draw attention to the host and all it signifies. It stewards the Holy Host, preserves its form and texture and material integrity, and frames its salvific function. Its affectability for practitioners and its ability to gather their sensory and cognitive attention emerge from this calculus of material engagements.

In ambient dwelling, recognition and understanding of the fourfold in any human-built thing "cannot be reduced to direct presence as it is also what remains concealed" (Rickert 2013, 244). This too is crucial for understanding the role of sensory artifacts in adoration. The monstrance in Eucharistic Exposition and the tabernacle in Eucharistic Adoration are artifacts that foreground presence; they argue, in and through their materiality, that Christ is present, here and now. The ineffable is present, but it is a presence that also withdraws. It is, in Heidegger's terms, a presence at times explicitly *concealed* (as in the tabernacle, hidden from view). This dynamic is central to religious experience for many humans around the world. Across religious traditions, gods manifest and reveal but also withdraw and recede. Gods are hidden and concealed within the things we build, and in their concealment they likewise gather.

Gathering and withdrawing, displaying and concealing are hard-won and long-standing rhetorical attunements to ways of dwelling. In Eucharistic Adoration, ambient dwelling is a function of any given parishioner's embodied comportments, sensory engagements, practices of meditative thinking, and everyday ways of engaging the ineffable. The sensory artifacts and spiritual infrastructures of Eucharistic Adoration foster ambient dwelling because rhetorical attunements "invoke less a subjective change of mind or emotional state than a transformation in our worldly situation" (Rickert 2013, 221).

This is the very point of adoration's sensory artifacts: they are purpose-built to gather, heighten, and shift everyday modes of dwelling; to promote meditative thinking—for the essence of dwelling is thinking—and to transform worldly comportments.

The fourfold, as conceptualized by Heidegger and invoked by Rickert, offers a fundamental way of understanding how sensory artifacts condition and emerge from dwelling. Sensory artifacts emerge from and shape the ways parishioners approach, experience, and interact with God, with others, and with themselves as spiritual beings. Attention to sensory artifacts, to the complex provenance of the artifacts themselves, and to what it means to contemplate, experience, and dwell requires different ways of thinking and doing rhetoric. Although Rickert's work is widely cited, his theory of ambient dwelling has rarely been been operationalized in empirical studies of rhetoric. But exploring ambient dwelling empirically is a way of taking up Hawhee's call for attention to sensory experience. Indeed, it is a way of seeking, tracing, documenting, and *dwelling with*—as researchers—some of the many ways rhetoric emerges as non-discursive, irreducible, ek-epistemological tunings to ambience (Davis 2010; Walsh et al. 2017).

Eucharistic Adoration is certainly rhetorical in *discursive* ways: through pedagogies of religious formation; through the verbal encouragements of priests, deacons, and other parishioners; through the recitation of formal prayers; and through the personal, internal dialogues of those in worship. These discursive forms of deliberation circulate continually; but as Rickert (2013, 222) illustrates, rhetoric "emerges from, works with, and is entirely permeated by our dwelling places considered both materially and discursively." The materiality of our dwelling "conditions us, affects us, attunes us in an originary way" (222); we circulate continuously in and among ambient this-now-here-ness. Rhetoric "never escapes from world into the social or symbolic; it is always worldly, a dynamic, emergent composite of meaning and matter" (222).

With his notion of attunement, Rickert (2013, 229, original emphasis) argued that things *gather*; he noted that the fourfold is inherent in everyday life; and he claimed that dwelling in and with the fourfold accounts for the fact that "*things make claims on us* that help constitute not just the various kinds of knowledge we produce but also our very ways of being in the world." This perspective, when coupled with more recent work on tuning to attunements (Rickert 2016; Walsh et al. 2017), accounts for *how* attunement *is*: how it shows up and withdraws, how we tune to fluctuations and intensities. The confluence of attunement, dwelling, and gathering inherent in Eucharistic Adoration is a specifically Roman Catholic way of being in the world, wherein living with sensory artifacts and engaging in extra-discursive deliberation are essential rhetorical practices for understanding the ineffable.

132 THE INEFFABLE IN THE TANGIBLE

*Figure 4.4. A young person kneels and makes the sign of the cross as a Eucharistic Procession moves down the street. Author photo.*

### KNEELING IN PUBLIC

I shot hundreds of photos over the course of my study, but in a situation like the one in chapter 3—when I left my camera equipment behind and failed to effectively document visually one of the most important moments of my study at Investigation and Foresight (I&F)—I made an error at a crucial moment. My camera was ready to hand, but I was unprepared for what I observed—did not even consider it a possibility, in fact—and though I was able to technically make one exposure, it is almost too embarrassing to share (figure 4.4).

Blurry and underexposed, the *visual* facets of one of my methods are, in the moment when they were most needed, underwhelming at best. The practices that were documented, however—in field notes and in this image—were central to my understanding of the ways sensory artifacts embody and evoke ambient rhetorics and the ways they emerge in and foster sensations, gather relations and affects, and manifest persuasion. Figure 4.4 is a poor photograph, but it makes *visible* something significant.

\* \* \*

Mark is a young priest, enthusiastic and passionate. His parish, St. Xavier, serves the campus community and surrounding neighborhoods of a mid-sized American college town. Shortly after he was awarded his parish, he expanded the route of the church's Eucharistic Procession.

Many parishes offer only one or two Eucharistic Processions each calendar year, and many also seem to avoid ostentatious public displays.

*Figure 4.5. Mark leading a Eucharistic Procession through the city. Author photo.*

Routes are short, hewing close to parish boundaries—sometimes a procession will simply follow the perimeter of the parish parking lot before heading back inside. The act of walking with the Holy Host, both inside and outside the sanctuary, takes only a few minutes. Such processions are tepid, almost a rote manifestation of the rite. For the impartial observer, they can be, frankly, disappointing. There is little glory or mystery in walking around a church parking lot for a few minutes and then returning to the mass.

Mark decided to do things differently.

The whole point of the procession, he explained, was to bring the body and blood of Christ, his material and spiritual presence, *to the public*—to *be* in public, to be visible and tangible. The route that Mark created covered the better part of a mile, winding through the nearby university, along major city streets, and through one of the city's most popular commercial districts. Mark led the faithful, holding the Eucharist high above his head, the monstrance glinting in early evening sunlight, unmistakable.

I observed one of St. Xavier's processions from start to finish. A group of about fifty parishioners joined Mark, four altar servers, and a cantor on a bright spring evening, weaving through the campus and surrounding neighborhood (figures 4.1 and 4.5). Alongside or just behind Mark, altar servers swung incensers, and each of four volunteers held one

Figure 4.6. Mark (with monstrance) leading a benediction at the base of the university bell tower. Author photo.

corner of a canopy that shaded both priest and Eucharist (figure 4.6). In a long, variegated train, parishioners walked, many carrying a folded printout with songs and prayers. St. Xavier's cantor led the faithful through devotional hymns and litanies.

Near the iconic bell tower in the center of the university campus, the procession paused and gathered around Mark in prayer. The conspicuous nature of the gathering—fifty or so people kneeling (if able) on the concrete and bricks at the foot of the campus's most recognizable landmark—drew the attention of many passersby. Standing in their midst, holding the monstrance aloft, his hands covered by the humeral veil, Mark's arms seemed to tire and shake. But his voice was steady, his tone reverent and confident. Converts to Catholicism are sometimes said to be "on fire" for the faith. Mark was not a convert, but he was on fire.

After a brief benediction, Mark led the group away from the bell tower and down the campus's main drag. A few blocks later, the intersection of two main streets marked the edge of campus and the beginning of a thriving commercial neighborhood. Mark stopped again, and participants kneeled and prayed. At the bell tower, Mark prayed for the well-being of students on campus; at the edge of campus, he prayed for the well-being of the wider community. At both stops, he emphasized the *presence* of Christ in the Eucharist, exposed and glorified in the monstrance. He brought the light of the faithful out of the sanctuary, out of the tabernacle, and into the city.

\* \* \*

As the procession moved through the commercial district, away from campus, and back toward St. Xavier, I stopped three different times to hurriedly dictate ideas and tap out field notes on my phone. I was documenting things quite well with my camera but added field notes too—I couldn't wait until the end of the observation. Consequently, during the last third of the procession, I often drifted away from the group, stopping on the sidewalk to jot 100 words or so before jogging ahead to rejoin them.

The third time I did this, I lagged far behind, perhaps a block and a half away from the procession. I hurried, but less urgently; for the first time I noticed—no longer immersed in the group of chanting and singing parishioners—some of the ways the procession was affecting the neighborhood.

Two young men stood on the stoop of a game shop, looking over their left shoulders and up the street at the trailing members of the procession. Three young women, half a block ahead, crossed the street, perpendicular to the procession; two asked about what they saw—"is that a parade or something?"—and the other replied "it's some religious thing." A man, picking through a recycling bin on the opposite side of the street, held a dented soda can, his mouth slightly open, his head turned over his right shoulder, watching the faithful.

I picked up my pace. Closer but still not part of the group, I hurried toward the storefront of a national sandwich chain as the late light fell. I glanced down the alley at the edge of the shop, looking to my left. A young employee was walking up the alley, away from the restaurant's dumpster, after taking out the trash. Turning the corner, the employee caught sight of the end of the procession. Wearing the company-issue green polo shirt and black apron, the employee immediately dropped to one knee and made the sign of the cross.

\* \* \*

What does it mean to kneel in public? What must one *feel* to do so? And what does it *feel like* to kneel in public?

For participants, kneeling on the uneven bricks at the base of the university clock tower or on the concrete at the edge of campus manifests participatory and performative embodiments of faith. Their acts are participatory because they have chosen to be there, to glorify the Eucharist together in their movement and embodiment. They have decided to experience their faith more fully, to join and collaborate with other parishioners in one of the church's most important traditions. But their acts are explicitly performative: one of the key reasons Mark led his procession through the campus and community was to testify—by discursive, sensory, and embodied acts—to the glory of Christ's real presence in the Eucharist.

When the group members kneeled together, when they walked along chanting, they performed their faith for others in the community—for the two young men outside the game shop, for the young women who wondered if they were seeing a parade, for the man searching for recyclables, for the cars passing by more slowly than usual, and for a sandwich shop employee taking out the trash.

Can the same be said of the employee who had knelt in public? We cannot know for certain what they felt, why they kneeled, or what doing so meant to them and their faith. We can assume that kneeling was indeed participatory and that doing so was also, at root, performative. The differences, however, are qualitative. Participation was self-directed, since others did not see the gesture and did not know another was, in some small way, a part of their procession. I am not arguing that one set of participations and performances is more effective or pure or orthodox than the other. Indeed, although there are crucial differences between these two examples of participations and performances, I am much more interested in what they mean when viewed together.

The Eucharist, as a sensory artifact yoked to and framed by a host of other sensory artifacts—the monstrance, the humeral veil, incense, the canopy, the litanies—*gathers*. It gathers and manifests a particular fourfold. It gathers the faithful, those for whom the material and sensory appeals of the Eucharist are, for whatever reason or complex of reasoning, suasive.

Moreover, *we were all gathered* by the embodied and multisensory enactment of the procession and by the sensory artifacts on public display. The man searching for recyclables is gathered by them; the sandwich shop employee too; the three young women crossing the street and the two men on the stoop; the people in cars passing by; me; and now, you. The sensory artifacts of Eucharistic processions are built for this gathering, and, so gathered, we dwell—even those for whom the response to such suasive and sensory artifacts and acts is ambivalence, uncertainty, or outright rejection.

This is what it means to dwell: we do not always choose the things and places with which and by which we dwell, and yet our dwelling is inescapably conditioned by those things and places nonetheless.

The Eucharist—*in* the monstrance, *held* through the humeral veil by Mark, *among* incense and chants and prayers, *with* worshipers, and *beheld* by passersby—gathers in its function as a sensory artifact purpose-built to glorify Christ, to draw attention to his presence, and in the process to persuade in all its extra-human, extra-cognitive, multisensory force. And in building, gathering, and persuading, the Eucharist manifests and embodies a form of dwelling, a specific world.

As practices, Eucharistic Expositions, Processions, and Benedictions facilitate embodied and sensory engagements with *the very presence* of the ineffable: adherents see, hear, smell, feel, and eventually taste what they believe to be Christ's body. But in bringing Christ to public presence, the Eucharist and the monstrance gather and condition all those proximate to the procession. One need not acknowledge, internally or externally, that "there is the body of Christ" to dwell with the presence of the ineffable. That is, perhaps, the key function of sensory artifacts: because they gather, they condition dwelling.

## CONCEALMENT AND WITHDRAWAL

Although the Eucharist in the monstrance draws attention to the *presence* of the ineffable, sensory artifacts also shape dwelling for Roman Catholics in *concealment* and *withdrawal,* thus inviting and shaping different notions of being with, connecting to, and embodying faith. Things that gather, that purposefully engage sensory experience, and that condition dwelling "are not simply present and relational, awaiting representation: rather, they constitute the impossibly convoluted and interactive stitchwork of being to which we have only partial access" (Rickert 2016, 229). Dwelling emerges from and is lived in this more complex confluence of presence *and* withdrawal.

Rickert (2016, 229) argues that dwelling occurs "as distributed forms of mutual conditioning" and that this conditioning is not reducible only to presence; dwelling emerges from all that brings something to be the way it is, the way it shows up (or not) in the world as an enactment of ambient this-now-here-ness. Visual methods can trace, document, and explore the sensory artifacts of Eucharistic Expositions and Processions. As I have demonstrated in a different context (McNely, Gestwicki, Gelms, and Burke 2013), such methods may document absent presences—the forces palpable in what is not readily available, what has receded from view, what may be concealed. By using photo-elicitation interviews with practitioners of Eucharistic Adoration—where the Eucharist is concealed in the tabernacle and where, during periods of longing and tests of faith, Christ may seem withdrawn—we can learn more about perceptions of presence and withdrawal.

\* \* \*

Jason is twenty-six, a member of a campus Catholic outreach group, and a daily practitioner of Eucharistic Adoration. Nearly every morning he enters the adoration chapel at St. Xavier (see figure 4.2) and spends an hour in Christ's presence—concealed yet exalted within the tabernacle that dominates the room. Jason's faith is sincere and infectious. But as he explained in our interviews, an hour of daily adoration is challenging.

After graduating from college, Jason wanted to stay connected to the church, but he didn't have a clear sense of how he might do so, outside of mass and general fellowship. Eventually, he found the Fellowship of Catholic University Students (FOCUS), a missionary group that works with college students around the world to meet them where they are. FOCUS missionaries lead study groups with students, plan and help local parishes with events, and mentor students individually. A recent graduate, Jason helped students navigate the challenges of leading a Catholic life while in school and away from home.

Jason's daily schedule is built around adoration, mass, and FOCUS outreach. His everyday life is quite different from that of most people working an 8-to-5 occupation—even that of very devout Catholics who attend daily mass. In interviews, Jason showed a keen understanding of his unique role as a missionary. Among the things he repeatedly brought to prayer in adoration was a concern for his own vocation—how he would live his life, professionally and spiritually, after his missionary experience ended.

Over three interviews, Jason described ways he has personally experienced Christ in the Eucharist. He has attended Eucharistic Expositions, Benedictions, and Processions—the practices in which Christ's presence in the Eucharist is inescapable, visually and materially palpable. He described a transformative experience during a Eucharist Procession in Steubenville, Ohio, the home of Franciscan University and the site of an annual Catholic youth conference. As a high school student, Jason first experienced extended sessions of Eucharistic Exposition and Benediction—two to three hours spent in Christ's presence.

The sensory experience in Steubenville was transformative: Exposition was accompanied by praise and worship music, which Jason felt heightened his connections to Christ. He described the smell of incense; at the conclusion of the service, he described the procession: "It's really, really powerful the way the Lord moves" through these sensory experiences.

The procession at Steubenville encircled—over and over, within the sanctuary—those kneeling in adoration. Jason's experience was shaped not by his own movements but in rooted contemplation, as the procession *moved around him*. "The Holy Spirit definitely moves a lot in those scenarios," he said, "and people are more open to the Holy Spirit there than [anywhere else] I've ever seen." As the procession moved through the congregation, Jason described seeing practitioners reaching out toward the monstrance. Then he described his own reticence to do so:

> As the priest is passing by me I'm like, you know, kind of this macho, like, egotistical, um . . . really, I won't say selfish but, like . . . too proud to do anything, but I just had . . . just finally had the nerve to actually, like, reach out and just touch the robe . . . of the priest, you know. At the same time, as soon as I did that, just kind of could feel like, this rush, um, of power just kind of like, go through me and instantly just knew like, wow, that was, that is God, like, that's not the pr . . . that's not the priest, but that is God. And it just struck me.

Jason described the effect the procession had on those near him. The sanctuary was full of sensations—visual, aural, olfactory, and haptic stimuli. He was moved, affectively, by a confluence of sensory engagements. His experience of God's presence was felt as an all-at-onceness, a onefold of sensory artifacts and practices: kneelers, musical instruments and signing, the pungent fragrance of incense, the visual force of the monstrance, physical acts of reaching out and opening, the texture of the priest's robes, the embodied presence of those near and around, and the continuous, circular movements of the procession. So much was gathered by the presence of Christ in the Eucharist.

In contrast, Jason described daily adoration, where Christ—and many of the sensory engagements on full display in the Steubenville procession—were withdrawn. In the Eucharist, Christ is concealed by the tabernacle. There is no incense burning, and all is muted and mundane—no praise and worship music, no audible prayers, no movement of a priest or altar servers or of other worshipers. The chapel is subdued, the spectacle withdrawn, the signifiers of godly presence tacit. For parishioners such as Jason, an hour of adoration in such an environment requires planning: one might bring and pray the rosary; one might bring along a Bible or a devotional text; one might bring a journal in which to reflect in writing on one's spiritual formation, struggles, or everyday challenges.

Despite the subdued atmosphere, adoration in a chapel or in a sanctuary is not silent. Concealment and withdrawal foster subtle sensory attunements and experiences, encouraging different forms of dwelling.

Participants noted greater sensitivity, for example, to awareness of pain and discomfort. Alone in the chapel, distanced from the pressures and expectations of everyday life, and focused on the *concealed* body and blood of Christ in the tabernacle, participants' thoughts drifted, their attentions drawn to the pressure on their knees or to kneelers with uneven padding. Distractions—the sound of the heater or air conditioner, the ways footfalls reverberate inside the sanctuary—caused a loss of focus, the realization that they are no longer alone with Christ. In the quiet chapel, it is easier to hear distant sirens or car tires sluicing through puddles on a rainy day. It is easier to tune out, to dwell on worries or things left unsaid or plans for later.

To minimize distractions or to turn them in productive directions, many participants read or wrote during adoration. I was surprised by the ways writing mediated adoration practices—how writing, often in spiritual journals, became a sensory practice that deepened experiences of the ineffable. Jason always brought his Bible, a devotional text of some kind (a spiritual autobiography, lives of the saints), and his journal. They served a prosaic purpose: sometimes spending an hour in meditative reflection is not possible, and the time can be productively turned toward other activities. After prayers, Jason might open his Bible: he'd read a passage and then use the text to redirect his adoration session. In my observations of chapel and sanctuary adoration, such practices were common among participants: many read quietly from a Bible, a Missal, or a book on the lives of the saints. Next to silent prayer and meditation, reading in the presence of the Eucharist was the most common activity I observed.

Many participants wrote as well. Field notes from one observation of Eucharistic Exposition—a Thursday evening service at St. Xavier—detail how some participants were reading and intensively *writing*:

> The young woman who sits criss-cross applesauce [in line for confession] . . . now has a journal in which she's writing. . . . I wonder why she writes in the presence of the Eucharist, what she writes, how she uses this time. . . . [ten minutes later] The young woman continues to write in her journal. She started on a left-hand page and is now more than halfway down the following page. She readjusts her sitting posture, looks up for a moment, then returns, intently, to her writing. She stops a moment, places the tip of the cap of her ballpoint pen to her lips, returns it to the journal. Raises the pen to her mouth again, appears to think some more, then returns to writing. . . . She's reading what she's written now. Runs a hand through her long blonde hair. Returns to writing.
>
> [Thirty minutes later, observing a different parishioner] The young woman laying down [prone, very near the altar] writes a LOT in a small

script on what appears to be a blank yellow piece of paper. [ten minutes later] The young woman who was laying down . . . now sits with her back to the wall, legs and feet out in front of her, still writing furiously. I'm dying to know what it is she's writing. The predominant sounds in the sanctuary right now are the flowing water [of the baptismal font] and the crackles of paper as this woman's hand moves across the pages sitting on the uneven surface of her thighs. She's . . . filling up pages.

I consistently observed parishioners, young and old, reading and writing in adoration chapels and in sanctuaries during Eucharistic Exposition. But discussing writing with participants during semi-structured interviews was challenging. Such writing was intensely personal and situationally meaningful.

Few participants were willing to share their journals. It was as if they had poured out their prayers on paper, and those prayers were intended only for God and for themselves. Jason, with his missionary zeal, however, was happy to share. He allowed me to borrow and photograph his journal; in a subsequent photo-elicitation interview, he reflected on what he wrote, where a given adoration session occurred for a particular journal entry (that is, in a chapel or during Exposition), and how he remembered feeling during a session. Pointing to a photograph of an entry written in the St. Xavier's adoration chapel, he said: "It was just like a, an outpouring, of just kind of my experience, what I was, like um, sort of struggling with, but, just questions that were going through my mind, like certain responses that I was having, just writing that down and I was thinking about it, praying with it." His journal helped him connect materially and spiritually to God. In so many of his adoration sessions, meditating and spending time with the Eucharist was not enough. Reading in God's presence, writing out his struggles, and making his prayers and desires concrete in his journal were crucial ways he connected with God—topographies of his spiritual journey.

In Jason's experience of adoration, key sensory artifacts gather elements of a fourfold dwelling. In any chapel-based adoration session, there is a stitchwork of scripture, Jason's bodily comportments toward the tabernacle, and his journal:

> If I'm meditating upon a particular [scripture] passage, through prayer [I'm] having a conversation with the Lord about it—writing down my thoughts and my feelings and what I am experiencing and just allowing that meditation to also be prayer that can be conversation that I can record, because I don't maybe want to forget it, or [I] want to go back to it in a time of desolation or dryness in prayer and say "oh yeah, I remember this, Lord. . . . This was a great time of prayer for me." And so it's there and it's tangible.

His journals contain frank reflections on his spirituality, composed in the adoration chapel. It is through writing and through the sensory artifacts of Eucharistic Adoration that *tangible* and tactical experiences and practices are embodied in acts that connect and dwell with an *intangible* spirituality. Writing is a material way of expressing feeling—its unique contours and topographies make visible and bring forth affective and cognitive compartments as a way of dwelling with God. The adoration chapel frames specific forms of writing rich with implications for spiritual identification and ontologies. As Christ is embodied in the Eucharist for parishioners, so are spiritual understanding and practice embodied in the materiality of writing.

\* \* \*

The sensory artifacts of Eucharistic Adoration gather things that come to presence—the transubstantiated Christ in the Eucharist; the material artifacts, environments, and practices that draw together attentions and experiences; and the people dwelling with and through such artifacts, practices, and experiences. But additional sensory artifacts such as spiritual books and personal journals help participants dwell with the concealment and withdrawal that are elemental to Catholic faith. As Rickert argues of ambient dwelling, "*Withdrawing is also a form of supporting*" (2013, 244, original emphasis). The world in which we dwell, our regional ontology, is "always more than what we make of it" (244).

Dwelling is an attunement to "what is noninstrumental, nonrepresentational," and concealment and withdrawal are thus "essential" (Rickert 2013, 244). Rickert argues that concealments have significant value, and his notion of ambient dwelling therefore celebrates presence as well as withdrawal and concealment: the latter "grants the world a kind of meaning or value that, while it cannot speak directly . . . nevertheless calls us in its holding sway and conditions every aspect of our being together" (244). Heidegger (1993, 163, original emphasis) argues that the sensory artifacts and environments built to gather the ineffable—even if they conceal—"ope[n] up a *world* and kee[p] it abidingly in force."

Heidegger's conception of building *is* dwelling, and dwelling—for both Heidegger and Rickert—is the fundamental way in which we *are* in the world and, indeed, in which we *world*. As Heidegger (1993, 358) has it, when we relate to things not within reach by thinking about or meditating on them—things withdrawn or concealed—we are actually "staying with the things themselves." More important, we *stay* the things themselves. There is a stewardship that fosters meditative pause, a persistence in thinking through and feeling with what is not present by gathering and being with what is. Spending time with the Eucharist, knowing that the object of desire is withdrawn or concealed, is thus a quintessential form of Heidegger's notion of "letting dwell" (361).

Building sensory artifacts, spaces of concealment, and meditative pause are all acts of letting dwell. Heidegger (1993, 362) argues that "only if we are capable of dwelling, only then can we build." Dwelling, he stresses, "is *the basic character* of Being" (362, original emphasis). In thinking about dwelling and building, we see more clearly how "building belongs to dwelling and how it receives its essence from dwelling" (362). And building and thinking, he adds, are inescapable from dwelling (362). They are insufficient for dwelling when considered as separate domains; but when brought to bear on one another, they belong to dwelling, insofar as they "remain within their limits and realize that the one as much as the other comes from the workshop of long experience and incessant practice" (362).

## THINGS BY WHICH WE DWELL

In our final interview, Jason told me about his plans and dreams. He hoped to fall in love, marry, and find a fulfilling career. After long hours in adoration, in mass, in counseling and mentoring college students, and in so many other activities related to his work as a FOCUS missionary, he'd come to understand that a vocation in the church was not to be. But he told me how, for Roman Catholics, marriage itself was a vocation. I had the sense, though, that his words were like dark clouds at a summer picnic. His voice was heavy with longing and the sadness of decisions already made. He badly wanted a life in the church but realized it was not possible. Yet he told me how much his life—after missionary service—would be spent in the church, how involved he would be, how he could still make it to adoration, although less frequently. I felt as though he was trying to convince himself.

While I listened to Jason's plans, I thought of how his normal, workaday life, regardless of where he ended up, would still be conditioned by the sensory artifacts of Eucharistic Adoration. By spending so much of his life to this point dwelling with Christ in the Eucharist through adoration practices, Jason had shaped his manner of dwelling for years to come. As I have argued elsewhere (McNely 2016), an ambient perspective on rhetoric moves us from considerations of rhetorical situations to rhetorical situatedness. Drawing on Heidegger, I argued that there is a fundamental sense in which we *are* our *there*. In an ambient understanding of rhetorical situatedness, our various *theres*—our conditioned comportments of dwelling in specific places with specific things—*move with us*, framing and blending with new *theres*, new comportments, new ways of dwelling.

This is what it means to be rhetorically situated. No matter where he is, there is an elemental sense in which Jason will continue to dwell—to steward and stay—with the things that have conditioned this important period in his life. Through the things with which he dwells, he will likewise *world* new *theres*.

Although I have drawn from Heidegger's later perspective on building and dwelling and from Rickert's notion of ambient dwelling, it is worth briefly revisiting *Being and Time* (2010), if only to illustrate how we are our *theres*. Rüdiger Safransky (1998) argues that *Being and Time* came in the wake of Heidegger's failed theological career, a break from Catholicism, a challenge to the phenomenological ideas of his mentor, Edmund Husserl, and the zeitgeist of the Weimar Republic. As Rickert might argue, Heidegger's ideas are firmly rooted in the *terroir* of his own regional ontology—one steeped in geopolitical turmoil, encroaching modernism, competing scientific and philosophical methodologies (such as phenomenology and psychoanalysis), and deep erudition about ancient Greek philosophy—particularly Aristotle's.

Often, Heidegger's pivotal notion of *Dasein* is translated into English as "being-in-the-world." But a transliteration of *Dasein* is closer to the way Heidegger uses the term in *Being and Time*. *Da sein* literally means "there being." Given the felicitous nature of German grammar, *Da sein* can literally mean "being there" as well. To do justice to Heidegger's distinction between the ontic (everything that exists) and the ontological (the being that *knows* it exists and that *cares* and *worries about* such knowing), *Dasein* in English could be rendered as "there Being" or "Being there," using the capital letter B to designate the ontological. This makes *Dasein* not only a *what*—a being that is *there*—but also a *how*, a being that ended up and dwells *there*.

Location, region, *terroir*—these concepts are central to dwelling. The later Heidegger is still *there*, with the earlier Heidegger. His *theres* move with him, combine with new *theres*, and produce new valences on Being. As Paul Dourish (2001, 110) intimates, *Dasein* is *Being there* in an embodied sense: one "is not simply embedded in the world, but inseparable from it such that it makes no sense to talk of [one] having an existence independent of that world." Dourish thus frames there Being/Being there with the force it deserves. But "being-in-the-world," as a translation of *Dasein*, carries a valence that is almost never addressed; it presumes that one can somehow, perhaps at some point, be out-of-the-world, too.

That opening, slim as it may be, entirely diminishes Heidegger's point. This is why, following Dourish, *it makes no sense whatsoever* to conceive of Being or dwelling as in any way independent, as in any way disentangled from one's *there*.

It makes no sense to disentangle one's ambient environs—the things and places and affects by which one dwells—from rhetoric. From where does suasion originate if not from our *theres*? *Dasein* is *there Being*, and *there Being* is not static. Heidegger, in *Being and Time*, says that despite our thrownness, despite our angst, despite our evasions, despite our worry, *Dasein* nonetheless engages the world. The choices we make and our engagements with past, present, and future *theres* are fundamental to how we dwell.

Dwelling happens in, among, with, and through the things that gather us as we gather them, in some particular *there*. And we are gathered across time and space, whether our things are present, concealed, or withdrawn. We are inseparable from our *theres*, even fleeting *theres* and their things—the third-floor sublet overlooking a busy street with the windows stuck open over one long summer, the twisting gravel driveway leading to Grandma's house, the smell of incense in the adoration chapel, the drawn-out shape of the Mary statue hanging from the wall, the quality of light in the bedroom on clear winter mornings. This perspective does not reinforce or even simply presume a traditional subject-object paradigm. Indeed, as Rickert (2016, 229) argues, our *theres* and our things are part of the very fabric of being, doing, and dwelling—a "stitchwork."

Our built things are relational and intra-active in both presence and withdrawal. They carry with them—and stay within us—embedded charges, affective forces, rhythms. The relationship between humans and space, between humans and building, "is none other than dwelling, thought essentially" (Heidegger 1993, 359). And dwelling may be seen, especially in light of Heidegger's *Discourse on Thinking*, as essentially *thought*. Not thought in the sense, necessarily, of explicit cognition but thought, too, of a different sort: meditative, reflective, affective. In what other manner can our things—concealed, withheld, or left behind—remain with us, continue to condition us? If the essence of building is "letting dwell" and the essence of dwelling is meditative, affective thought, then the concealment and withdrawal of presences is fundamental to the stitchwork of dwelling.

In that interview with Jason, I felt as if his changing *theres* would not necessarily obstruct or obscure his waning *here*. Instead, they would be woven into an expanding tapestry of sensations, affects, presences, and withdrawals. In "Building Dwelling Thinking," Heidegger's (1993) bridge abides in the fourfold, establishes locales, and circumscribes boundaries. The boundaries, though, denote "not that at which something stops, but . . . that from which something *begins its essential unfolding*" (356, original emphasis). Jason's future vocation, perhaps as a devout Roman Catholic with an ordinary career, a loving spouse, and healthy children, will establish new *theres* and new boundaries. He will have less time for daily adoration, and he might miss monthly opportunities for Eucharistic Exposition and Benediction because of a child's soccer practice or the school open house. But in the sense of dwelling developed here, the boundary shapes how and where his life unfolds. Boundaries are thresholds of the presences and withdrawals of sensory and affective engagements. The boundaries that circumscribe Jason's life are sure to change; so too will new forms of presence and withdrawal emerge and become part of the stitchwork of his ambient engagements. At the boundary, sensory artifacts and everyday affects, old and new, condition dwelling.

In Eucharistic Adoration, presence, withdrawal, sensation, affect, and boundaries weave in and out of engagements with the ineffable. Practices of ambient dwelling are both physical and metaphysical. Feeling pressure on your knees or pain in your lower back while praying in an adoration chapel are sensations intimately yoked to experiences of God. The smell of incense, the bright golden gleam of the monstrance, the texture of a priest's robes, the singsong litany of holy names chanted during Eucharistic Benediction—these sensory artifacts and acts are physical ways of signaling the presence of the metaphysical in one regional ontology. It reflects something of Roman Catholic practice around the world, but it is not that practice exactly. How the Eucharist was experienced and received in adoration at three parishes in one medium-sized city in the midwestern United States cannot and should not represent the regional ontologies of similar practices in Sausalito or Volgograd or Lagos. You already know this. All qualitative research is limited in scope, its purview particular and small and intimate. And yet in the best ethnographies we see something of our own experience; we make connections to participants across times and places. Our *theres* mesh in some way with theirs.

But allow me to make a more radical argument for the significance of qualitative research: ambient dwelling and its rhetorical force is indeed generalizable. The things by which Jason and others dwell are physical and metaphysical; their suasive power yearns toward the mystical. God emerges, for Jason, through the things by which he dwells. But ambient dwelling presupposes only the stitchwork of human and non-human sensation, affects, comportments, and suasion. Our "dwelling is activity conditioned by the land and the things in the world" (Rickert 2013, 243). We can, like Jason, dwell with metaphysical things, with sensory artifacts built to engage and heighten an understanding of ineffable presence.

But we can (and do) dwell with mundane things, from which no gods are called forth but through which our sensations, affects, comportments, and suasive potentials are nonetheless conditioned. We are our *theres*. The things by which we dwell may have no metaphysical import in our regional ontology. And such things may yet emerge as mystical, surprising, breathtaking, full of wonder. Ambient dwelling can attune us to a mysticism without metaphysics. *All* regional ontologies are full to bursting with presences, concealments, withdrawals, boundaries, and thresholds that disclose sensory engagements, that condition comportments, that function as the elemental ground of rhetoric. This is generalizable. This is also best studied in the minute particular.

Every regional ontology, every way in which things show up and *world*—for this person, in this place, at this time—has its individual variations (Walsh et al. 2017). Following Jenny Rice, we might ask: What have we to gain, as researchers and theorists of rhetoric, by tuning into individual variations, by attending to the small and close in addition to the distant and vast? Such variations are inherent to the particular *theres* of a given ambient environment, "charged moments within an ecosystem" that "possess their own trajectories" (quoted in Walsh et al. 2017, 434). In "reading individual variations," Rice argues, we neither get nearer to intimacy nor move further from objectivity; instead, "we are merely encountering the different voices, different registers, of an ecosystem" (434). We are encountering, in other words, ambient this-now-here-ness.

This is nothing like objectivity; indeed, it is more complex, more generalizable. The ancient aphorism provides guidance: *individuum est ineffabile.* The individual is ineffable. The individual variations of *everyone's* ambient dwelling are inexhaustible. This is the way the minute particular is generalizable. Attending to individual variations, Rice argues, increases our capacity to experience vulnerability (quoted in Walsh et al. 2017, 435). And to be vulnerable is to be entangled (435). "The parts of an ecosystem are vulnerable not in the sense of being *objects* of force," she notes, "but instead of being caught up in the *movements* of force" (435, original emphases).

We are vulnerable—entangled, caught up in sensations and affects and suasive forces—and we are open to influence, to originary suasion (Walsh et al. 2017, 435). We become implicated, affected, sometimes persuaded by our entanglements. And "we" are not the only ones—not "we" humans but any *there Being*. How can it be any other way if we are our *theres*? Rickert argues that rhetoric "springs from these relations and iterations" (cited on 449). It simply cannot be extracted from our *theres*, for "rhetoric is not just a human invention." Indeed, the inverse is the case: "human existence is already interior to a rhetoric forged by life and world" (449).

The individual variations we encounter in any regional ontology are the different voices and registers that emerge from—but do not stand in for or represent—ambient dwelling. "Individual variations are not illustrative of the ecology in which they are also entangled," Rice argues (quoted in Walsh et al. 2017, 436). She continues, "We must allow objects to *object* to their status as examples merely waiting to be aggregated" (436, original emphasis). Any given individual variation is just that—an emergence of fathomless particularity among any possible *there Being* in enactments of this-now-here-ness.

# 5
## WALKS, TALKS, *GELASSENHEIT*

**NIGEL**

I walk to work most days. I live in a shabby bungalow but pay rent below market rates for the neighborhood, which I chose because it's an easy stroll to campus. I walk in the rain and snow and when the wind chill is 10 degrees below zero. I'm attuned to the streets I walk on my way to campus, the rhythms of everyday life here. The uneven driveways and sidewalks. The shady stretches and sunny patches. The sometimes muffled, sometimes flat, sometimes delicate sounds of movement all around me—screen doors slapping, basketball games spilling from front-room televisions, yapping dogs, winter footfalls. Sometimes, at the intersection of Park and Sunset, it smells like peanut butter cookies, the kind my mom made. She rolled the dough into a small ball, dropped it on a baking sheet, mashed it flat with the meaty palm of her right hand. She'd grab a fork and create a hash pattern in the dough, pushing the tines this way, then that.

Sometimes, at the intersection of Park and Sunset, I smell peanut butter cookies and think of that hash pattern. I hear kids in the playground at Christ the King School when the weather is nice. I hear crows calling from trees and power lines. I see wet newspapers, walkers in tights, three crushed solo cups in a sidewalk tableau—two red, one blue, as if a shell-game confidence man was whisked away mid-hustle by the rapture. Cars splash through puddles, a lovely white bark peels from trees, the whirr of a table saw stretches down a long driveway from the detached garage of a house on Tremont. Two college-age women are drinking cheap bottled beers on the porch of their rented house. A young man flicks a cigarette from the stoop of Wildcat Market; smoke tendrils twist around his jeweled dreadlocks.

One unusually warm evening in early February, I left my office late, close to 7:00 p.m. I wanted to focus on the sounds of my neighborhood on the walk home. I hear sniffs, the freewheel clicks of a bicycle hub, a muffled stray yell from inside a house. The clack of a motion sensor as a light switches on. Easy springy footfalls from someone out for a run. Sirens. I hear an email chime coming from my backpack as my phone picks up a pocket of Wi-Fi. Loud, steady HVAC and electrical hums behind fraternity houses. Car doors open and close; once, I hear one creak, metal scraping metal. Wood on wood thuds of a fly-leaf table being moved by two men and a woman from the back of a pickup. The scrape of table legs against the truck bed.

"Help me on this side," one of the men says.

"I'm sick of dealing with this thing," says the other.

The woman laughs nervously.

The plastic wheels of a garbage can, rolling across the sidewalk. A car drives by, windows cracked, two bars of a song I don't know. Dogs whining, straining at leashes. A chain-link gate opens and springs closed, clinking. A fan whirrs from an HVAC unit bolted to the side of a duplex. A front door opens on Beaumont, and a screen door creaks, pushed forward a few inches by a woman in a red pantsuit.

She coos, "Nigel. Nigel."

I slow, hear nothing for a stretched and languid moment, all those other sounds suddenly mute in the dark.

"Nigel kitty. Tsk tsk tsk. Niiigel."

I pass in front of Nigel's house, worried that I'll spook him, that I'll keep him from dinner or cuddles. I keep walking and hear once more, behind me now:

"Nigel kitty."

* * *

In chapter 4, I explored sensory artifacts purpose-built for practices of meditative thinking and for directing affective comportments toward the mysteries of the ineffable. The sensory artifacts of Eucharistic Adoration bring attention to presence and withdrawal by virtue of their extraordinary visual, material, and sensory capacities for gathering. They are purpose-built to be extraordinary, to foreground the ineffable, the distant, the fathomless, the mysterious. They are designed and built for such purposes, experienced in and through a particular form of dwelling. But we dwell with all manner of things, most of which are ordinary, practical, and close. While it is implicit in any discussion of Heidegger's notion of dwelling, there is an additional, crucial valence—to dwell is to think deeply about, to ruminate upon, to sit with. We dwell with all manner of things and organisms—we live with them, we sit with them, we think with and through them in everyday ways of living.

We are our *there*, and our *theres* are brimming with things that have capacities for visual, material, and sensory suasion.

In this chapter, I explore the individual variations in one form of dwelling and the suasive potential of the ordinary, the everyday, the immediate things with which we dwell. It is nearly axiomatic that meaningful consideration of the things near us—of our most mundane things—is most difficult. Thomas Rickert's theory of ambient rhetoric challenges us, as scholars and teachers of rhetoric and writing, to better attend to the things by which we dwell in everyday life. It challenges us to consider ways our *theres* condition our comportments, attune us as rhetors, and affect us in the most mundane manner.

"That which is ontically closest and well known," Martin Heidegger (2010, 43) argues, "is ontologically the farthest and not known at all, and its ontological signification is constantly overlooked." The ontological significance of the things with which we dwell—the things that shape our comportments—is rarely considered, despite the intimate, everyday proximity of those things. Despite Rickert's challenge, apprehending even a fraction of our ambient environs—the very ground of rhetoric—is exceedingly difficult. As a way of understanding our *theres*, Rickert suggests the term *attunement*, the typical English translation of Heidegger's *Befindlichkeit*.

I often read attunement as a verb. When walking through my neighborhood that warm February evening, I *attuned* to the world—I focused on the sounds of my environs as I passed through them, I registered what I could, and I reflected on how they related to me and to one another. But this understanding of attunement is limited. Rickert expanded and refined his notion of attunement, which is a much richer rhetorical concept than a notion of attunement-as-a-verb.

*Befindlichkeit*, in everyday German, is typically translated as mood or condition. Condition works well as both a noun and a verb, and both mood and condition describe states of being; it is this sense of attunement that is crucial to apprehending and studying ambient rhetoric. Rickert makes clear: attunement "names the *how* of a situation—how it will show up for someone, how it will matter" (quoted in Walsh et al. 2017, 449, original emphasis). Attunement frames the "disposition of a situation from within it as opposed to without" (449). And dispositions, he adds, are neither passive nor active but conditions of involvement (449). Moods condition us, involve us. "I am in the mood for . . ." is a statement of involvement in some situation, a sharing of openness, an articulation of a stance or comportment. Moods and conditions can fine-tune actions or dispositions. We tune into attunements.

This is a rhetorical way of being in ambience. We are always already *in* the world rather than on it (Ingold 2008), and thus we are "part of the world, inseparable from the world, beworlded and bethinged" (Rickert 2016, 230). Moods, too, are worldly and worldish—they emerge from the stitchwork of our *there* Being, and they condition ongoing comportments. Involvement does not presuppose control or intention. Rickert describes how "mood is an *a priori* possibility emerging from the situation as an attuning within that situation, not an emotional charge leaping from one person to the next" (quoted in Walsh et al. 2017, 449). A person is always attuned—that is, immersed, involved, entangled in ambient this-now-here-ness (449). Any inquiry into attunement discloses the ontological, "opens up our understanding of being-in-the-world more profoundly, providing a deeper sense of what life and world are" (449). Ontological questions are thus about deep relationality (449).

Attunement names involvement, disposition, and condition. And what any organism or thing *is* "already encapsulates its environment; the environment is already included in its basic structure and the particularities of its lifeways" (Walsh et al. 2017, 450). Before differentiating between beings, Rickert says, we must first differentiate "between ways of being, the manner in which they are *there*" (quoted on 450, original emphasis). "An organism," he adds, "cannot be prior to its ways of being in the world" (450). These ways of being take shape in the *there*, and *thereness* "is not pre-given and pre-formed" but rather "something that emerges with and through an environment" (450). "There is no 'being,'" he argues, "prior to a way of being-in-the-world where world is already iterated and internalized in how that entity takes shape and pursues life" (450). We are our *theres*. All that is ontic exists in relations, "and where there is relationality, there is meaning" (451).

Attunement also names nearnesses. Our involvements are entangled with that which is near us, with us, in us—that with which we dwell. At the end of chapter 4, I argued that Jason's way of dwelling with the Eucharist during his time as a missionary is a *there* that will move with him, that will continue to condition and iterate within new *theres*. In the brief vignette with which I began this chapter, I described other forms of nearness, some proximal and some much more distant—physically and temporally—yet *experienced* as near, relational, and iterative, still a part of my situated attunement, condition, and entanglement. I smell peanut butter cookies, proximally, and a nearness is likewise called across physical and temporal distances: sensory response triggers other sensory and affective responses—I am in my childhood kitchen in California, I see cookie sheets and stainless-steel fork tines, I puzzle over the hash pattern. A proximal sensory engagement recalls and iterates distant relations of nearness, across time and space and many different *theres*. I am sucked in, and time is unstuck (McNely 2019).

This is an example of what tuning into attunements accomplishes, rhetorically: recognition and recovery of relations, a scene of iterations, and awareness of nearnesses in our *theres*. Rhetoric, Rickert argues, "is the tuning and turning of attunements" (quoted in Walsh et al. 2017, 453).

\* \* \*

How do we explicitly tune and turn attunements? How do we engage, in a scholarly way, the mundane nearnesses of our *theres*? How do we reconcile attunements to the things with which we dwell, the things that dwell in us and move with us into new *theres*, new relations, and new iterations? Chapter 3 and chapter 4 each offered partial answers to this question by modeling visual ethnography to focus on specific aspects of ambient this-now-here-ness: material suasion, factorial rhetorics, sensory artifacts, and ambient dwelling. This chapter offers another approach for engaging ambience *as* ambience: multisensory autoethnography.

Below, I provide an overview of autoethnography and describe how I've adapted it to the study of ambient rhetorics. Multisensory autoethnography is an empirical way of exploring ambience using Heidegger's notion of *Gelassenheit*, or releasement. I describe the ways releasement is both a theoretical and a practical mode of turning toward and tuning into ambience. By practicing releasement in fieldwork, we can meet the challenge of approaching nearnesses, of "coming-into-nearness" of the things by which we dwell. I use fieldwork vignettes—written and visual—from one study of ambience, a systematic investigation of the everyday entanglements I experienced in a mundane and ordinary environment: my daily pedestrian commute to and from work. These vignettes explore and evince individual variations and mutual vulnerabilities. They suggest openings, disclosures, intra-actions, involvements, and moods. They demonstrate how and why the Nigels in our respective lives matter.

\* \* \*

On a late spring evening of warm winds and blood orange skies, flying pollen and blooming greens, a plump tabby trotted along the Beaumont sidewalk, belly swishing side to side.

"Hey, kitty. Are you Nigel?"

He had to be. I squatted and tucked my Kindle into my back pocket.

"Come 'ere, buddy," I said, aware that Nigel's family might be looking out the front window.

He came within arm's reach and gave up a scratchy meow. I rubbed his head, behind his ears, and stroked the length of his back. He seemed to like that, so I did it again. Hair jumped off his body and lingered in the warm air and late light. Most days, as I passed this way, I thought of Nigel. As I was drafting this chapter, I opened my field notes and searched for "Nigel"; his name came up eight times, on four different days over the course of my project. Nigel was a specter during fieldwork—I often wondered where he was, whether he was warm inside. Meeting him was worth the wait. His rough and scratchy voice chirped and bounced as he walked back and forth, rubbing his cheeks and sides against my jeans. I offered a few more strokes and said, "Bye, Nigel. See you soon!"

I walked away down Beaumont, then turned for one more look; Nigel sat with his tail curled around his front paws, looking back at me.

### AUTOETHNOGRAPHY AND AMBIENT ATTUNEMENT

Autoethnography seems ready-made for studies of rhetoric and writing—a research methodology wherein the researcher is the primary instrument and participant, exploring the self in society. The approach, despite increasing use and awareness, is still something of a scholarly interstice. Suspicions about its use, rigor, and application are common in the social sciences and humanities. Much of the trepidation stems from questions of validity and reliability. The skeptic asks: how can a study with an "n of 1" be rigorous? How can a methodology focused on a single self in society provide any kind of generalizable insights? How can methods and findings be replicated?

These are reasonable questions, but they stem from research paradigms that assume objectivity and replicability. Just as moods and attunements and conditions vary in nearly infinite ways, so too do knowledges about the world. Sometimes the most effective ways of understanding phenomena are not borne through the gold standard of clinical trials or from stratified sampling of surveys with 1,000 respondents or from quasi-experimental approaches. Autoethnography today seems to be facing many of the same challenges faced by qualitative researchers in the 1970s and 1980s.

I have neither the space nor the inclination to defend autoethnography as a methodology writ large. Instead, I argue that autoethnography is an appropriate and fruitful approach for exploring research questions driven by ambient rhetorical theory. The individual variations of one's ambient environs are *so* situated and nuanced that other common methods—such as ethnography, survey-based studies, or even oral histories—while technically possible to conduct with fidelity to situated experience, may not be feasible in practice. As Jenny Rice (quoted in Walsh et al. 2017) argues, studying individual variations does not necessarily have the goal of *representing* the individuals or environments under scrutiny but instead simply serves to make such voices heard.

This entails a different perspective, therefore, on what research *is* and what it *does* for theorists, researchers, and teachers of rhetoric and writing. Rice (quoted in Walsh et al. 2017, 436) suggests that any tuning to individual variations establishes mutual vulnerability. To be vulnerable is not only to be entangled but to be aware of that entanglement and thus to be open to suasion and risk, to circulations of force, change, and mutual intelligibility (435). Among the formative definitions of autoethnography is Deborah Reed-Danahay's assertion that it assumes "the researcher's vulnerable self, emotions, body, and spirit" (quoted in Muncey 2010, 30). She adds, crucially, that autoethnography "questions the notion of a coherent, individual self" (30). Considering Rice's and Rickert's work, autoethnography is thus a methodology par excellence for empirical inquiry into mutual vulnerability and entanglement, attunement, and ambient dwelling.

Autoethnographic scholarship exists on a spectrum, with evocative approaches at one end and analytic approaches at the other. Carolyn Ellis and Arthur P. Bochner (2000; Ellis, Adams, and Bochner 2011) have helped define evocative autoethnography. They argued that autoethnography is "an autobiographical genre of writing and research that displays multiple layers of consciousness, connecting the personal to the cultural" (Ellis and Bochner 2000, 739). In practice, in the work of Ellis (2004), Ellis and Bochner (2000), and other evocative autoethnographers (see, for example, Bochner and Ellis 1995; Denzin 2013; Goodall 2006; Pelias 2007; Poulos 2008; Tillmann 2009), an emphasis is placed on the *written* contribution made by the researcher, often at the expense of the transparent protocols and methods of most social science research. Evocative autoethnographies place a premium on richly rendering the experience of the research subject and evoking that experience to share and shape knowledge.

To connect with others, Tessa Muncey (2010, 30) argues, we need to understand the inner stories of people in all walks of life. For many evocative autoethnographers, however, traditional qualitative approaches are unable to sufficiently render inner stories. Indeed, even some autoethnographers are unable to meet the challenges of the form, which requires deep introspection and reflexivity, keen observations of one's environs, and a willingness to rigorously question one's assumptions and decisions (35). Ellis's early work was intended to "extend ethnography to include the heart, the autobiographical and the artistic text" (35). Evocative autoethnography often includes narrative techniques that mirror creative nonfiction and disrupt the genre norms of traditional social science research. Evocative autoethnographies are so prevalent in published scholarship that many researchers conflate this form of practice with autoethnography itself.

But Muncey notes that there are several forms of autoethnographic practice between the evocative and the analytic. Moving along the continuum, from the evocative and toward the analytic, we can include performative autoethnography (which may manifest as nontraditional forms of writing or presentation, including art, dance, song, or plays), narrative inquiry (which hews more closely to fiction or creative nonfiction than it does to social science reporting), gendered stories (which build from and extend feminist theory with the aim of making visible political and power imbalances), and phenomenological autoethnography (which draws from traditions of phenomenological social science to explore the self in society). As a response to the dominant position of evocative autoethnography among sociologists and anthropologists, the *Journal of Contemporary Ethnography* (*JCE*) published a special issue in 2006, led by Leon Anderson's "Analytic Autoethnography." Anderson made the case for more systematic and methodologically transparent autoethnographic research practices, situating autoethnography within traditions of symbolic interactionism and arguing that autoethnography can be practiced in a manner similar to ethnography.

Although Anderson's work has been scrutinized by autoethnographers from across the spectrum (including critical responses published in the *JCE* special issue), his argument was well-founded: the predominance of evocative autoethnography obscured and even precluded other implementations of the methodology. Anderson (2006) proposed five features of an analytic autoethnography: the researcher must be a complete member of the regional ontology under scrutiny (379); the researcher must demonstrate analytic reflexivity regarding the "mutual informativity" of the self in their milieu (383); there must be narrative visibility of the researcher's self—this point addresses the tendency of traditional ethnography to promote "a hidden and yet seemingly omniscient presence" (383); there should be an expression of dialogue with informants beyond the self to distinguish autoethnography from autobiography; and there must be a commitment to an analytic agenda, such that the researcher do more than simply document experience, using data instead to develop, refine, or extend social theory (387). In practice, Anderson suggests, analytic autoethnography is a contemporary form of self-reflexive, analytic ethnography. It is grounded in traditional ethnographic practices with valences stemming from the careful and systematic analysis of the self in society.

Ultimately, analytic autoethnography "lies at the intersection of biography and society: self-knowledge that comes from understanding our personal lives, identities, and feelings as deeply connected to and in large part constituted by—and in turn helping to constitute—the sociocultural contexts in which we live" (Anderson 2006, 390). Although analytic autoethnography will not ameliorate social scientific researchers who cannot accept any study of the self by the self, the systematic and analytic nature of Anderson's approach can mollify the concerns of many researchers. With an analytic approach, autoethnography can incorporate the kind of methodological rigor and transparency expected of other common forms of qualitative research, such as case study or ethnographic methodologies.

Kathleen Stewart's work models a productive middle way along the continuum of autoethnographic practice. Like many contemporary autoethnographers, Stewart has deep experience with ethnography. But Stewart's prose, whether in reporting findings from a traditional ethnographic study (1996) or autoethnographic work (2013), is, well, incredibly *evocative* (see especially *Ordinary Affects*, 2007). Her renderings of society and of the self in society are lush, reflecting the irreducibility of her research subjects, places, events, and affects. Autoethnography can be *both* systematic and evocative, *both* transparent and irreducible, *both* analytic and epistemologically ambivalent.

Stewart's (2013, 659) work also models how autoethnography is readymade for studies of rhetoric and writing: "autoethnography can be a way of doing something different with theory and its relation to experience." It is a methodology that is unsettling to many researchers, but for many more, it is a relief (659). Autoethnography draws attention to the processual nature of fieldwork and making sense of fieldwork phenomena *by writing*. In autoethnography, Stewart contends, "you write from a place in which the world is reacting to something: it's animated, incited, thrown together into something; you react to this thrown together world" (660).

Such writing is analytic; it is theory work. The descriptive detours common to autoethnographic reporting "note the incommensurateness of the elements [of experience] throwing themselves together" (Stewart 2013, 661). Writing itself "might become a hinge onto the commonplace labors of becoming sentient to whatever is happening" (661). Autoethnography is "a way of calling up the textures and densities of worlds of all kinds formed out of this and that—identities, situations, scenes, sensory conditions, bodies, meanings, weights, rhythms, absence" (667). It is "a hinge onto a moment of some world's legibility" (667). It is a methodological *poiesis*, another way of making ambience visible.

The "the textures and densities of worlds of all kinds" can be brought forth in and through visual fieldwork too. Elizabeth Chaplin (2011) was perhaps the first scholar to propose a visual autoethnography when she suggested that a photo diary might be a sound and systematic way of generating autoethnographic field notes. She argues that autoethnography has a responsibility to convey feeling, affect, and sensation (246), so the combination of images and prose may richly render research subjects and sites. She positions her own work as a middle way between the evocative and analytic ends of the autoethnographic continuum, arguing that theory can indeed be developed from the methodology while also rejecting any compunction to do so in a way that attempts to tie up or generalize the work.

Chaplin (2011) also illustrates ways in which autoethnographic projects may be relatively small in scale compared to ethnography. Her own study unfolds over three weeks of fieldwork, wherein she developed a better sense of two different versions of herself: "[Writing] autoethnography is the 'working me,' and the [visual] diary as itself is the 'off-duty me'" (253). These two forms of fieldwork come together analytically as ways of turning toward and tuning to Chaplin's everyday life. They are complementary, as her "images can say things that words can't"; taken together, her visual and written fieldwork provide richer details about her experience than either could alone (260).

Autoethnography can accommodate experimental prose alongside systematic fieldwork, visuals alongside words, and rich descriptions alongside (and *as*) theory generation. My own autoethnographic work has been inspired by Stewart and is driven by the desire to empirically explore new materialist and ambient perspectives on rhetoric and writing. But rather than the approach suggested by Chaplin, wherein photography complements an autoethnographic protocol by acting as a visual diary, I have incorporated visual methods into the methodology as a documentary pursuit, in at least two senses.

First, I have designed and executed analytic autoethnographies that include systematic visual documentation of the phenomena under scrutiny (see McNely 2016). Images were made each day during the study, composed and framed in the same manner. In this way, photographs systematically make phenomena visible and trace changes over time, acting as an archive of visual data from which to compare other forms of fieldwork, such as field notes and analytic memos. But I have also used photography as a documentary pursuit in the more popular sense of the term *documentary photography*, wherein a photographer or visual researcher uses images to trace and make visible a specific topic, subculture, or phenomenon (see McNely 2018, 2019). In this sense, the act of conducting visual fieldwork may be systematic but not uniform or circumscribed.

When conducting fieldwork, I am aware of the general phenomena I would like to better understand and document, but I am unsure of how they will show up in the world, in which contexts and times, with what kinds of emotions, intensities, or nuances. These senses of documentary photography, or, to avoid confusion with photojournalism, documentary fieldwork, may be accomplished simultaneously: the methods can document the specifics of a particular ontology or way of dwelling—"seared with reality" (Pinney 2011, 89)—while also evoking emotion, complexity, and nuance in each environment.

Ultimately, visual autoethnography is a methodology well suited to studies of attunement (as a noun). As I describe in the next section, empirical studies guided by new materialist and ambient theories of rhetoric are best developed as *multisensory* efforts. We need data collection methods and research protocols that include all the senses, or as many of the senses as are practical given the phenomena under scrutiny. Ambience is multisensory. Documenting ambience in praxiographic studies calls for multisensory methods and protocols.

## TURNING AND TUNING TO EVERYDAYNESS

Studying ambience empirically is personal. As a researcher and teacher of methods and methodologies, I wanted to design a protocol that would allow me to investigate ambience rigorously and systematically. But as I often tell my students, something like "ambience" is simply too expansive to study credibly. How do we get our arms around something so all-encompassing, so difficult to pin down? We narrow, narrow again, then narrow some more. We reduce irreducibles. The first item to eliminate was an IRB protocol. How would I credibly describe my study of ambience to an Institutional Review Board? No IRB approval means no human subjects save one: me. Autoethnography, then, was my first narrowing move in studying ambience.

The second way of narrowing scope was by activity. I have done this in previous visual autoethnographies: the borrowing and lending practices in one Little Free Library (McNely 2016) and phenomena in a specific environment—plastic bags along the borders and interstices of El Paso, Texas (McNely 2018). As I noted at the beginning of this chapter, for most of the year I walk to work. My commute, thirty minutes each way, immersed me in ambient environs that are simultaneously familiar and near, irreducible and distant. Narrowing by activity, then, was both feasible and tractable: I was already making the commute, and I could construct a protocol for making it strange and for systematically collecting data during an activity I was doing anyway.

Next, I designed a protocol to research ambience. Each day during the month of February, I would walk to my office and walk home, Saturdays and Sundays too. Each day, I would write two field note entries—one "inbound," reflecting on my commute to the office, and one "outbound," reflecting on my return home. During each leg of my commute, I would make at least one image. Field notes and documentary photographs thus comprised the two primary data collection methods I engaged systematically over the course of the study.

Each day I also carried a directional microphone, a portable audio recorder, and a tripod. With the tripod, directional microphone, and digital camera, I often composed brief videos. With the directional microphone and portable audio recorder, I often made brief recordings of ambient soundscapes. With the tripod, digital camera, and a shutter remote, I often made long-exposure photographs during the early February days when light was scarce. Finally, I wrote weekly analytic memos to synthesize and reflect on fieldwork. This humble research protocol generated rich data: 56 field note entries comprising over 30,000 words, 4 analytic memos comprising more than 3,500 words, 412 photographs, 19 videos, and 14 audio recordings. Narrowness in research design need not preclude depth in data collection.

My protocol explicitly engaged sensory experience in several ways. I explored sensory engagements and affects: the plump, stinging redness of my fingers in my office as they gradually warmed while I typed my field notes after trudging through snowy, below-freezing conditions; the smell of peanut butter cookies; the sad expression on the grill of a Volkswagen Beetle under heavy snow. My photographs evoke music, movement, the scent of incense and cigarettes and stale beer, the crunch of snow under one's feet. My videos focused on movements too, on materiality and ephemerality: leaves twisting on brittle stems; squirrels twitching on garbage cans; warm exhaust meeting the freezing air, billowing, stretching, dissipating. Audio recordings documented the sounds of my commute: boots crunching a layer of new snow; bird song and sirens, helicopters and car horns; yelling kids; HVAC systems droning. In field notes and memos I reflected on sensory experiences, combining and comparing them in my mind and in my writing as a way of grasping cognitively what needs no grasping at all in its everyday wholeness. This underscores the challenges of studying ambience: the attempt to reduce, even temporarily, irreducibles. I had to constantly fight a desire for salience.

After the study, I analyzed my data systematically. My project, in other words, meets the standards of autoethnographic rigor suggested by Leon Anderson (2006). However, I have chosen to write about this experience in an evocative key.

The project challenged my typical pedestrian comportment—closed off, focused, in my own head rather than open to the world. Sarah Pink (2012b, 28) argues for a conception of place as open, which "is crucial for [an] understanding of the openness and potentialities of practice." But to be receptive to the openness of place, to the worldish disclosures of beings and things of all kinds, required a change in my practices. My comportments toward my walk, toward my neighborhood, toward the sensory engagements in which I am habitually enmeshed also needed to open. And so I opened. On some days, such openings were forced: the decision to focus only on sounds during one walk home. Such reductions were a practical necessity—there is just too much of the world to tune and document, even on something so mundane as a 1.7-mile walk. But on some days, these constraints were heuristic and productive.

One morning, before leaving for campus, I stood in my kitchen holding a steaming cup of espresso, staring out at the back lawn—dormant and yellow-green, scattered with the few remaining fall leaves I never gathered. A small orange-and-white cat trotted along the far property line, then cut a diagonal across the fallow grass toward the large wooden fence that separates my yard from my neighbor's. At the foot of the fence, the little cat dipped paws and head into a declivity I did not know existed. Its body turned to liquid and pooled under the fence, a fleshy and stringy U that poured through to the other side.

As I walked to work that day, I followed my protocol, but I also could not help thinking about the cat in my backyard. Disclosures and recognitions. Spaces and affordances. Open comportments. Could I be like that cat? Open to worldish disclosures and opportunities? Sensitive to unseen openings? Able to contort myself so that my embodied comportment adjusts seamlessly to what is offered, to what I am already enmeshed and entangled within? One way readers might judge the "validity" and "rigor" of my multisensory autoethnography is to determine how well my descriptive analysis (rendered in both writing and photographs) answers such questions. Developing a protocol for studying ambience was important, but learning how to open myself, to be vulnerable to the disclosures of ambience, was even more crucial.

### MUTUAL VULNERABILITY, *GELASSENHEIT*

In Richard Marback's (2008, 50) conceptualization of mutual vulnerability, researchers in rhetoric should attend to the "availability and vulnerability of spaces, bodies, and objects to each other." Agency, for Marback (2008, 61) (as for Gries 2015), has no discrete origin but rather "lives in the event as the availability, the responsiveness, of ourselves and objects to each other." Marback's (2008, 49) understanding of agency is grounded in rhetorics of sensations and embodiment. Although he was responding to a concrete event (racist vandalism in Detroit), his notion of "event" can be extended to any given this-now-here-ness, any given *there*, recognized or not, understood or not, embraced or evaded; "the event" describes nothing more than our fundamental entanglements in any moment. What do things do to us, to our bodies, in our everyday environs, in everyday events? To make sense of sensations, Marback argues, we should recognize and explore mutual vulnerability. But "the search for meaning," he adds, "need not lead us to stable answers" (52).

Mutual vulnerability means finding comfort in instability, remaining open to the many possible intra-actions in which we are immersed, whether we're cognizant of them or not, whether they unfold in a recognizable event or whether they seep into us, unnoticed, during everyday life. Embodied and material rhetorics actively engage vulnerability as an ongoing moment, a happening: "Vulnerability to the moment of a rhetorical event is more than openness to circumstance. Vulnerability is an activity, a making do in the conjoined mental and physical worlds of embodied expression" (Marback 2008, 60). Mutual vulnerability is a mode of *there Being*. Worlds are thrown together through infinitesimal and factorial influencings, intra-actions, and diffractions—all, at some level, entangled in and as mutual vulnerability.

Rice (in Walsh et al. 2107), too, argues that we may be mutually vulnerable in any given environment. Our vulnerability may sometimes come as a surprise, but we can signal it, as Marback argues, through openness, a willingness to be available and tuned to disclosures of worldish ambience. My research protocol, the looping film clip in my mind of the neighbor cat dipping into unseen space—contorting its body, open to possibility—and my own desire to be that way, these are praxiographies of vulnerability.

But there is another kind of vulnerability and openness needed to study ambience: the work, on us and in us, of theory. I needed grounding in theoretical comportments suitable to guide both fieldwork and analysis. Rickert's work represents the overarching impetus and guiding theoretical framework for my study. The theories guiding my methodological decisions too. But to tune attunements, to develop and practice an open comportment, to enact mutual vulnerability as a doing, I called on another theory of openness congruent with Rickert's discussion of mood and condition: *Gelassenheit*. *Gelassenheit*, or *releasement*, is both a theoretical and a practical opening onto the world's disclosures, a praxiography of mutual vulnerability.

In his *Discourse on Thinking* (1966), Heidegger argues for the importance of meditative thinking and a new perspective on the ontic—everything that exists—which presupposes an openness to the mystery and being-potential of any given thing: releasement. The utility of meditative thinking is relatively straightforward, but the notion of releasement is more philosophically and practically nuanced. The two concepts are closely related, however, so I will take them in turn before commenting on how they relate to multisensory autoethnography, mutual vulnerability, and tuning to ambience.

Heidegger (1966) begins with popular tropes of contemporary thought. Modern society, he argues, is in full flight from thought—at least the kind of thought he wishes his audience to consider. We see thinking all around us, but such thinking is largely *calculative*—the kind of thinking that involves plans and investigations that yield definite results (46). "Calculative thinking," he says, "computes," and its computations seek and find new and improved economic and practical results (46). "Calculative thinking," then, "races from one prospect to the next. Calculative thinking never stops, never collects itself" (46). Calculative thinking differs from meditative thinking because it does not *ponder*.

Heidegger (1966) acknowledges that calculative thinking is necessary, but not to the exclusion of meditative thinking. Some people think meditative thinking somehow floats above reality, inheres in a different realm than the here and now. He concedes that meditative thinking requires practice, requires a concerted shift from calculative thinking, but he argues that meditative thinking is available to anyone. It is not ethereal and ungraspable but eminently practical. Humans are always already thinking beings and, thus, meditating beings (47). Meditative thinking need not be seen as separate but rather as embedded in the here and now: "It is enough if we dwell on what lies close and meditate on what is closest; upon that which concerns us, each one of us, here and now; here, on this patch of home ground; now, in this present hour of history" (47).

In Heidegger's time, the impediments to meditative thinking were mass media—television, advertisements, ubiquitous photographs. Today, we are encouraged to think transactionally in the social media feeds and streaming media ever beckoning from the shiny rectangles in the palms of our hands. The achievements of the natural sciences, the inundations of mass media, the commodification of our time and attention conspire to inhibit reflection; calculative thinking does not meditate, and we, following the spirit of the age, thus "forget to ponder" (1966, 30). A future without meditative thinking is grim; Heidegger could see clearly, in 1955, that humans "will be encircled ever more tightly by the forces of technology" (51). These forces will be felt everywhere, in every minute of the day, operating outside one's will and control, shaping us.

These forces, as impediments, do not preclude reading or taking notice; indeed, we read and write now more than ever. But it is one thing to take notice—to read a headline, to retweet the latest absurdity or outrage, to like or comment on a rant—and something else entirely to understand and to ponder (Heidegger 1966, 52). We are unprepared for the pace of change, the swift and powerful currents of calculative and transactional thinking that dominate modern society (52). Although delivered in 1955, these remarks seem at once prescient and exhausting. We can see that we were unprepared for the pace of change, and yet we are, most of us, tired of hearing the argument, tired of being shamed.

Heidegger's lecture shifts at this point, perhaps because he too sensed that his audience could stand only so many reminders of their own tendencies toward calculative thinking or worse: not thinking at all. So he offers an alternative. "Perhaps the answer we are looking for," Heidegger (1966, 53) suggests, "lies at hand; so near that we all too easily overlook it. For the way to what is near is always the longest and thus the hardest for humans. This is the way of meditative thinking." Heidegger knows it is foolish to attack the technologies that have become essential to our lives, so he instead argues for both/and: we can use our technologies, and we can leave them be. We can do both.

Heidegger (1966) argues, in the same manner as so many contemporary mindfulness gurus, that we should be more intentional about our use of technology and about the ratios of calculative to meditative thinking in our everyday lives. He suggests a perspective well-grounded in philosophy and rooted in everyday experience: we can develop comportments toward technology that express both engagement and withdrawal at the same time. He calls this comportment *die Gelassenheit zu den Dingen*, "releasement toward things" (54). In modern German, *Gelassenheit* is typically used to express composure, calmness, unconcern, or even tranquility; in its older connotations, it carries a related meaning: "the sense of letting the world go and giving oneself to God" (54; note from John Anderson).

But translations of Heidegger's *Gelassenheit* typically use the word *releasement* because it is not a common English word and thus is "free from too specific connotative meanings" (1966, 54; note from John Anderson); it is used to evoke a state of difference, an opening toward the world that is unusual and reserved for a particular kind of thinking and being, which is what Heidegger intends. Note too that *Gelassenheit* is oriented *toward the world* and toward the *things* of the world. Heidegger's use of *Ding* carries with it a sense of gathering—we gather things in our everyday lives, and we are *gathered by things* as well. *Gelassenheit*, then, suggests a comportment of openness toward things, toward their being and their capacity to gather.

This is why Heidegger is so interested in developing a distinction between calculative and meditative thinking before he introduces the notion of *Gelassenheit*. If our everyday comportment toward things is calculative, then the being or being-potential of any given thing will be circumscribed by its usefulness. If the use-value of any given thing is not readily apprehended, then its being is immediately (but not irrevocably) reduced and set aside. Such a comportment, while certainly necessary in many aspects of everyday life, is also nearly closed; it perpetuates subject-object divisions and positions humans as set apart from the things by which we dwell. Heidegger argues, again, with prescience that the meanings of our technological objects are unclear.

Indeed, such objects *hide* their meanings from us (Heidegger 1966, 55). But if we understand that the meanings are there—that, as Steven Shaviro (2014) argues, the being of any given thing is inexhaustible—then "we stand at once within the realm of that which hides itself from us, and hides itself just in approaching us" (Heidegger 1966, 55). Heidegger argues that ontologies of ontic things may not (or may never) be fully disclosed, and yet we can nevertheless relate to those ontologies with meditative thinking, with an open comportment, with releasement. "That which shows itself and at the same time withdraws is the essential trait of what we call the mystery," he says (55). The mystery here is not necessarily metaphysical but rather that which we do not fully understand or apprehend—the meanings that another being conceals from us, for example. But a meditative comportment—an intentional mode of *there Being*—can enable "us to keep open to the meaning hidden in technology, *openness to the mystery*" (55, original emphasis), openness to the facets of being that we do not yet (or do not yet fully) understand.

Releasement grants us "the possibility of dwelling in the world in a totally different way" (Heidegger 1966, 55). It promises us "a new ground and foundation upon which we can stand and endure in the world of technology without being imperiled by it" (55). The notions of openness and releasement forming the ground or the foundation of a new comportment toward the world and its things are prerequisites for meaningfully engaging and tuning to our ambient environs, which are in turn the very ground of rhetoric (Rickert 2013). But releasement does not happen naturally for most of us (Heidegger 1966, 56). Instead, releasement and openness "both flourish," Heidegger says, "through persistent, courageous thinking" (56), meditative thinking.

Heidegger's "Conversation on a Country Path about Thinking" (1966) composed from notes written in 1944–45, develops the themes of *Gelassenheit* and openness in a more philosophical key. In many ways, it embodies the semantic, linguistic, and technical challenges that make so much of Heidegger's work opaque for so many. But the "Conversation" is essential for understanding and developing *Gelassenheit* as a theory and praxiography for encountering ambience. First, it extends meditative thinking through a more complex notion of *waiting*; second, it develops further relations and nuance between nearnesses and distances.

The setting of the "Conversation" is straightforward. A Teacher, a Scholar, and a Scientist converse, in medias res, while walking along a country path. This setting places the interlocutors away from the concerns, cares, and trappings of everyday life, even as the conversation unfolds among the most mundane acts—walking, thinking, listening, and speaking. The discussion begins with questions about the nature of humankind and the most effective manner of posing and answering such questions. The Teacher, for example, suggests that understanding the essence of thinking "can be seen only by looking away from thinking" (Heidegger 1966, 58). This exchange, at the beginning of the dialogue, establishes an important methodological thread: the best way to approach the essence of something may be by moving away from, or adjacent to, the commonly perceived locus of that essence. To explore thinking, we might look away from thinking. To explore willing, we might consider non-willing. To explore representation, we might force ourselves not to re-present.

Readers familiar with Heidegger's philosophical method will recognize this tactic: in *Being and Time* (2010), for example, the language used is sometimes discomfiting because it is designed to disrupt the common nomenclature of philosophical inquiry and thus distance us from entrenched ways of approaching phenomena. Although exchanges in the dialogue may seem obtuse, they are designed with this method in mind. The Scientist says to the Teacher and the Scholar: "You want a non-willing in the sense of a renouncing of willing, so that through this we may release, or at least prepare to release, ourselves to the sought-for essence of a thinking that is not willing" (Heidegger 1966, 59–60). Stated another way, we must willfully look away from willing to approach the essence of thinking without willing, and we must do so without re-presenting Being—that is, approaching and discussing Being in the same ways we always have.

This change in method and this distancing from formal philosophical propositions and nomenclatures lead the interlocutors to the first major discovery of the dialogue, one that is significant to Heidegger's theory of releasement. The Teacher responds to the Scientist's statement about "willfully look[ing] away from willing" by suggesting that he has "uncovered something essential" (Heidegger 1966, 60). We must first *will* any release, any openness; but in so doing, we pause and then allow what may come. We *will*, and then we stop willing.

As John Anderson argues in his introduction to *Discourse on Thinking* (1966, 23), we must wait *upon* rather than wait *for*. The former presupposes openness, whereas the latter presupposes expectation. This is where Heidegger's disruptive method is crucial: waiting itself is typically understood as a *human* activity. Most often, we wait *for*. But waiting *upon*, or, to interpolate Heidegger, *looking away from waiting*, transforms the typical understanding of the act: waiting *upon* is a waiting in which we know not what *for* or *why* we wait. Rather, we wait in openness, and what appears is a gift—unexpected, unwanted, yet undertaken for what it is. The subtle change in prepositions, the slight shift in view, transforms subjective human expectation to acknowledgment of what *is* (23).

The Teacher suggests that as we wean ourselves from willing we stay "awake for releasement" (Heidegger 1966, 61). The Scholar asks whether this itself is an awakening, but the Teacher notes that "on our own we do not awaken releasement in ourselves" (61). Another paradox of willing and non-willing, opening ourselves and experiencing releasement, waiting *for* versus waiting *upon*. The Scientist asks whether releasement "is effected from somewhere else"; the Teacher says it is "not effected, but let in" (61). To allow anything in, we must first find or create an opening, and only in openness can we approach Being.

*Gelassenheit*, then, involves waiting (upon) in openness and vulnerability; rather than being released *from* something—everyday cares and worries, the expectations of loved ones and society—we are instead released *to* Being. Releasement is both theory and practice. Anderson (1966, 26) argues that *Gelassenheit* contains "a kind of steadfastness which is related to a resolve for truth, and which when fully comprehended is to be called 'in-dwelling.' " Meditative thinking is not *just* an opening up but a *resolve* to wait in openness—a practice, a comportment, a form of dwelling. "In meditative thinking," Anderson adds, one "opens to Being and resolves for its disclosure" (26). This resolve is "not an exercise of subjective human powers" but rather "taking a stand which reveals Being, a kind of dwelling in Being" (26).

Heidegger's discussion of meditative thinking and releasement evinces a theoretical orientation toward—and practice of—listening, waiting, and encountering ambience. It describes a comportment toward one's relations with the ontic. Heidegger is not suggesting a contemplative or spiritual practice (to be clear, he is not discounting such approaches either) but rather an opening up of human thinking, a releasement toward the non-human environments in which humans are immersed. The methodological implications of this perspective on waiting and opening become clear as the "Conversation" continues.

The Teacher, Scholar, and Scientist engage in what seems a pedantic discussion of representation. The challenge of exploring essences, a common theme in Heidegger's work, is avoiding the trap of simply re-presenting concepts with the same baggage with which we approached them. In doing so, we find no essence at all but only the silt and residue of previous thought. The Scientist and the Scholar are troubled because they have no previous conceptual or philosophical framework for re-presenting to their own minds what releasement might look like; they realize instead that it cannot be re-presented (Heidegger 1966, 62). To this the Teacher assents; rather than try to re-present the concept, "we are to do nothing but wait" (62). Waiting upon is a methodological move, one that does not force encounters or presuppose re-presentations.

We wait *for* nothing. Waiting has no expectation. Releasement stems *from* nothing. Instead, we open and wait upon what comes. We resist re-presentations, for in re-presenting, we objectify appearances. And when we objectify appearances, we place the resulting *objects* at a distance from us, into a stable horizon of knowing and perceiving, knower and perceived, us and them.

The Teacher, Scholar, and Scientist come to realize that appearances and objects are not the same and that the horizon is not in front of us, at a distance, but rather surrounds us, encircles us, envelops us, and *moves through us*. Their discussion brings the two facets of releasement together—waiting and proximity. Waiting upon "lets re-presenting entirely alone. It really has no object," the Scholar notes (Heidegger 1966, 68). In waiting upon, "we leave open what we are waiting for," says the Teacher (68). This kind of waiting "releases itself into openness," the Teacher adds, "into the expanse of distance," says the Scholar, "in whose nearness it finds the abiding in which it remains," says the Scientist (68). "Openness itself," says the Scholar at this point, "would be that for which we could do nothing but wait" (68). In openness, thinking itself, says the Scientist a moment later, "would be coming-into-the-nearness of distance" (68).

Some re-presentation is necessary, unfortunately, to follow the path of the Teacher, Scholar, and Scientist and the path of my argument—through philosophy, my ambient environs, and my daily commute. Neither the Scholar nor the Scientist—nor, for that matter, Heidegger himself—offers up a Zen koan here. The writing is obtuse, but the ideas are simple: meditative thinking—the ability to ponder, to wait upon what comes—is a practical approach to that which has been distanced in subject-object dualism, in anthropocentrism, and in technological determinism. We exist among distancing practices of routine and habitus, of norms and expectations, of calculative or transactional modes of thought. But these are abstractions. Such distances can be seen plainly: in an automobile, on an ordinary commute, distances are brought near; but wrapped in tons of metal, plastic, and glass, we are separated from the world, literally sealed off, moving on the world instead of in and through it. We are distanced from what is near.

Releasement presupposes waiting—waiting *upon* rather than waiting *for*. This has important methodological implications for studying ambient rhetoric because "waiting moves into openness without re-presenting anything" (Heidegger 1966, 69). Aside from the initial decision to wait, we cannot *will* ourselves into releasement; by waiting, however, we let ourselves into it (69). This is not the same as saying that we let ourselves into the essence of Being. Despite our habitual distancing practices, "We are not and never could be outside of" Being (72). Waiting in openness, as a methodological move, thus releases us from our distancing practices (73). And we encounter the nearness of distanced objects, beings, and environments.

In releasement, what we habitually distance *moves toward us* (Heidegger 1966, 74). Near the end of the dialogue, the Scholar suggests that a fragment from Heraclitus might encapsulate the nature of thinking about Being. The fragment contains only one word, Αγχιβασιη, which the Teacher translates as "going toward" (88). The Scholar responds that its literal translation is "going near" (89). This second translation evokes the sense that one can come near to something in waiting alone, but the Teacher adds a third translation: "moving-into-nearness" (89). To this, the Scientist suggests a final interpretation: "letting-onself-into-nearness" (89). What we perceive as distant and what we distance from ourselves through our everyday practices is always already near us. That nearness cannot be simply re-presented. It can, however, be engaged, sensed, and experienced in releasement. We open and in so doing let ourselves into what is near, into nearness itself.

*Gelassenheit* is both a theory of relations and a practice of opening to ambience. It is *as* a theory of opening and of collapsing distances that *Gelassenheit* conditions practice and realigns one's bodily comportments. Although Rickert's theory of rhetorical ambience and attunement draws heavily from Heidegger, he rarely invokes the *Discourse on Thinking*. This is no criticism; instead, by approaching Rickert's work orthogonally, methodologically, we can see how rich and open his framework is for rhetorical theory. Exploring ambience empirically, with a methodological comportment of releasement, fosters rigorous investigation of suasive relations and intra-actions of all kinds; it allows us to be open, vulnerable, an unexpectant toward those relations and their variations; it allows us to come nearer to that which we distance in our everyday practices; and it allows us to tune attunements.

In releasement, we open outward and let ourselves in to a world bursting with disclosures. Releasement is not metaphysical; it is simply an opening up, a waiting upon, and a moving into nearness of that which surrounds us, envelops us, moves through us, and conditions our ways of being and acting in the world.

### COMMUTING IN RELEASEMENT

What follow are four fieldwork vignettes that demonstrate methodological engagements with ambience. These are praxiographies of releasement—tuning and turning toward the sensory and affective engagements of one ordinary commute. They evince the complexity of nearnesses and of ambient affectivity, and they offer evidence of rhetoric's stratigraphic abundance—the layers of worldly affectivity that serve as the ground for rhetorical being. Fieldwork photographs offer sensory engagements; they were composed in moments of openness, in moments of waiting, in affective vulnerabilities that often arose and dissipated in fractions of seconds. They make their own arguments about releasement and mutual vulnerability, offering perspectives on nearness that stand alongside and intra-act with written perspectives.

My movements through one ordinary neighborhood were also movements through what Stephanie Springgay and Sarah E. Truman (2017, 16) call "geological forces and land-centred knowledges." In describing the contemporary rhythms of my city, I acknowledge forms of memory and movement that precede and condition any current understandings of my environs. Despite the city's attempts at fixity, the landforms and biosphere are ancient, with material and biosocial histories that are buried under paved streets and cinderblocks. Drawing on Kathryn Yusoff (2015), Springgay and Truman (2017, 26) note that the term *geosocial* draws attention to "the ways that the geological and the social are knotted, while also attending to different geologic scales. While the earth has typically been understood as a geologic surface upon which social relations occur, geosociality for Yusoff insists on the imbrication of geological formations and social formations. In other words, both are materialized simultaneously." The geosocial histories of my neighborhood, though unseen and largely unappreciated, nonetheless contribute to understandings of the city and its surroundings.

Springgay and Truman also invoke Aninishinaabe scholar Vanessa Watts (2013, 29), whose notion of "Place-Thought" draws attention to "the earth's aliveness and agency." Watts argues that "Place-Thought is based upon the premise that land is alive and thinking and that humans and nonhumans derive agency through the extensions of these thoughts" (2013, 21). The land is alive and thinking thoughts beyond our comprehensible timescales. The landforms don't belong to me, to the city, to the nation in which I live; Lexington's street names and routes are ephemeral from the perspective of geosociality and Place-Thought.

Moreover, the city's current boundaries, thoroughfares, policies, and practices are not only recent in terms of geosocial timescales; they are wholly artificial, imposed upon landforms and histories of use driven by settler colonialism. The streets of my city pave over misery and treachery too. Jennifer Clary-Lemon (2020, 1) has argued that "rhetoric and composition's new material gaze has not, as of yet, reconciled that it chooses not to include the work of Indigenous scholars and writers in thinking through material epistemologies and ontologies." She asks, "How might the material turn be enriched by the overt acknowledgment of Indigenous materialism, rather than surreptitious borrowing?" (2). My study acknowledges the geosocial histories of Lexington, its embedded and rich histories of Place-Thought, its history of settler colonialism and imperialism, and the hauntingly absent presence within these landforms of Indigenous cultures whose artifacts and forms of dwelling have been invisibilized and buried by backhoes, construction cranes, asphalt, concrete, and racist policies of consumption and conquest.

The Lexington, Kentucky, that I moved through is a recent invention in geosocial time, the usurped home of Indigenous peoples who dwelled in this area for nearly 14,000 years before colonial settlements. At the time Lexington was claimed as settler territory in 1775, the Chickasaw, Cherokee, Yuchi, and Shawnee peoples also had claims in Kentucky. Their histories have been largely overwritten in Lexington, by the city's very infrastructure. Indigenous materialisms, however, are inseparable from the city's geosocial history and its Place-Thought. My walks through Lexington are walks through occupied lands that remember and think.

**Possum Tails**

*February 13, Outbound*
There was heavy snow last night. This morning's walk was sure-footed, the snow unblemished on many sidewalks, traction good in the fresh fall, no ice. I work late, heading home in the creeping dark, ten minutes to seven. Outside my building, I look up and see the dying remnants of a purple sky and wispy cotton candy clouds. I make my way through campus, and near its edge I notice that I've lost myself, I've lost these last four or five minutes. I've noticed nothing. I scold myself, tell myself that I'm supposed to be paying attention.

As I ready to cross Rose, I look left and right, like a good citizen. I have plenty of time to cross before the cars I see, far down the hill, will reach this spot. Halfway across the street, though, I see that two cars have just turned the corner to my right and are heading down the hill, swiftly. One buzzes by me, but the other slows, then flashes headlights to encourage my crossing. I do, but before I'm across the car is rolling toward me. It seems like it wants to buzz me, to show me who's boss, to teach me a lesson. As I reach the sidewalk, the car is next to me, close, and the driver punches the gas hard, speeding down the street. I'm not sure what the point of this display is. I slowed them down for two seconds? I offended the driver by not waving a "thank you" for flashing headlights at me? I wish people in cars would ignore me.

I weave through a courtyard in between sorority and fraternity houses. This is my typical route—direct, quiet, built for pedestrian traffic. I look up and see three young women walking toward me on the small, paved path, deep in conversation. Each wears tan, knee-high boots and puffy

*Figure 5.1. Wind and waves. Author photo.*

coats; the woman in the middle is swaddled in a giant tartan scarf. They stop talking to each other as I draw near.

On the other side of the courtyard, on Colombia Avenue, thirty or so sorority members stand on the sidewalk in sweatshirts and pajamas, wrapped in blankets and robes. There has been a fire alarm, and they wait across Colombia Avenue—one of the busiest streets on campus—for an all clear. I hear one say "that guy has a video camera." Another yells "take a picture of me." A third says "take a picture." Another says "hey you with the camera . . ." but she trails off when it becomes clear that I don't want to take a picture of them. I walk up the street and hear sirens behind me now. The sorority girls peal in unison. A couple of minutes later, I hear more sirens.

The sidewalks are dodgy now. Thousands of students have walked the neighborhood since this morning, and the compressed snow congeals, hardens itself against the indignity of footfalls. Near Wildcat Market, two different young men, at two different times, move onto the snow and ice so I can have the little single-track path that's clearest. That's nice of them. Pedestrians in this neighborhood, I think, don't engage in the kind of dick-size displays I saw earlier from motorists. I turn right onto Beaumont, where it's easier to walk down the middle of the street than to continue along the icy sidewalk.

I see a cat about forty feet ahead. It steps from the sidewalk into the street. The curve of its spine looks wrong. Maybe it's not a cat. I quiet my footfalls and slow down a bit, hoping to get close enough to see. It's halfway into the street—it's definitely not a cat, and I'm hoping, willing it to be a raccoon. It looks up the street, away from me, waiting, thinking. Twenty feet away now. I'm quiet, walking in the middle of the street on bare pavement, carefully, rolling heel to toe, heel to toe. It turns its head and looks right at me—raccoon—then moves, deliberately but in no rush, across the street and headfirst into a sewer opening.

*February 24, Outbound*

I'm not sure what time it is when I leave my office, but it's light outside. The days are longer. It's cold, but the sun is still bright, the sky still blue. I can feel spring when I look into people's faces—there's a looseness in their shoulders, wrists, and hands.

A bluegrass three piece plays on the little stoop of Wildcat Market. I linger for a couple of minutes, listening, watching the tendons bounce in the forearms of the banjo player, muscles flex in the thin throat of the stand-up bass player as he sings. I think about photographing them, not for this project but because there's something in this little tableau that I want to remember and see again. I don't shoot, though.

A few blocks later, on Beaumont, I shoot a driveway, mostly because the sun is setting, the light is warm, and I've wanted to capture the occupant's "keg barbecue" for some time. There's a house on Sunset that has a yellow "Don't Tread on Me" flag draped over the windowpane glass in the front door. I've wanted to shoot that for a long time, too.

Around the corner, on Tremont, I look down a long driveway. At the end, something moves near the garbage bins, slow and languid as honey. A possum works away in bright early dusk, its lean white tail an exclamation point on the blacktop. I stand and watch. It waddles toward me down the driveway, alongside a parked sedan, then hangs a left, picking its way through the shrubs beneath a low and wide bay window. I'm crouched now, hoping to get a shot. The possum looks my way, looks and sees. Its pace quickens and I squeeze the shutter. Around the corner and into the backyard, the possum is gone.

Closer to home, I pass a house with *NBC Nightly News* on an oversized wall-mounted flat screen. People still watch the news?

*February 26, Outbound*

It's 8:25 p.m., in the high teens outside. Just past Wildcat Market, the "Don't Tread on Me" flag is lit from behind, the yellow nylon glowing through the

*Figure 5.2. Traces. Author photo.*

glass windowpanes of the front door, spilling canary-tinted light onto the stoop and front walk. I have to take this shot. It's a long exposure but not *that* long. But the shutter stays open, stays open, stays open. I'm not doing anything wrong, but this feels strange—my DSLR on a tripod, pointed at the front door of a stranger's house in the dark, me standing there watching it, watching the door, watching for movement in the front window. I rehearse what I'll say if someone comes stomping out of the house, asking "what the fuck are you doing with that camera." "I'm doing a project on the neighborhood, and I thought your flag was really interesting. Want to see the shot?" No one comes out. No one stomps but me.

The neighborhood is muted after dark. The birds must be sleeping. Dogs must be curled up on couches. Nigel must be grooming himself on someone's lap. Quiet raccoons and possums and cockroaches are out. Someone is always out.

My fingers and toes are cold. I blow into my hands and stomp my feet.

**Subtle Reclamations**

February 1. It's 62 degrees at 4:00 p.m., with sun breaking through high, white, puffy clouds. Babies smile in strollers. Runners wear shorts and tanks. Students on campus hang hammocks, bare feet grazing dormant grass. The timing of this heat wave feels both odd and hopeful, like taking a wrong turn but seeing something new along the way.

*Figure 5.3. Subtle reclamations. Author photo.*

There's a tree near the corner of Tremont and Kastle that is slowly spilling over the sidewalk. I look up and down Tremont. No cars coming; a woman with a stroller walks away from me in the distance. I lie down on my stomach in the street, alongside the curb, and bring my camera to my left eye. But this is no good. I sit on the curb. This puts me next to the tree, but I know that I am both next to and on top of it, its prying roots a record of time and space in a strong, fleshy network deep below the neighborhood. I run my hand along a section of its trunk that overlaps the sidewalk curb. Cold, rough, and alive. And painted yellow in spots, the curb indistinguishable from the tree itself to the city vehicles that signal caution in reflective paint.

Jane Bennett's (2010) *Vibrant Matter* includes this remarkable assertion from Charles Darwin (1881, 205): "Worms have played a more important part in the history of the world than most persons would at first assume." Worms make history because they make vegetable mold, which provides the fertile ground for plants of all kinds to take root. By making the earth a hospitable place for human agriculture, these worms indirectly make possible "the cultural artifacts, rituals, plans, and endeavors of human history" (Bennett 2010, 96).

Worms thus "inaugurate human culture" as they work "alongside people and their endeavors" (Bennett 2010, 96). For Darwin, the agency of worms is not intentional, but their exertions contribute to human history nonetheless (96). According to Bennett, "Darwin describes the

Walks, Talks, Gelassenheit 177

*Figure 5.4 and 5.5. Subtle reclamations. Author photos.*

activities of worms as one of the many 'small agencies' whose 'accumulated effects' turn out to be quite big" (96). She updates this notion, arguing that "worms participate in heterogeneous assemblages in which agency has no single locus, no mastermind, but is distributed across a swarm of various and variegated vibrant materialities" (96).

These small agencies and vibrant materialities surround us, indifferent to our plans, designs, and intentions. As I walked to work, I

*Figure 5.6. Subtle reclamations. Author photo.*

considered the slow and subtle agencies of mature trees in the neighborhood. Their vibrancy is muted by their slowness, their continuous movements invisible in our everyday. But their effects are myriad and accessible to those willing to look and wait.

Uneven, buckled concrete is an effect of a tree's slow agency, of its subtle, subterranean, subversive movements. Trees slowly reclaim space, folding over and down the tops and sides of curbs. Humans respond, painting trees yellow where curbs should be, smoothing new concrete around roots, or adjusting routes altogether. The neighborhood's collective human-non-human relations are slow, subtle reclamations.

**Sounds, Intensities, Rhythms**

I've been to China three times—once to Shanghai and twice to Changchun, in northeastern China's Jilin province. In total, I've spent three months and a handful of days living in China, speaking rudimentary Mandarin, teaching, writing, and making photographs of everyday life.

The distances between Lexington, Kentucky, and Changchun, China, are many and obvious. On a run at 4:30 a.m., the first full day of my third trip, in the full light of a morning without daylight savings time, the soundscape of Changchun enveloped me and I acknowledged it for the first time—recognized and welcomed how its sounds resonated through me, in me.

The pace of my thinking kept up with the pace of my feet running over cracked sidewalks, packed dirt desire paths, and uneven brickwork. The soundscapes of everyday life in Changchun—and my responses to them, acknowledged or not—showed me the profound distances between home and here. The visual and cultural and everyday distances were in no way diminished, but it dawned on me for the first time just how much the *sounds* of China affected me, resonated within me, as if drawing a line on a map to illustrate the distances, my profound displacement from my ordinary life in Lexington, even as I was involved in something ordinary—my daily early morning run.

I slowed and jogged by a light rail station, thinking. Signage in simplified Chinese, endless apartment blocks, an urban landscape nothing like my Lexington neighborhood—none of these things worked on me as deeply as the sounds. The sounds showed me differences.

I walked and thought about my dog, Mo, who is often with me on morning runs. I thought about the sounds she'd hear in Changchun, with her regal, upright, triangular basenji ears. Jackhammers, hammers striking iron pipes, metal clanking on metal, falling bricks—the incessant din of a country constantly building, growing, bursting. Sweeping sweeping sweeping—bamboo brooms in the streets and gutters—swish swish swish. Squeaky, rusty bike chains. Cab horns. The hollow echo of furniture moving across the tile floor in the apartment above me. Shuffling shoes on sidewalk bricks. A little girl, holding hands with her mom and grandma, counting to four in the sweetest singsong—*yī, èr, sān, sì, yī, èr, sān, sì*—each word timed with a stomping foot, left, right, left, right. The fluid, sometimes languid, sometimes musical tones of Mandarin, a language, to my ears, like a Heraclitean river whose notes I sometimes recognize long after they've flowed by. The vocalizations I make in hushed tones on my own, far enough away from others that I'm not self-conscious, working on the aspirated sound of a word such as "*cai*" (草). The sounds of men, especially older men, generating phlegm from deep inside their chests, hocking little glistening treasures on the sidewalks in morning light. University students standing at the top of the arena grandstand before 6:00 a.m., holding textbooks, pacing, repeating phrases in English over and over, drilling pronunciation with odd constructions: "You know that I know these things. You know that I know these things. You know that I know these things."

Meno—a former student of Gorgias (according to Socrates)—is credited with an incisive axiom on invention: "How will you go about finding that thing the nature of which is totally unknown to you" (quoted in Solnit 2005, 4). Rebecca Solnit (4) argues that this question concerns

*Figure 5.7. Sounds and rhythms. Author photo.*

much more than invention, that it is, indeed, "the basic tactical question of life." To answer it, one must lose oneself. To be lost, she argues, channeling Walter Benjamin, is to be fully present, to "be capable of being in uncertainty and mystery" (6). Although spatially and situationally aware, there were many times in China when I felt lost, in the best possible way. Lost among the soundscape of Changchun, vulnerable to everything around me, I moved much closer to that which is distanced in everyday life—the myriad sounds that shape me, condition me, even when I'm not listening, hearing, or paying attention.

"Noise. Noises. Murmurs. When lives are lived and hence mixed together, they distinguish themselves badly from one another"—so begins chapter 3 of Henri Lefebvre's *Rhythmanalysis* (2013, 27), in which an apartment window a few stories above Rue Rambuteau in Paris, facing Centre Pompidou, is a metaphor for proper distance from the sounds and rhythms of everyday life. "In order to grasp and analyse rhythms," he argues, "it is necessary to get outside them, but not completely" (27). To grasp a rhythm, he adds, "it is necessary to have been *grasped* by it; one must *let oneself go*, give oneself over, abandon oneself to its duration" (27, original emphasis).

The window, with its little balcony overlooking the bustle of Rue Rambuteau, allows one to be both inside and outside, near and far simultaneously. This argument is reminiscent of Michel de Certeau's in *The Practice of Everyday Life* (1984): at street level, one is immersed in "the

*Figure 5.8. Sounds and rhythms. Author photo.*

multiplicity of noises, murmurs, rhythms" (quoted in Lefebvre 2013, 28). But with the right vantage point, de Certeau argues, we can better see the "spatial acting-out of place" (de Certeau 1984, 98)—movements en masse, routes, spatial affordances. Both Lefebvre and de Certeau seem to be saying that we need to distance ourselves from what is immediate and, in doing so, bring ourselves closer to what has been distanced. Perhaps we need to find a space in which we can get lost, some middle ground—a balcony that lets us hear rhythms among the din.

Travel may bring awareness to the everyday rhythms we've tuned out. We are so accustomed to our everyday soundscapes that the rhythms no longer register. Although the rhythms persist, affect us regardless, we become closed to their variations by virtue of nearness and routine. Opening onto the rhythms of nearness proves difficult without willing it so. But distance, being lost in a soundscape so different from my everyday life, brought me back to what was near and gave me a way of engaging my everyday soundscape with intent, with a willing releasement toward the rhythms and murmurs I had unintentionally tuned out.

Back home, I imagine a drone hovering ten or fifteen feet above me, pacing my commute, with sensitive, omni-directional microphones documenting the soundscape of my neighborhood. We would hear raindrops, water rolling down tree trunks and rushing like little streams in aluminum gutters, feet slapping and splashing in muddy puddles. Helicopter blades cutting at the atmosphere, skating low across the neighborhood's treetops, carrying the sick and dying to the university hospital. A crow calling. Three young men toss a football on Pennsylvania Court, music blaring from a house nearby. It sounds a little like James Taylor, but that can't be right. A train blares in the distance. Snow shovels scrape sidewalks, ice scrapers scrape windshields.

On the third day of February, walking home, I pass two boys—perhaps ten and twelve—on Tremont, heading toward Tates Creek Road. The younger boy sticks his shovel into a mass of solid ice at the end of his driveway, the blade perpendicular to the ground, ill-suited to the job, like the blade of a butcher's knife hacking at a manhole cover. The older one tosses his shovel into the snow on the front lawn. He says "hey" as I come near. I say "hey" back. The sound of the younger boy's steel shovel striking ice and asphalt follows me up the road and across Tates Creek, soundtracking my commute. Closer to home, in the parking lot of Christ the King Cathedral, a nun talks to a woman and her daughter, an impatient toddler. I hear the nun say "that's why he's never there, that's exactly why." The woman, after a thoughtful pause, says "I know." Her daughter, pleading, says "mom-eeeee."

There are sounds in my head when I walk. Do these count? I can't be open to everything all the time. It's too difficult. I'm happy in my own head, comfortable. But complacent too. Closed to disclosures. Still, I made notes whenever I could remember the songs running through my head: Ke$ha, "Timber"; the Black Keys, "Girl Is on My Mind"; Thug Life, "Pour Out a Little Liquor"; Nirvana, "Dive"; Mad Season, "River of Deceit."

I step onto the porch at 7:45 a.m. on February 7, closing the locked door behind me, skipping a couple of steps to catch up to Abbey, my daughter. It's 11 degrees, and millions of tiny, ethereal snowflakes flutter in the breeze. I walk with Abbey to school, and we talk about *Gilded*, a young adult book she began reading a few days before. She tells me that in the book, a Korean American girl moves from Los Angeles to Seoul after the death of her mother and discovers that she's a demigod of some sort. Abbey loved the Percy Jackson books—more demigods—so this sounds similar.

She finished the book in three days, she says, helped by a snow day. I've started it but am far behind.

"How far?" she asks as we turn onto Hart.

"I've read only three chapters," I say.

"There's already a second book. Has Mom read it?"

"I don't think so."

We talk about the Korean words we already knew (*kimbap, bibimbap*) and the new ones in the book (*haraboji, tteok*).

At the back door of her school, as I head down the sidewalk toward campus, she calls out: "I want to be Gandalf the Grey for Halloween."

I'm sure I've misheard her, so I ask "what?"

"I want to be Gandalf the Grey for Halloween," she says and smiles, teeth and braces exposed to the cold winter air.

"Okay, sounds awesome!" I say.

For the next two or three blocks, I'm in my head again, thinking about how on previous mornings I had bracketed Abbey out of my field notes. I walked her to school on Wednesday, but I didn't really "count" my time with her as part of my commute. How silly. She is as much a part of my commute as helicopter blades, muddy puddles, or unseen slugs. My rhythms, when I walk with her to school, are her rhythms too. Hers are mine.

### "THE [BODY] AT THREE MILES AN HOUR"

In *Wanderlust*, Rebecca Solnit's (2000, 14) history of walking, Jean-Jacques Rousseau is her entry point for exploring "walking as a conscious cultural act rather than a means to an end." Walking is integral to human *being*, as much an ontological foundation of humankind as language or consciousness.

Aristotle's peripatetic school of philosophy is so named because the philosophers who studied there walked up and down a colonnade, a "peripatos," as they philosophized (Solnit 2000, 15). Solnit notes that in English, "The word *peripatetic* means 'one who walks habitually and extensively'" (15). The name of Aristotle's school "links thinking with walking" (15). The Sophists were even more prodigious—"wanderers who often taught in the grove where Aristotle's school would be located" (15). And the Stoics were "named after the stoa, or colonnade, in Athens, a most unstoically painted walkway where they walked and talked" (16).

Even Socrates—who in Plato's *Phaedrus* argues against writing, against rhetoric, and even against *trees*—does so on a walk. On advice from Acumenus, Phaedrus resolves to walk outside the city walls because "it's more refreshing to walk along country roads than city streets" (Nehamas and Woodruff 1995, 1). The two men walk together, and Socrates leads the way, physically and intellectually (2). Examples abound—Wordsworth, Kierkegaard, Nietzsche, Rimbaud, Woolf, Kant, Beauvoir, Dickens, Gandhi—minds primed at three miles an hour,

*Figure 5.9. Openings at three miles per hour. Author photo.*

walking streets and sidewalks and hilly paths, their pedestrian rhythms one with their inventional milieu.

"Never did I think so much, exist so vividly, and experience so much, never have I been so much myself—if I may use that expression—as in the journeys I have taken alone and on foot," wrote Rousseau (1953, 158). Solnit (2000, 21) argues that unstructured, associative thinking is the kind most often connected to walking, and it suggests walking not as an analytical but "an improvisational act." For Solnit, Rousseau was "one of the first who thought it worthwhile to record in detail the circumstances of his musing," and he left an indelible record of the relationship between his walking and thinking (22). This is why, she argues, walking elucidates the "mind at three miles per hour" (14). What of the body?

There are sounds in my head when I walk. There are thoughts in my head when I walk. There are books and articles and rebuttals written in my head when I walk. Maybe, though, not "in my head." I don't walk with my head but with my toes, ankles, calves, knees. I swing my arms, twist my trunk. There are sounds in me, around me, passing through me. When I walk, I feel wind, mist, sleet. When I walk, I feel bass, treble, empathy. When I walk, I feel arguments, metaphors, dialogues—in my gut, in my chest.

For Kierkegaard, the streets of Copenhagen were a Burkean Parlor. But rather than take a seat in the room, next to the fireplace, Kierkegaard

Figure 5.10. Openings at three miles per hour. Author photo.

preferred to walk by and listen from the sidewalks. His walking, according to Solnit (2000, 24), was "a way to be among people for a man who could not be with them, a way to bask in the faint human warmth of brief encounters, acquaintances' greetings, and overheard conversations." "Walking provided Kierkegaard, like Rousseau, with a wealth of casual contacts with his fellow humans, and it facilitated contemplation," she adds. (24).

Kierkegaard wrote: "This very moment there is an organ-grinder down in the street playing and singing—it is wonderful, it is the accidental and insignificant things in life which are significant" (quoted in Solnit 2000, 24). Solnit suggests that "perhaps it is because walking is itself a way of grounding one's thoughts in a personal and embodied experience of the world" that it facilitates the kind of writing found in the personal, descriptive work of Rousseau and Kierkegaard (26). "They were in the world but not of it," she adds (26). As if perched on a balcony, tuning to the rhythms and intensities of the street below, grasping at this-now-here-ness as if trying to carry water in cupped hands.

Country path, city streets, mountain passes. Walking is in-between *and* here. The Teacher, the Scholar, and the Scientist in Heidegger's *Discourse on Thinking* (1966) are in the world but not of it—on a country path, between settlements, literally and figuratively. Nothing settles when walking. The mind at three miles an hour is like the sea floor grazed by a fin—all billowy clouds and sediments sent swimming, reaching up and out and over. "A solitary walker," Solnit (2000, 26) writes, "is unsettled, between places, drawn forth into action by desire and lack, having the detachment of the traveler rather than the ties of the worker, the dweller, the member of a group."

Postmodern theory, Solnit (2000, 28) argues, elides the body. The postmodern subject "doesn't engage in physical endeavor or spend time out of doors." But walking "returns the body to its original limits again, to something supple, sensitive, and vulnerable" (29). "The path is an extension of walking," she adds; "the places set aside for walking are monuments to that pursuit, and walking is a mode of making the world as well as being in it" (29). Walking "is how the body measures itself against the earth" (31). In *The Gay Science*, Friedrich Nietzsche (1974, 322) suggested that "on lonely mountains or near the sea . . . even the trails become thoughtful."

On city streets, even the sidewalks become thoughtful given an open comportment, given releasement. As Frederic Gros (2014, 21) explains, "Nietzsche walked all day long, scribbling down here and there what the walking body—confronting sky, sea, glaciers—breathed into his thought." The walking *body*.

Heidegger (1968) asked, what is called thinking? The trail, the sidewalk, the sky and sea are called thinking. "For thinking," Gros (2014, 23) argues, "one needs a detached outlook, to be at a distance, to have clear air. One needs to be unconstrained to think far." Is this so? Very likely not, at least in no literal sense. One can think far without walking. One can think far in polluted air. But we must distance ourselves in some sense in order to open up, to release, to clear, to think meditatively. In seeing trails or sidewalks or alleys, for example, as thoughtful—as full of thought as I am in my own head and body—something rounds into focus, something clears, something is illuminated, something lightens.

"It may be that the world yields more of itself to the whimsical saunterer than to the serious observer," Gros argues (2014, 165). Is this so? It may be, insofar as it shifts perspective from walker/thinker to mover/feeler. Comportment, once again. An opening onto a world's disclosures. Waiting upon in motion—disclosures that may be cognitive, disclosures that may be affective, disclosures of things so near they can only be approached from a distance. Disclosures of distances that may only resolve into focus through that which is near, in mutual vulnerability.

*February 17, Outbound*
I wrote all day, something better than draft prose. It started raining this afternoon, and it's still drizzly when I head into the darkness at 6:45 p.m.

On Beaumont, I fall into a groove, not thinking of much, not tuning to much. The neighborhood is cold and quiet. Snow and ice melt, flowing in little torrents down storm drains. Nigel must be snuggled up warm, curled on a lap, taking in the heat of a radiator.

On Tremont, I blow into my hands and stomp my feet. A white SUV is backed into someone's driveway. On its side I see "Kerr Brothers Funeral Home" in large black letters. As I pass the driveway, I see the front door of the house, its screen door propped open.

I walk up the little hill on Tremont, and I am also standing in the cul-de-sac of a subdivision in suburban Atlanta in 2008, watching the white SUV pull slowly away with my dad's body. I am here, in my neighborhood; I am at my dad's house. A representative from the funeral home, in even tones and assured movements, prepares the body for transport. He leaves the clothes as they are. House slippers too. He pulls the fitted sheet from under the mattress at all four corners, then wraps it over the body, first one side and then the other, like folding a flag. He gathers fistfuls of fitted sheet at the shoulders, nods his head at me to do the same, near the calves. Together, we move the body from the bed to a gurney. The body wrapped in this banal shroud is belted in place with brown straps. He kicks the wheel stop, moves down the hall. The screen door is propped open, and body and gurney and slippers and sheet are wheeled onto the porch, along the front walk, and into the back of an SUV. And that's it. That's it.

I'm here, and I'm in suburban Atlanta the rest of my walk home.

*Coda*

# 6
## WRITING WITH LIGHT

Around the corner from my house lives a family with two station wagons—a silver 1990s Volvo and a newer azure blue Subaru. One wagon is often parked in the street, the other in the driveway. On the rear bumper of each, dead center, is a green sticker with "Lie Down in the Light" printed in crisp white capitals. I cannot remember when I first noticed these stickers—perhaps during the autoethnography of my pedestrian commute or perhaps shortly after the conclusion of that project. I have no idea to what the stickers refer, nor do I want to know their intended meaning. I haven't Googled them, and I won't. I'm content to take them as they are. Little green rectangles with bold white letterforms.

The stickers have a literal meaning, and the clause is imperative. I picture dappled sunlight filtered through high country evergreens in an open space too small to be a meadow. A breeze through the trees gently shakes limbs and boughs, and the sunlight falls and shimmers in a luminous pond, shallow and warm over California sweet grass, clover, and wildflowers. I lay there, warmed by dappled light, and stare softly at fluffy clouds that scatter and skip across the late spring sky. "Lie Down in the Light" is a command. It is also sound advice.

Ultimately, I did all I could think to do: I sat down on the tarmac and made a photo. "Photography is naively believed to reproduce visual actuality," Janet Malcolm (2023, loc. 1777) argues. "In fact," Malcolm says, "the images our eyes take in and the images the camera delivers are not the same. Taking a picture is a transformative act" (loc. 1777). So it goes. "The connection among all things was lightness" says Jean Genet's narrator in *The Thief's Journal* (1964, 78).

\*\*\*

In his introduction to the English translation of Heidegger's *Poetry, Language, Thought* (2013), Albert Hofstadter makes a subtle contribution to Heideggerian scholarship. The challenges of translating Heidegger into English are well documented—as Hofstadter explains, "to find the

*Figure 6.1. Lie Down in the Light. Author photo.*

right English words one has to learn to think German thoughts" (xvii). Heidegger's play on etymologies, his use of related sounds and spellings, and his proclivities for repurposing and reworking common German words (to work around and outside of the heavily freighted baggage of technical philosophical jargon) are legendarily difficult for readers in German and in translation. In *Autumn*, the Norwegian novelist and essayist Karl Ove Knausgaard (2017a, 131) expresses what many have felt when reading Heidegger: "This spring, in the evenings when I lie reading Safranski's book about Heidegger, I just don't get his philosophical explications, I don't understand what they mean even when I exert myself to the utmost. It's worse when I try reading Heidegger's own writings. Even when I consider that Heidegger writes about being a human being and I am a human being too, so that his thoughts and insights also pertain to me, it doesn't help: I just don't have it in me." I first read the *Discourse on Thinking* long after earning my PhD. Once I finished it, I immediately began reading it from the beginning once again, including the introduction. Over the course of several days, I wrote up my annotations of the book: I needed 8,257 words to explain Heidegger's ideas to myself. Knausgaard eventually sees some light: "When I read Safranski's biography of Heidegger in the evenings, I understand nothing of his philosophy, but I understand *him*, in the sense that what makes up his life doesn't seem foreign and complicated but fathomable and meaningful" (132, original emphasis).

In Hofstadter's fourteen-page introduction to *Poetry, Language, Thought* (Heidegger 2013), he gives a little more than four full pages to the challenges of translating the words *ereignen* (in contemporary German: to unfold, to occur) and *das Ereignis* (an event, a happening). Heidegger connected *ereignen* to another historical verb, *eräugnen*, to show or to "place before the eyes" (the verb stem is related to *das Auge*, eye; xix). The pronunciation of these two words is similar for some speakers of German, so the sounds and the valences of meaning come together nicely for Heidegger. In his later work, *ereignen* embodies the "joint process by which the four of the fourfold are able, first, to come out into the light and clearing of truth, and thus each to exist in appropriation of and to each other" (xx). Hofstadter adds that "the mutual lighting-up, reflecting, *eräugnen*, is at the same time the mutual belonging, appropriating, *ereignen*" (xx).

Hofstadter makes a distinction between the early Heidegger and the later Heidegger and the early and late perspectives on *ereignen*. For the early Heidegger—the phenomenological Heidegger—*ereignen* is associated with "truth as evidence, opening up, clearing, lighting, the self-showing of beings in overtness" (2013, xx). But his later perspective gives way to *ereignen* as "the *disclosure of appropriation*," a fourfold in which mutual appropriation "*lightens* all the four into their own" (xxi, original emphases). From this perspective, Heidegger's *lichtend*, usually translated as "clearing," becomes "lightening" in Hofstadter's translation; "lightening" embodies "at once and in inseparable union the senses of: to illuminate, to clear, to make nimble and easy" (xxi).

Hofstadter's translations "survived the critical scrutiny of Heidegger himself" (Heidegger 2013, xxi). Heidegger scholars have long focused on "the clearing," the typical understanding of *lichtend* in English. Perhaps what is obscured in that translation, however, are moments of lightening—illuminations, certainly, but also simply *lightness*: as if a heavy backpack is dropped to the earth after a long trek, boots and socks peeled off, one's tired and beaten feet practically floating in the air, unencumbered. This is quite different from "the clearing," which suggests a grand philosopher stepping into the clearing of Truth or, even more pointed, that philosopher *clears space, creates* the clearing with insight. This image of "the clearing" has followed me since graduate school, and I don't think I'm alone in having had this impression of the philosophical clearing.

But as I read Heidegger's later work more deeply and as I worked to learn German, I realized that I had it wrong or, at least, not fully right.

It is fine to simply lie down in the light. Truth claims, essences, and technical arguments fall away like a heavy backpack. In contemporary German, *lichtend* means "thinned out"—something said of plants, of trees, of smog, of crowds, of traffic. When things thin out, they are easier to distinguish in their individual quiddity. Forest, trees, and such. Light works its way in. The way becomes easier. It's fine if we just let things be and wait awhile. If we open up to the thinned spaces. If we *wait upon*, with no expectations.

In "The Origin of the Work of Art," Heidegger (2013) discusses problems of translation, noting Roman obfuscations of the original (and for Heidegger, *originary*) Greek experience of being. These translations represent a cultural, historical, and philosophical crucible. For after the translation of the Greek *hupokeimenon* (the core of things), *hupostasis* (an underlying substance), and *sumbebekos* (accident, accidental properties of a thing) into the Latin *subiectum, substantia,* and *accidens,* "the interpretation of the thingness of the thing is established which henceforth becomes standard" (23). Consequently, Heidegger argues, "the Western interpretation of the Being of beings stabilized" as well (23). This seemingly straightforward transposition of terms from the Greek to the Latin was not innocent: "*Roman thought takes over the Greek words without a corresponding, equally authentic experience of what they say, without the Greek word*" (23, original emphasis). The Greek *experience* of being is in the sense of *presence* in things, and this is lost in the Latin translation. As a result, "the rootlessness of Western thought," Heidegger says, "begins with this translation" (23).

I claim nothing so dramatic in the subtle shift of *lichtend* to lightening and thinning—it includes the sense of clearing. But perhaps by deemphasizing clearing—*the clearing*—the later Heidegger's ideas emerge in a new key, one grounded not in developing or discovering *the Clearing* of philosophical truth but rather in a nimble, lightened sense of being in the world, being with the world, *there* being.

\* \* \*

In 1962, after several false starts and scrapped plans, Martin Heidegger finally visited Greece. Finally, because Heidegger's most important philosophical ideas begin and end in Greece. Finally, because despite previous tickets and itineraries, his anxieties got the best of him, and he turned back at the last minute. In 1962, he departed from Venice en route to Greece; being there, he was filled anew with anxieties—will the land match (in its surroundings, smells, sights, and sounds) the ideal he had developed in his mind over the years?

No. Not at first anyhow. According to his journals, the Corfu he saw was not *his* Corfu (ancient Kephallenia), the Ithaca he saw was not *his* Ithaca. But finally, in Mycenae, "this world penetrated into him after all" (Safranski 1998, 402). Then came a visit to Delos: "The name of the island said it all—it meant 'the manifest, the apparent'" (402). Delos was quiet, unmarred by tourists, ruins shining under a brilliant blue Mediterranean sky. "The veiledness of a former beginning spoke from everything," Heidegger wrote (402). Of this day, Rüdiger Safranski writes: "Now comes the great moment. The mountains, the sky, the sea, the islands all around 'are rising,' showing themselves in the light" (402). They beckon Heidegger "into a feast of visibility as 'they cause that which is present in one way or another to emerge and become visible'" Safranski adds, quoting Heidegger (402). Heidegger's Greece resolves into focus, *his* Greece overlaid in visibilities and affects and memories and desires on top of the ambient viscosity of Delos itself.

The next day, in Athens, Heidegger's frustrations and anxieties returned. He arrived at the Acropolis in the early morning, ahead of the tourist crowds, but then later went to Delphi, "whose sacred precinct swarmed with people" (Safranski 1998, 403). The tourists there "were ceaselessly taking photographs" instead of revering the "feast of thinking" before them (403). In his journals Heidegger wrote that these tourists had not only lost their memory, they had lost their very ability to remember (403). In contrast is Heidegger's memory: what he experienced at Delos, in the suddenly lightened veiledness of former beginnings, was "the surprising moment of pure presence" (403).

A lightening of the presence of things, a second-order apprehension of a Greek experience of things—"lighting up, reflecting, mutual belonging, appropriating, *ereignen*" (Heidegger 2013, xx). Heidegger's judgments notwithstanding, no one can say whether the tourist photographers were not also surprised by pure presence, were not also engaged, in their own way, with the feast of thinking at Delphi. Heidegger and the tourists share something important: they each attempt to generate some kind of fixity on and interpretation of the experience. Delphi disclosed differential worlds to its visitors on that day in 1962, and the visitors responded differentially, with their own enactments.

For Heidegger: a feast, a rising, a great veil pulled back. For tourists: an oracle, a landmark, layers of historical experience. Heidegger fixes his thoughts in his journal; he writes about the light and the lightening. The tourists fix their thoughts with photos on silver halide crystals; they literally capture reflected light, a lightening; they write with light.

It's possible that Heidegger was merely grumpy that day at Delphi, upset with the throngs obscuring his view. Or perhaps he bristled at the ease and seeming carelessness of tourists' snapshots—at the burgeoning, democratizing technology of visual reproduction. But Heidegger's appreciation for the value of visual phenomena in manifesting and presenting disclosures of being was well established by 1962.

"The Origin of the Work of Art" was originally delivered as a lecture in 1935, repeated in early 1936, published in 1950, republished and revised over the following decade with an addendum, and stabilized in its current form in 1960. A significant argument in this long essay focuses on Vincent Van Gogh's painting of his own boots (what Heidegger describes as "peasant's boots"). Heidegger's analysis turns on the ability of visuality and visibility to bring elemental disclosures of being to light, literally. As in so much of his philosophy, he works around the cultural baggage of technical jargon, describes existence "without any philosophical theory" (Heidegger 2013, 32).

His methodology is to turn first to a visual figuration of common equipment—leather boots—and then to an architectural work: a temple set within and apart from the landscape. Heidegger takes the Van Gogh painting and describes its features as thoroughly as possible. Indeed, he *sees through* the painting itself to the phenomena depicted. As Roland Barthes (1981, 6) writes of photography, "A photograph is always invisible: it is not it that we see." Heidegger eventually makes his way to the materiality of the painting itself but only after seeing *through* it for several pages, imagining the (imaginary) world of the peasant whose boots rest, worn, on the floor.

The visual phenomenon discloses, for Heidegger. Van Gogh's painting helps us come nearer to the use and usefulness of boots, and not simply *those* boots. In Heidegger's (2013, 35) terms, we discover the equipmental quality of equipment not by observing the boots in situ or observing them in use but by "bringing ourselves before" the painting. "The painting spoke," he writes, and "in the vicinity of the work we were suddenly somewhere else than we usually tend to be" (35). The painting does not simply help us visualize the boots and their character. Instead, "The equipmentality of equipment first genuinely arrives at its appearance through the work [the painting] and only in the work" (35)

The painting overflows with disclosures, allowing us to see the equipment anew. We're distanced just enough to bring us nearer to the boots' being. The painting's capacity to make the boots *visible* in a different way lightens, brings us close, thins the clutter. We see the ordinary anew: "This entity [the boots] emerges into the unconcealedness of its being"

(Heidegger 2013, 35). In and through the painting, it comes "to stand in the light of its being" and "the being of the being comes into the steadiness of its shining" (35). The philosophical baggage is lightened, a veil is drawn back, an essential and elemental character emerges, into the light.

At Delphi, Heidegger is troubled by the tourists and their snapshots, by their seeming inability to reflect in a meditative way on the "feast of thinking" before them (quoted in Safranski 1998, 403). But for the better part of the previous two decades, Heidegger argued that visual phenomena can speak, can disclose something elemental, can bring us near to the light of being. So what gives? Does Heidegger, in his journals, contradict his philosophy? Not necessarily—I'm sidestepping the distinctions between *kinds* of visual phenomena. Heidegger seems to make a grand distinction between painting and photography, and in this he is not alone. But the differences between, say, oil painting and film photography notwithstanding, *both forms of visual production may overflow with disclosures.*

This is what Heidegger missed in 1962 but what decades of meditative thinking on the potential of photography have demonstrated. Again, I turn to Barthes (1981, 21)—photography is affective, and affect is irreducible: "I see, I feel, hence I notice, I observe, and I think." At Delphi, the tourist sees and feels. From seeing and feeling, they notice, observe; they are pulled by affects, by a change in mood, by an encounter. Any meditation on that charge, discomfort, or wonder—however quick, however slight—is a form of thinking, is meditative thinking. A photograph, Barthes argued, may be *pensive* (38), may itself be full of thought. The tourists take what is given to them—little slivers of Grecian space-time, little experiences of their *there* that travel home with them.

Snapshots can overflow with disclosures, real and imagined (Hariman and Lucaites 2016). What was captured and transported may resurface to new effect: remembered disclosures, new disclosures, remembered affects, new affects, and meditation on what was and is and what might be. In his "Letter on Humanism," Heidegger (1993, 237) argues that the "dimension of the *ecstasis* of ek-sistence" is Being, such that "everything spatial and all space-time occur essentially in the dimensionality that Being itself is." *Ecstasis,* standing outside oneself. A snapshot is essentially this: a way of standing next to oneself, outside oneself, to situate and enmesh and remember oneself in a particular *there.*

What are Heidegger and the tourists at Delphi doing? Attempting to apprehend and understand Being as manifest in the oracle, as manifest in the relationship between word and world, as manifest in a particular space-time, in a particular *there.* For Heidegger, thinking is our way of attending to these relationships, of standing outside everyday being to draw nearer to what is distant. But Heidegger also demonstrates that we can think with and through visual phenomena. For the tourists, snapshots are a way of standing out to apprehend and draw nearer to the monumental *there* of Delphi. Heidegger and his companions see, feel, notice, observe, and think. They make inscriptions. They are affected by their *theres*, they engage their *theres*, and they take something away. They both write with the light as a way of lightening the disclosures of being.

Both Heidegger and the tourists, both writing and photography, *fix the light*, lie down in the light.

In his 1960 addendum to "The Origin of the Work of Art," Heidegger (2013, 82) encourages us to "keep in mind the Greek sense of *thesis*—to let lie forth in its radiance and presence." We need to keep this in mind, he argues, to apprehend his sense of "fixing in place" throughout the essay (81). A fixing in place is a "setting-into-work," an idea that correlates with " 'to place' and 'to set' " and with " 'to lay' " (81). The Greek sense of *thesis* includes a special kind of fixity: "a setting up in the unconcealed" (81). To place, to set, to lay all "have the sense of bringing *here* into the unconcealed, bringing *forth* into what is present, that is, letting or causing to lie forth" (81, original emphases). In fixity, Heidegger means not "rigid, motionless, and secure" but rather "admitted into the boundary," to the light and the bringing forth of being (82).

Heidegger's (2013) sense of boundary, as I discussed in chapter 4, is a threshold of the presences and withdrawals—concealing and un-concealing—of sensory and affective engagements with beings of all kinds. And fixing in place is not a mere "letting happen" (82). Hofstadter argues that "laying forth, placing here, bringing here and bringing forth" are all embodied in *work* and *working* (82). Whether conceived as a "something bringing itself forth out of itself into presence" or a person "performing the bringing here and bringing forth of something" or, even better, an interplay of both, any fixing in place is an active way in which "something that is present presences" (82).

Something is un-concealed, lightened—what Kathleen Stewart (2007, 30) calls "a something waiting to happen"—and a world is seen anew. *Poiesis* and *techne*, as I discussed in chapter 1, are ways we let "what is present come forth into unconcealedness" (Heidegger 2013, 84). We write and bring forth; we make photographs and bring forth; in both we attempt to draw nearer to something un-concealed, to apprehend and imagine and "fix" disclosures. To interpolate Barthes, the photographic fixity of absolute particulars is wondrous because what is brought into the light, fixed with light, refuses to stay put.

Heidegger's companions at Delphi carve slivers of space-time, fixing on film a moment that occurs only once; but photography as a *techne* of *poiesis* reproduces the moment to infinity (Barthes 1981, 4). And these slivers of space-time, Heidegger might be happy to consider, "cannot be transformed (spoken) philosophically" (5). A photographic image—made by someone open to and surprised by presence, by a lightening, by a wondrous recognition of ambient this-now-here-ness—is inescapably *deictic*. In other words, the language of philosophy, which Heidegger sought to avoid, cannot adequately explain the tourists' photographs; but when such photographs are taken with an open comportment—meditatively, in releasement, as a waiting upon disclosures of being, as a response to sensory affects, in mutual vulnerability—the philosophical context of the image is now both fixed and unfolding. Photography cannot help but be involved (in Heidegger's and Rickert's sense of involvement) in ambience, in "all the objects in the world" (6).

\* \* \*

In *M Train*, a luminous meditation on love and loss, Patti Smith (2015, 86) asks "why can't things be just as they are?" We lose our things, the people we love die, places wash away in hurricanes and mudslides. "These things happen," she writes of myth, mystery, and reality—"the undeniable domino effect of being alive" (108). Even so, the realization that "these things happen" never obfuscates our surprise at loss, our yearning for what was, our dreams of what might be. "We want things we cannot have," she writes, "we seek to reclaim a certain moment, sound, sensation. I want to hear my mother's voice. I want to see my children as children. Hands small, feet swift" (210).

We cannot have these things as we once had them, and still we have them. Heidegger goes to Greece. His trip is hit and miss. He was there, and he wrote. His unwelcome companions at Delphi were there, and they captured what they saw and felt in photographs. They were *there*, and they made their Greece visible. Smith can no longer hear her mother's voice, and yet her voice is something we have, brought forth in Smith's writing. And Smith (2015), with her Polaroid Land Camera and peel-apart instant film, documents sites of sensation and loss—her favorite café, now closed; her husband, now deceased; Rockaway Beach after Hurricane Sandy; herself, in a different time. "I stood there as time stretched into the guise of a horizon," she writes; "I wasn't overcome with sorrow—more a sense of wonder" (258).

Heidegger, the tourists at Delphi, Smith, me, you—we're constantly making our desires visible, constantly bringing forth our participation with the stuff of everyday life, from the mundane to the sublime. We gather and we are gathered; we venture out into a world already active and full and wondrous and imposing; we are conditioned by our surroundings, and we bring forth and make visible new conditions of interaction and engagement. The world withdraws and conceals, and this too fosters attunement. We are *there beings* and are *there feeling*—sensations, affects, emotions, and moods are gathered, made visible, and concealed too. We withdraw from the world, we conceal something of ourselves. We also open to the world, to ambience, to nearness and distance.

### WRITING WITH LIGHT

The word *photography* is derived from the Greek words φῶς (*phos*, sometimes φωτός, *photos*) and γράφή (*graphy*). Together, the Greek words combine light (φῶς) and writing (γράφή). My favorite understanding of the word *photography* is *writing with light* or simply *writing light*. Because γράφή can also mean drawing and because the related verb γράφω (*grapho*) means to write, to draw, and to paint, many photographers and critics have preferred *drawing with light, light drawing*, or *painting with light*. As a writing researcher, I'm biased: *writing with light* is elegant.

From the moment of its invention, photography distinguished itself from painting and drawing; photographic impressions were far less mediated by human agency and interpretation than by chemical and material agencies. As photography developed, so too did understanding of human agency in image production: the stitchwork of human + chemical + material dramatically transformed chemical reactions into *work*, in the Heideggerian sense. The connection to writing is clear: photography and writing document, fix, and move in endless permutations. Both technologies perform the most banal functions and enliven the most inscrutable emotions. Both inscribe an absolute particular that moves in and out of time, that embodies and defies death, that folds time and space upon itself.

Both photography and writing make worlds visible and legible in acts of *poiesis*. They are each in their own way also sublime *technes* for engaging experience, sensation, affect, and ambience. For Heidegger (1993, 361), *techne* is a practice of visibility, a "letting appear," a record and trace of something un-concealed. In photographs, that something literally lies in the light—the photographic image is always a reflection of light on *something* that is really present. And *techne* works with and reimagines what is present. Practiced together, writing and photography interoperate in ways that can strengthen the strengths of each, creating stratigraphic layers of inquiry, understanding, and imagination. When multisensory methods of investigation are added—the documentation of soundscapes, for example—the ways we might study and understand writing and rhetoric as *poiesis* can flourish.

\* \* \*

Alex Ronan was supposed to be doing something else. "I was on deadline for a story," he says, but he was distracted by the Metropolitan Museum's online collections, where he saw, again and again, "elaborate paintings of women in ornate dresses [that] featured eyebrow situations that reminded me of my favorite celebs in the late-90s and early aughts" (Tindle 2018). Despite the looming deadline, the @historyofoverplucking Instagram account was born. The images collected and curated by Ronan evolved into an archive of a very specific visual trope: skinny eyebrows. Scrolling through the account's time line offers up pop stars in 2000, a screenshot from *The Art of Zandra Rhodes*, a still from the 1990s sitcom *Friends* with Jennifer Anniston's character, Rachel, frozen in a look of deep confusion, skepticism, or ponder.

The account's description reads "Everybody makes mistakes." Ronan's curation is satirical, but the collection is valuable nonetheless. From the perspective of visual cultures research, it visibilizes historical and cultural norms of beauty. From the perspective of visual rhetoric, it illustrates the extent to which argumentation and persuasion are embodied in gendered situatedness and performance. Skinny eyebrows as signifiers of chic fashionableness; tendons, wrists, fingers, muscles engaged in meticulous, painful extractions of body hair, shaping and grooming a particular look that communicates to others something of who these people were or are. From the perspective of visual methods, Ronan has ingeniously repurposed widely available visual material to illustrate a cultural, social, and rhetorical trend. Your mileage may vary, of course, but for now, it's *there*.

Between August 29 and September 30, 2017, a young woman used Instagram to document the verbal and physical harassment to which she is subjected on an almost daily basis. The account, @dearcatcallers, includes twenty-two images and six posts with explanatory text. Each image is a selfie, framed so the men who have catcalled her are clearly visible. The images often include broader environmental contexts about where and when a given instance of harassment occurred. "This Instagram has the aim to create awareness about the objectification of women in daily life," she writes in the initial text post (@dearcatcallers 2017). "By making the selfie," she adds, "both the objectifier and the objectified are assembled in one composition."

Power dynamics are subverted—she stands in front of those who have harassed her; she reframes the situation: "#dearcatcallers," she writes, "it's not a compliment." We might characterize the woman who created the account as a social activist, a "#feminist," a courageous citizen, a visual researcher. She uses everyday tools and technologies—a smartphone, Instagram's public platform—to make visible the bias and harassment she faces in everyday life, in her very embodiment, by simply being a woman in public space. She makes arguments with words, images, and embodied acts that demonstrate the bias in her everyday environs and that subvert that bias by making it visible on her terms.

On February 12, 2018, in front of the Uzbek consulate in New York City, a group called Voices 4 staged a queer kiss-in. In the statement for the event, Voices 4 wrote: "Appealing to 'traditional' values, the governments of Uzbekistan, Tajikistan, and Azerbaijan have been abusing their respective powers, rounding up, detaining, assaulting, and physically abusing LGBTQIA+ people. In some cases, law enforcement have started registering LGBTQIA+ people, blackmailing and torturing detainees, forcing them to give up the names of their LGBTQIA+ friends and peers. We at Voices 4 utilised this historical protest format to demand the governments of Uzbekistan, Azerbaijan, and Tajikistan immediately stop the genocide" (*Dazed Digital* 2018). *Dazed Digital* brought public awareness to the event, quoting from some of the attendees who read prepared statements. But it is the intimate street portraits of queer couples kissing that transform this event from a localized protest into something timeless. Nick DeLieto's photographs isolate couples from the crowd, the soft focus of the black-and-white images evoking the work of Elliot Erwitt—queer inversions of the famous V-J Day photograph taken in Times Square.

The details might prick Barthes's attention: wet hair and raindrops, an ascot tied above a crewneck sweatshirt, a man whose wire-rimmed glasses are misty and covered over but for whom this doesn't matter in the least, his eyes closed in an embrace with a man whose nose presses into his cheek as they kiss. The small project is part street photography, part portraiture, part documentary work. These combined perspectives coalesce in the images; they bring forth a series of small moments that make visible unspeakable oppression and genocide. They document a protest, and at the same time they stand alone as arguments and artifacts of fundamental human connection, of desire, of identity.

The murder of George Floyd by Minneapolis police on May 25, 2020, was recorded by seventeen-year-old Darnella Frazier with a smartphone, at close range. I remember the grainy footage of Rodney King's beating, shot by George Holliday from his apartment balcony on March 3, 1991. Looking at each video is an act of looking *through* videography to the horrific realities of human beings powerless to resist brutal state-sanctioned violence and racism. The beating of Rodney King was sickening—two officers strike King over and over with batons, they kick him as he crawls in agony on the pavement; at least five other officers stand, surrounding King, watching.

But the video of George Floyd belies malignant calm on the face of officer Derek Chauvin, his body at ease as he kneels on Floyd's neck—grinding his face into the pavement, restricting his air flow, killing him in broad daylight. Chauvin knelt on Floyd's neck for two minutes and fifty-three seconds *after* Floyd had become unresponsive. The sight of Floyd, lifeless on the ground, contrasts sharply with the self-possessed comportment of Chauvin, who looks comfortable, relaxed, his hands in his pockets. But what of this video, this document? I had looked *through* the footage to the inhumanity of the Minneapolis police, to the long histories of police violence toward Black Americans, to the complicity of white Americans, to the promise of the Black Lives Matter Movement, to the desperate necessity of changing the racist policies and systems so prevalent in the "land of the free." But seventeen-year-old Darnella Frazier had the courage to record state violence with her smartphone; she stood perilously close to murderers and didn't hide; she wasn't on a balcony, using a zoom lens; she was there as George Floyd died.

\* \* \*

We are all photographers. Each of us carries sophisticated digital cameras with network affordances that were simply unthinkable when Sarah Pink's *Doing Visual Ethnography* first appeared in 2001. Thanks to any number of digitization projects, we have access to the visual archives of some of the world's most well-funded and supported museums. Creative-commons licensed images and sophisticated search tools afford the trivially easy compilation of visual materials of nearly any phenomenon in a nearly endless array of configurations. Industrial research firms such as Frog Design have built tools for running visual surveys. They ask, for example, "what do your cooking spaces look like" and then quickly receive photos from around the world, giving them a visual baseline for exploring spatial and material arrangements in cross-cultural home environments (see McNely 2015a). Instagram's hashtags provide easily accessible archives of user-generated images focused on the most narrow and esoteric phenomena, social acts, and cultural interests imaginable (see McNely 2015b). The easy access to both visual archives and the means for incorporating visual methods into research practices begs the question: Why are we so reticent to write with light?

We tend to favor illuminative *writing*, the generation of text, even when visual phenomena are the subject of our inquiry. When we do incorporate visuals into our work, we typically do so in illustrative—and often teleological—ways. We use images that exist in the world and write about them; when we do occasionally incorporate photography into our research and scholarship, our images illustrate and index our written arguments, rarely making arguments of their own. Even as we have turned, in our rhetorical theories, to a greater focus on sensation and affect, our methodologies and methods have remained grounded in critique.

Only recently have rhetorical scholars begun to take seriously the soundscapes that condition our environments (Ceraso 2018; Hawk 2018; Stone 2015) or the ways haptic and tactile interactions are suasive and rhetorically predicative (Walters 2014). Recent work in new materialist and object-oriented rhetoric is turning our attention toward sensations, their relationships to affects, and the import of physical environments, material entanglements, and extra-discursive semiotics to rhetorical theory. These are important developments, but our methodologies are not keeping up with our theories. Critique will take us only so far. To explore more deeply the grounds of rhetoric, our methodologies need to develop too.

And methodological work *is* theory work. Theory cannot be disentangled from methodology, and methodology is the activation of theory. Clay Spinuzzi (2003) argues that methodologies embody the theories, values, and aims that drive scholarly inquiry and thus shape our methods—the actual practices we use in specific research projects. Theory and methodology are thus reciprocal and recursive, constantly conditioning and enlivening one another. Our predominant theories implicitly say something about the methodologies we value and the methodologies we choose not to practice. But our predominant methodologies circumscribe the theories we can develop.

Methodological innovation, therefore, is inescapably yoked to theoretical innovation. Throughout this book, I have argued for visual and multisensory methodologies and methods. Our methodologies *are* our theories. They are ways of thinking about, questioning, and invoking theory; they are ways of investigating, testing, and making theory. In studies of rhetoric and writing, our visual and multisensory methodologies have so far been limited. This limits the questions we ask, which in turn limits our ways of *seeing* and *making visible* our objects of study.

## CLEARINGS, OPENINGS, LIGHTENINGS

In everyday language, a clearing is an open space. As a verb, clearing (or to clear) creates an opening of or onto space, whether space is conceived literally (a meadow in the woods) or figuratively (creating space for new ideas in one's mind). "To be clear" means also "to make clear," "to make lucid." And lucidity embodies something bright, luminous, filled with light. Every clearing is potentially an opening onto lucidity. Methodological innovation *clears* and in doing so provides openings onto new theoretical insights. Further, methodological innovation is also a lightening of the way toward new theories. It can literally lighten our load—instead of forcing the same methodologies to carry ever greater forms of theory work, new methodologies suggest nimble and lightened ways into different theoretical perspectives.

Mobile information flows, access to big data, and the processing power to do things with both have reached the point where projects such as "Phototrails"—revolutionary just a few years ago—are not only possible but relatively simple to execute (http://phototrails.net/exhibition/). The recent (and related) object-, thing-, sensation-, and affect-oriented turns in rhetoric have led to discussions of plants as suasive taking up a significant portion of a recent special issue of *Rhetoric Society Quarterly* (Walsh et al. 2017). New materialist approaches are here; and they demand new methodologies, new methods, and new pedagogies. We're innovating theoretically, but we're straining the bounds of the methodologies from which and through which those theoretical innovations can extend. Rethinking our methodologies and methods—as theory work—can, in turn, help us continue to innovate theoretically in rhetoric and writing.

We can better *picture* writing and rhetoric. As I described in chapter 1, we still have not meaningfully responded to Linda Brodkey's call to rethink how we picture writers, writing, and rhetors more broadly. As I have argued throughout this book, rethinking the practices, systemic contexts, sensations, and ambient environments of composing requires more than a shift of theoretical perspective. By taking up Brodkey's call and by literally enacting (and developing) new methodologies and methods for picturing writers and writing, we can develop new understandings of the ways writing and rhetoric is embedded within and constitutive of everyday life for people in myriad situations.

Picturing writing requires us to confront the "meaning and enigma" of visibility itself (Berger 1980, 45) and the relationships between visibility and visuality. For too long, our scholarship and teaching has been wedded to notions of visuality and to modes of visual critique. By turning our focus instead to methodologies and methods that *make visible* the practices and places of writing, we can engage both visibility and visuality. We can, for example, explore the very topographies of writing that are central to a participant's work. By presenting arguments in our scholarship—in both visual and textual forms—about the topographies of participant writing practices and the spaces in which those practices occur, we open to what, how, where, and why writing matters.

I have explored methodologies and methods for picturing writing and rhetorics as in situ, praxiographic engagements with writers and rhetors in a variety of contexts—academic, professional, and personal. But responding to Brodkey's call to picture writers and writing is not limited to such approaches or to explorations of writing practices. Indeed, the variety of rhetorical practices calls for better documentation and understanding of all forms of everyday suasion, and picturing rhetors and rhetoric is a methodological move with explicit epistemological and ontological aims.

For example, Janice Fernheimer and her colleagues and students have created the Jewish Kentucky Oral History Collection with the explicit goal of preserving and *making visible* Jewish individuals and communities in Kentucky and in the American South. Nathaniel Rivers and I (McNely and Rivers 2014) used a new materialist approach to chile farming in southern New Mexico as a way of making visible the many actors—human and non-human, networked and physically present—involved in contemporary farming. Scholars in rhetoric, writing, and technical communication have drawn from Bruno Latour and actor-network theory to trace inter-agentivity; with visual and multisensory methodologies and methods, we can more effectively picture and thus build theory about such actors. Jim Ridolfo's (2015) work in digitizing Samaritan manuscripts is yet another form of scholarship in which key texts and actors are made visible; from this work, Ridolfo developed a more nuanced theoretical understanding of digital delivery. These projects of visibility foreground *techne* and *poiesis* and help us better picture writers, writing, and rhetorical practice.

Visual and multisensory approaches build from and extend new materialist and object-oriented theories of rhetoric. Picturing communication environments lends important insights into material suasion and the ways our ambient environs condition writing and rhetorical work. As Scot Barnett and Casey Boyle (2016, 1) have argued, "Things provoke thought, incite feeling, circulate affects, and arouse in us a sense of wonder." In chapter 3, I argued that visible and proprioceptive phenomena hail us, and in such acts they facilitate the development of rhetorics factorially. The participation of non-human things in such everyday work environments results in complex rhetorical events and practices with variables that are difficult to surface and trace using traditional fieldwork methods alone.

With visual ethnography, however, documenting those variables and tracing their permutations and products over time becomes more feasible. A wall-length whiteboard and the evanescent (and stabilized) writing that circulates there becomes a focal point of the many differential attunements of several actors. At Investigation and Foresight, the whiteboard was a fundamentally suasive participant in unfolding rhetorical events. The way Mike, Michelle, and Jenn tuned to the heterogeneous materiality of their environs was foundational to their rhetorical practices and thus their acts of *poiesis*, the work they developed and brought forth. As Rickert, Barnett and Boyle, Gries, and many others have demonstrated, the things around us, with us, and in us matter in an originary way. With visual and multisensory methodologies, the "universe of things" (Shaviro 2014) is impossible to bracket or ignore. We *have* to attend to them because they are inseparable from rhetoric.

Our things *gather* and participate meaningfully in our being there, in our feeling there, and in our speaking and acting there. As I demonstrated in chapter 4, it is not only the ideas and philosophies and beliefs that gather us; we are gathered through the concatenation of ideas and beliefs with specific spaces and artifacts that coalesce in sensory, affective, cognitive, and rhetorical practices. Material artifacts often gather these variables. A young person in an alleyway, seeing the monstrance held aloft, is gathered by the Eucharistic Procession—the literal procession of the here and now and the ongoing procession of spiritual belief and practice.

Things *gather* in practices such as Eucharistic Adoration because for the faithful, they signal and embody the ineffable. Sensory artifacts such as the monstrance or the tabernacle are not merely objects; they are *things* in the Heideggerian sense. They are purpose-built to engage the senses and to be spiritually and ideologically suasive. They overflow with disclosures. As I described in chapter 4, different participants in Eucharistic Adoration brought different backgrounds to the practice, experienced the practice differently in situ, and brought different feelings away from their practice. Their differential practices are grounded in their differential positionalities, to be certain, but ambient rhetoric shows us that the very disclosures of things with which we dwell are differential too. Sensory artifacts are built in and from ways of dwelling, encourage ways of thinking meditatively, and embody ways of understanding intangible phenomena. With visual and multisensory methods, we *must* attend to things; in so doing, we can better explore ambient dwelling, what Rickert describes as a central mode of attunement and the ground of rhetoric.

Methodologies provide *a clearing*—not *the clearing* of philosophical insight but a thinning, a lightening, a way of illuminating phenomena and inter-agentivity. Methodologies create openings for theoretical development. Methodologies foster lucidity, a lightening of the way toward better understandings of our objects of study. And methodologies bring distances nearer.

Much of what is most distant from our understanding paradoxically lies nearest to us in everyday life. Sensory experiences, the contours and topographies of our everyday spaces and acts, daydreaming, walking, catching sight of clouds in a rain puddle, everyday soundscapes—these may be the subject matter of multisensory methodologies. *Gelassenheit*, or releasement, is a mode of opening toward the lucidity of our ambient environs, of recognizing and practicing mutual vulnerability. Releasement is a way of tuning individual variations in each environment, of exploring attunement as a noun that situates us and conditions rhetorical involvements, that acts as the literal ground of rhetorical being. Rickert (2016, 230) argues that we are "beworlded and bethinged"; empirically studying such entanglements can be accomplished with visual and multisensory approaches. In using such approaches, our theories are enriched.

Opening up in releasement to the world's disclosures is a methodological move, but it is also equipment for living, for dwelling.

## ONE LAST PHOTO

*February 28, Outbound*

My final bit of fieldwork for the (commute autoethnography) is both welcome and bittersweet. Jim [Ridolfo, a colleague] asked if I wanted to grab a beer. I did, and I told him we'd need to do so around 5:00 p.m. At 5:10, Jim and I persuaded Matt, an English department colleague, to join us at Country Boy Brewing. We walked over together, and Jan [Fernheimer, a colleague] joined us a bit later.

*Figure 6.2. One last photo. Author photo.*

I have one beer; I listen, smile, and laugh. When my glass is empty, I say "so long" to Jim, Matt, and Jan. I stop at the office to grab my things and my camera and head home at 6:20. Outside, I hear squirrel claws scraping across tree bark near the White Hall classroom building. Campus and its neighborhoods are quiet and still. I see no one walking through the Greek row courtyard, and I notice that my shortcut through the parking lot is more lot than parking. Perhaps students have gone home for the weekend?

On Columbia, I stop to shoot a picture of a Jeep Wrangler parked on a side street. Its license plate reads "SPOYLD." This seems almost too good to be true.

\* \* \*

Since this is my last chance to visually engage some of the things I've attuned to over the last four weeks, I stop and take a photo of a front porch I noticed early in the project. This porch is illuminated by two floor lamps that cast a neat glow on either side of the door. My photo turns out to be doubly interesting: reflected in the home's glass storm door is the facade and entryway to the house across the street.

On Beaumont, there's a woman trimming hedges in front of a house for sale. The light is fading fast, and as I walk by, she turns to me and asks "does this look better to you?" She is thirty or thirty-five and wears baggy silver track pants and a loose crewneck sweatshirt in navy blue. Her hair fights itself in a loose bun on the top of her head and falls in strands heading every which way. Her mascara has run, sweating, and she holds a pair of rusty trimming shears in her right hand; her left hand on her hip, she shifts her weight to her right foot, hard.

She has almost finished trimming the three or four bushes to the left of the walk. It's clear how much better these trimmed bushes look when compared to the overgrown and haggard bushes to the right. I tell her so.

She says: "Good, cuz I worked my *ass* off on this. I told my mom, I says, 'No one's gonna want to buy a house with these raggedy, overgrown bushes in front.'"

"Yeah, you're right. They look very nice—much better."

"I'm juss tryina shape 'em, you know? To clean 'em up some."

"It's working. These look a lot better than those."

"I'm so glad. You have a good one."

"Thanks. You too."

I walk away wishing I'd photographed the hedges.

\* \* \*

Near the top of Tremont's hill, the house with the colorful glass bottles in the kitchen window again catches my eye. Daylight is nearly gone, and kitchen lights illuminate the colored glass from within. I stop to take a shot, even though the homeowner, a woman with close-cropped gray hair, is in the process of taking out the garbage. She doesn't notice me.

Farther up Tremont, across Kastle, two men are on a front porch, discussing a woman. Their speech is slow and slightly slurry. One sits on the stoop, smoking, while the other stands; he has a scruffy, straw-colored ponytail that fans out like a ragged broom on top of a dark blue Carhartt hoodie.

On Cochran, almost home, I stop to shoot one last photo—of the cathedral's adoration chapel, illuminated from inside and out.

# REFERENCES

@dearcatcallers. 2017. "Image Post." https://www.instagram.com/p/BYYSF_lIjQp/, August 29, 2017.
Ahmed, Sara. 2010. *The Promise of Happiness*. Durham, NC: Duke University Press.
Anderson, John. 1966. "Introduction." In *Discourse on Thinking*, edited by Martin Heidegger, 11–39. New York: Harper Colophon Books.
Anderson, Leon. 2006. "Analytic Autoethnography." *Journal of Contemporary Ethnography* 35, no. 4: 373–95.
Arnold, Jeanne E., Anthony P. Graesch, Enzo Ragazzini, and Elinor Ochs. 2012. *Life at Home in the Twenty-First Century: 32 Families Open Their Doors*. Los Angeles: Cotsen Institute of Archaeology Press.
Arola, Kristin L. 2010. "The Design of Web 2.0: The Rise of the Template, the Fall of Design." *Computers and Composition* 27: 4–14.
Ashmore, Malcolm. 1989. *The Reflexive Thesis: Wrighting Sociology of Scientific Knowledge*. Chicago: University of Chicago Press.
Backman, Jussi. 2015. *Complicated Presence: Heidegger and the Postmetaphysical Unity of Being*. Albany: State University of New York Press.
Banks, Marcus. 2001. *Visual Methods in Social Research*. London: Sage.
Barad, Karen. 2007. *Meeting the Universe Halfway: Quantum Physics and the Entanglement of Matter and Meaning*. Durham, NC: Duke University Press.
Barnett, Scot. 2016. *Rhetorical Realism: Rhetoric, Ethics, and the Ontology of Things*. London: Routledge.
Barnett, Scot, and Casey Boyle, eds. 2016. *Rhetoric, through Everyday Things*. Tuscaloosa: University of Alabama Press.
Barrios, Barclay. 2004. "Of Flags: Online Queer Identities, Writing Classrooms, and Action Horizons." *Computers and Composition* 21: 341–61.
Barthes, Roland. 1977. *Mythologies*. Translated by J Cape. New York: Hill and Wang.
Barthes, Roland. 1981. *Camera Lucida: Reflections on Photography*. Translated by Richard Howard. New York: Hill and Wang.
Bateson, Gregory, and Margaret Mead. 1942. *Balinese Character: A Photographic Analysis*. New York: New York Academy of Sciences.
Becker, Howard S. 2004. "Afterword: Photography as Evidence, Photographs as Exposition." In *Picturing the Social Landscape: Visual Methods and the Sociological Imagination*, edited by Caroline Knowles and Paul Sweetman, 193–97. London: Routledge.
Benjamin, Walter. 2011. *A Short History of Photography*. Translated by Stanley Mitchell. Oxford: Oxford University Press.
Bennett, Jane. 2010. *Vibrant Matter: A Political Ecology of Things*. Durham, NC: Duke University Press.
Berger, John. 1977. *Ways of Seeing*. New York: Penguin.
Berger, John. 1980. *About Looking*. New York: Vintage International.
Bernhardt, Steven. 1986. "Seeing the Text." *College Composition and Communication* 37: 66–78.
Bezemer, Jeff, and Gunther Kress. 2008. "Writing in Multimodal Texts: A Social Semiotic Account of Designs for Learning." *Written Communication* 25, no. 2: 166–95.

Blair, Carole. 1999. "Contemporary US Memorial Sites as Exemplars of Rhetoric's Materiality." In *Rhetorical Bodies*, edited by Jack Selzer and Sharon Crowley, 16–57. Madison: University of Wisconsin Press.
Bochner, Arthur P., and Carolyn Ellis. 1995. "Telling and Living: Narrative Co-Construction and the Practices of Interpersonal Relationships." In *Social Approaches to Communication*, edited by Wendy Leeds-Hurwitz, 201–13. New York: Guilford.
Bødker, Susanne, and Clemens Nylandsted Klokmose. 2011. "The Human-Artifact Model: An Activity Theoretical Approach to Artifact Ecologies." *Human-Computer Interaction* 26: 315–71.
Bogost, Ian. 2011. "Seeing Things—Oooiii." https://vimeo.com/29092112.
Bogost, Ian. 2012. *Alien Phenomenology, or What It's Like to Be a Thing*. Minneapolis: University of Minnesota Press.
Bourdieu, Pierre. 1977. *Outline of a Theory of Practice*. Translated by Richard Nice. Cambridge: Cambridge University Press.
Boyle, Casey, James J. Brown Jr., and Steph Ceraso. 2018. "The Digital: Rhetoric Behind and Beyond the Screen." *Rhetoric Society Quarterly* 48, no. 3: 251–59.
Brighenti, Andrea Mubi. 2010. *Visibility in Social Theory and Social Research*. New York: Palgrave Macmillan.
Brodkey, Linda. 1987. *Academic Writing as a Social Practice*. Philadelphia: Temple University Press.
Brown, Roger. 2011. "Photography as Process, Documentary Photographing as Discourse." In *Visual Research Methods in the Social Sciences: Awakening Visions*, edited by Stephen Spencer, 199–224. London: Routledge.
Bryant, Levi R. 2011. *The Democracy of Objects*. Ann Arbor, MI: Open Humanities Press.
Bryant, Levi R. 2014. *Onto-Cartography: An Ontology of Machines and Media*. Edinburgh: University of Edinburgh Press.
Burke, Kenneth. 1961. *The Rhetoric of Religion*. Boston: Beacon.
Caldwell, Kate. 2010. "We Exist: Intersectional In/Visibility in Bisexuality and Disability." *Disability Studies Quarterly* 30, no. 3–4. https://dsq-sds.org/index.php/dsq/article/view/1273.
Carter, Michael. 1988. "Stasis and Kairos: Principles of Social Construction in Classical Rhetoric." *Rhetoric Review* 7, no. 1: 97–112.
Ceraso, Steph. 2018. *Sounding Composition: Multimodal Pedagogies for Embodied Listening*. Pittsburgh: University of Pittsburgh Press.
Chaplin, Elizabeth. 1994. *Sociology and Visual Representations*. London: Routledge.
Chaplin, Elizabeth. 2011. "The Photo Diary as an Autoethnographic Method." In *The Sage Handbook of Visual Research Methods*, edited by Eric Margolis and Luc Pauwels, 241–62. London: Sage.
Chávez, Karma R. 2018. "The Body: An Abstract and Actual Rhetorical Concept." *Rhetoric Society Quarterly* 48, no. 3: 242–50.
Christensen, Inger. 2018. *The Condition of Secrecy*. Translated by Susanna Nied. New York: New Directions.
Clary-Lemon, Jennifer. 2020. "Gifts, Ancestors, and Relations: Notes toward an Indigenous New Materialism." *Enculturation* 30. https://enculturation_net/gifts_ancestors_and_relations.
Clifford, James, and George E. Marcus, eds. 1986. *Writing Culture: The Poetics and Politics of Ethnography*. Berkeley: University of California Press.
Cole, Teju. 2017. *Blind Spot*. New York: Penguin Random House.
Coole, Diana, and Samantha Frost, eds. 2010. *New Materialisms: Ontology, Agency, and Politics*. Durham, NC: Duke University Press.
Daniels, Inge. 2010. *The Japanese House: Material Culture in the Modern Home*. New York: Berg.
Darwin, Charles. 1881. *The Formation of Vegetable Mould through the Action of Worms, with Observations on Their Habits*. London: Murray.

Davis, Diane. 2010. *Inessential Solidarity: Rhetoric and Foreigner Relations*. Pittsburgh: University of Pittsburgh Press.
Davis, Diane. 2017. "Rhetoricity at the End of the World." *Philosophy and Rhetoric* 50, no. 4: 431–51.
*Dazed Digital*. 2018. "Intimate Photos of a Queer New York Kiss-In." February 12, 2018. http://www.dazeddigital.com/politics/article/38996/1/intimate-photos-of-a-queer-new-york-kiss-in.
de Certeau, Michel. 1984. *The Practice of Everyday Life*. Translated by Steven Rendall. Berkeley: University of California Press.
Deleuze, Gilles. 2002. *Francis Bacon: The Logic of Sensation*. Translated by Daniel W. Smith. Minneapolis: University of Minnesota Press.
Denzin, Norman. 2013. *Interpretive Autoethnography*. Los Angeles: Sage.
Derrida, Jacques. 2010. *Copy, Archive, Signature: A Conversation on Photography*. Translated by Jeff Fort. Stanford, CA: Stanford University Press.
Dickinson, Greg, Carole Blair, and Brian L. Ott, eds. 2010. *Places of Public Memory: The Rhetoric of Museums and Memorials*. Tuscaloosa: University of Alabama Press.
Dourish, Paul. 2001. *Where the Action Is: The Foundations of Embodied Interaction*. Cambridge, MA: MIT Press.
Dyer, Geoff. 2007. *The Ongoing Moment*. New York: Vintage.
El Guindi, Fadwa. 2004. *Visual Anthropology: Essential Method and Theory*. Walnut Creek, CA: Altamira.
Ellis, Carolyn. 2004. *The Ethnographic I: A Methodological Novel about Autoethnography*. Walnut Creek, CA: Altamira.
Ellis, Carolyn, Tony E. Adams, and Arthur Bochner. 2011. "Autoethnography: An Overview." *Historical Social Research / Historische Sozialforschung* 36, no. 4: 273–90.
Ellis, Carolyn, and Arthur P. Bochner. 2000. "Autoethnography, Personal Narrative, Reflexivity." In *Handbook of Qualitative Research*, edited by Norman K. Denzin and Yvonna S. Lincoln, 733–68. London: Sage.
Emig, Janet. 1982. "Inquiry Paradigms and Writing." *College Composition and Communication* 33, no. 1: 64–75.
Enos, Richard Leo, and Roger Thompson, eds. 2008. *The Rhetoric of Saint Augustine of Hippo: De Doctrina Christiana and the Search for a Distinctly Christian Rhetoric*. Waco, TX: Baylor University Press.
Evans, Jessica, and Stuart Hall, eds. 2005. *Visual Culture: The Reader*. London: Sage.
Faigley, Lester, and Stephen Witte. "Analyzing Revision." *College Composition and Communication* 32, no. 4: 400–414.
Finnegan, Cara A. 2001. "The Naturalistic Enthymeme and Visual Argument: Photographic Representation in the 'Skull Controversy.'" *Argumentation and Advocacy* 37, no. 3: 133–49.
Fleckenstein, Kristie S. 2009. "Decorous Spectacle: Mirrors, Manners, and *Ars Dictaminis* in Late Medieval Civic Engagement." *Rhetoric Review* 28, no. 2: 111–27.
Freedman, Aviva, and Graham Smart. 1997. "Navigating the Current of Economic Policy: Written Genres and the Distribution of Cognitive Work at a Financial Institution." *Mind, Culture, and Activity* 4, no. 4: 238–55.
Gallagher, Victoria J., and Kenneth S. Zagacki. 2007. "Visibility and Rhetoric: Epiphanies and Transformations in Thelifephotographs of the Selma Marches of 1965." *Rhetoric Society Quarterly* 37, no. 2: 113–35.
Genet, Jean. 1964. *The Thief's Journal*. Translated by Bernard Frechtman. New York: Grove.
George, Diana. 2002. "From Analysis to Design: Visual Communication in the Teaching of Writing." *College Composition and Communication* 54, no. 1: 11–39.
George, Diana, and Mariolina Rizzi Salvatori. 2008. "Holy Cards/Immaginette: The Extraordinary Literacy of Vernacular Religion." *College Composition and Communication* 60, no. 2: 250–84.

Goodall, Bud H. L. 2006. *A Need to Know: The Clandestine History of a Cia Family.* Walnut Creek, CA: Left Coast Press.

Gorkemli, Serkan. 2011. "Gender Benders, Gay Icons, and Media: Lesbian and Gay Visual Rhetoric in Turkey." *Enculturation* 10. https://enculturation.net/gender-benders.

Graham, S. Scott. 2015. *The Politics of Pain Medicine: A Rhetorical-Ontological Inquiry.* Chicago: University of Chicago Press.

Graham, S. Scott, and Lynda Walsh. 2019. "There's No Such Thing as a Scientific Controversy." *Technical Communication Quarterly* 28, no. 3: 192–206.

Graves, Michael. 2009. *Preaching the Inward Light: Theory and Practice of Early Quaker Rhetoric.* Waco, TX: Baylor University Press.

Gries, Laurie E. 2015. *Still Life with Rhetoric: A New Materialist Approach for Visual Rhetorics.* Logan: Utah State University Press.

Griffiths, Alison. 2002. *Wondrous Difference: Cinema, Anthropology, and Turn-of-the-Century Visual Culture.* New York: Columbia University Press.

Gros, Frederic. 2014. *A Philosophy of Walking.* Translated by John Howe. New York: Verso.

Halliday, Lisa. 2018. *Asymmetry.* New York: Simon and Schuster.

Handa, Carolyn. 2001. "Letter from the Guest Editor: Digital Rhetoric, Digital Literacy, Computers, and Composition." *Computers and Composition* 18, no. 1: 1–10.

Haraway, Donna. 2016. *Staying with the Trouble: Making Kin in the Chthulucene.* Durham, NC: Duke University Press.

Hariman, Robert, and John Louis Lucaites. 2001. "Dissent and Emotional Management in a Liberal-Democratic Society: The Kent State Iconic Photograph." *Rhetoric Society Quarterly* 31, no. 3: 5–31.

Hariman, Robert, and John Louis Lucaites. 2016. *The Public Image: Photography and Civic Spectatorship.* Chicago: University of Chicago Press.

Harman, Graham. 2009. *Prince of Networks: Bruno Latour and Metaphysics.* Victoria, BC: Re.press.

Harman, Graham. 2011. *Tool-Being: Heidegger and the Metaphysics of Objects.* Chicago: Open Court.

Harman, Graham. 2016. *Immaterialism: Objects and Social Theory.* Cambridge: Polity Press.

Harman, Graham. 2018. *Object-Oriented Ontology: A New Theory of Everything.* New York: Pelican Books.

Harper, Douglas. 1998. "An Argument for Visual Sociology." In *Image-Based Research: A Sourcebook for Qualitative Researchers,* edited by Jon Prosser, 24–41. London: Falmer.

Harper, Douglas. 2004. "Wednesday-Night Bowling: Reflections on Cultures of a Rural Working Class." In *Picturing the Social Landscape: Visual Methods and the Sociological Imagination,* edited by Caroline Knowles and Paul Sweetman, 93–113. London: Routledge.

Harper, Douglas. 2012. *Visual Sociology.* London: Routledge.

Hashimov, Elmar, and Brian McNely. 2012. "Left to Their Own Devices: Ad Hoc Genres and the Design of Transmedia Narratives." In *Proceedings of the 30th ACM International Conference on Design of Communication—SIGDOC '12,* edited by Mark Zachry, 251–60. New York: Association for Computing Machinery. https://doi.org/10.1145/2379057.2379105.

Haskins, Ekaterina V., and James Zappen. 2010. "Totalitarian Visual 'Monologue': Reading Soviet Posters with Bakhtin." *Rhetoric Society Quarterly* 40, no. 4: 326–59.

Hawhee, Debra. 2015. "Rhetoric's Sensorium." *Quarterly Journal of Speech* 101, no. 1: 2–17.

Hawhee, Debra. 2016. *Rhetoric in Tooth and Claw: Animals, Language, Sensation.* Chicago: University of Chicago Press.

Hawisher, Gail E., Cynthia L. Selfe, Brittney Moraski, and Melissa Pearson. 2004. "Becoming Literate in the Information Age: Cultural Ecologies and the Literacies of Technology." *College Composition and Communication* 55, no. 4: 642–92.

Hawk, Byron. 2007. *A Counter-History of Composition: Toward Methodologies of Complexity.* Pittsburgh: University of Pittsburgh Press.

Hawk, Byron. 2018. "Sound: Resonance as Rhetorical." *Rhetoric Society Quarterly* 48, no. 3: 315–23.
Heidegger, Martin. 1966. *Discourse on Thinking*. Translated by John M. Anderson and E. Hans Freund. New York: Harper Colophon Books.
Heidegger, Martin. 1968. *What Is Called Thinking?* Translated by J. Glenn Gray. New York: Harper Perennial.
Heidegger, Martin. 1977. *The Question Concerning Technology and Other Essays*. Translated by William Lovitt. New York: Harper Perennial.
Heidegger, Martin. 1993. *Martin Heidegger: Basic Writings*. San Francisco: Harper San Francisco.
Heidegger, Martin. 2010. *Being and Time*. Translated by Joan Stambaugh. Albany: State University of New York Press.
Heidegger, Martin. 2013. *Poetry, Language, Thought*. Translated by Albert Hofstadter. New York: Harper Perennial.
Hocks, Mary E. 2003. "Understanding Visual Rhetoric in Digital Writing Environments." *College Composition and Communication* 54, no. 4: 629–56.
Houck, Davis W., and David E. Dixon, eds. 2006. *Rhetoric, Religion, and the Civil Rights Movement, 1954–1965*. Waco, TX: Baylor University Press.
Ingold, Tim. 2000. *The Perception of the Environment: Essays on Livelihood, Dwelling and Skill*. London: Routledge.
Ingold, Tim. 2008. "Bindings against Boundaries: Entanglements of Life in an Open World." *Environment and Planning A: Economy and Space* 40, no. 8: 1796–1810.
Ingraham, Chris. 2017. "The Suddener World: Photography and Ineffable Rhetoric." *Philosophy and Rhetoric* 50, no. 2: 129–52.
Ingraham, Chris. 2018. "Energy: Rhetoric's Vitality." *Rhetoric Society Quarterly* 48, no. 3: 260–68.
Jacknis, Ira. 1988. "Margaret Mead and Gregory Bateson in Bali: Their Use of Photography and Film." *Cultural Anthropology* 3, no. 2: 160–77.
Jones, Madison. 2019. "Sylvan Rhetorics: Roots and Branches of More-than-Human Publics." *Rhetoric Review* 38, no. 1: 63–78.
Kalin, Jason. 2017. "Gathering Memories with Augmented Reality." In *Augmented Reality: Innovative Perspectives across Art, Industry, and Academia*, edited by Sean Morey and John Tinnell, 119–34. Anderson, SC: Parlor Press.
Kalin, Jason, and David Gruber. 2022. "Rhetoric, Methodology, and a Question of Onto-Epistemological Access." *Philosophy and Rhetoric* 55, no. 2: 127–51.
Knausgaard, Karl Ove. 2017a. *Autumn*. Translated by Ingvild Burkey. New York: Penguin.
Knausgaard, Karl Ove. 2017b. *Winter*. Translated by Ingvild Burkey. New York: Penguin.
Knausgaard, Karl Ove. 2018a. *Inadvertent*. Translated by Ingvild Burkey. New Haven, CT: Yale University Press.
Knausgaard, Karl Ove. 2018b. *My Struggle: Book Six*. Translated by Don Bartlett and Martin Aitken. New York: Farrar, Straus and Giroux.
Knausgaard, Karl Ove. 2018c. *Summer*. Translated by Ingvild Burkey. New York: Penguin.
Knowles, Caroline, and Paul Sweetman. 2004a. "Introduction." In *Picturing the Social Landscape: Visual Methods and the Sociological Imagination*, edited by Caroline Knowles and Paul Sweetman, 1–17. London: Routledge.
Knowles, Caroline, and Paul Sweetman, eds. 2004b. *Picturing the Social Landscape: Visual Methods and the Sociological Imagination*. London: Routledge.
Kostelnick, Charles. 1988. "A Systematic Approach to Visual Language in Business Communication." *Journal of Business Communication* 25, no. 3: 29–48.
Kress, Gunther. 2005. "Gains and Losses: New Forms of Texts, Knowledge, and Learning." *Computers and Composition* 22, no. 1: 5–22.
Latour, Bruno. 1988. *Science in Action: How to Follow Scientists and Engineers through Society*. Cambridge, MA: Harvard University Press.

Latour, Bruno. 1994. "On Technical Mediation." *Common Knowledge* 3, no. 2: 29–64.
Latour, Bruno. 2007. *Reassembling the Social.* Oxford: Oxford University Press.
Lauer, Janice M. 1984. "Composition Studies: Dappled Discipline." *Rhetoric Review* 3, no. 1: 20–29.
Law, John. 2004. *After Method: Mess in Social Science Research.* London: Routledge.
Lefebvre, Henri. 2013. *Rhythmanalysis.* Translated by Stuart Elden and Gerald Moore. London: Bloomsbury.
Levy, Deborah. 2018. *The Cost of Living.* London: Bloomsbury.
Lewis, Camille. 2007. *Romancing the Difference: Kenneth Burke, Bob Jones University, and the Rhetoric of Religious Fundamentalism.* Waco, TX: Baylor University Press.
Liggett, Helen. 2003. *Urban Encounters.* Minneapolis: University of Minnesota Press
Lucaites, John Louis, and Robert Hariman. 2001. "Visual Rhetoric, Photojournalism, and Democratic Public Culture." *Rhetoric Review* 20, no. 1–2: 37–42.
MacDougall, David. 1997. "The Visual in Anthropology." In *Rethinking Visual Anthropology,* edited by Marcus Banks and Howard Morphy, 276–95. New Haven, CT: Yale University Press.
Malcolm, Janet. 2023. *Still Pictures.* New York: Farrar, Straus and Giroux.
Malinowski, Bronislaw. 2015. *Argonauts of the Western Pacific.* London: Routledge.
Marback, Richard. 2008. "Unclenching the Fist: Embodying Rhetoric and Giving Objects Their Due." *Rhetoric Society Quarterly* 38, no. 1: 46–65.
Markel, Mike. 1995. "Using Design Principles to Teach Technical Communication." *Journal of Business and Technical Communication* 9, no. 2: 206–18.
Markel, Mike. 1998. "What Students See: Word Processing and the Perception of Visual Design." *Computers and Composition* 15, no. 3: 373–86.
Maxwell, Anne. 2013. "Modern Anthropology and the Problem of the Racial Type: The Photographs of Franz Boas." *Visual Communication* 12, no. 1: 123–42.
McKinnon, Sarah L., Robert Asen, Karma R. Chávez, and Robert Glenn Howard, eds. 2017. *Text + Field: Innovations in Rhetorical Method.* State College: Pennsylvania State University Press.
McNely, Brian. 2010. "Exploring a Sustainable and Public Information Ecology." In *Proceedings of the 28th ACM International Conference on Design of Communication—SIGDOC '10,* edited by Junia Anacleto, Renata Pontin Fortes, and Carlos J. Costa, 103–8. New York: Association for Computing Machinery. https://doi.org.10.1145/1878450.1878468.
McNely, Brian. 2011a. "Informal Communication, Sustainability, and the Public Writing Work of Organizations." In *2011 IEEE International Professional Communication Conference,* 1–7. New York: IEEE. https://doi.org/10.1109/IPCC.2011.6087195.
McNely, Brian. 2011b. "Sociotechnical Notemaking: Short-Form to Long-Form Writing Practices." *Present Tense: A Journal of Rhetoric in Society* 2, no. 1. http://www.presenttense journal.org/volume-2/sociotechnical-notemaking-short-form-to-long-form-writing-practices/.
McNely, Brian. 2013a. "'That Light-Bulb Feeling': An Interview with Clay Spinuzzi." *Present Tense: A Journal of Rhetoric in Society* 3, no. 1. http://www.presenttensejournal.org/volume-3/that-light-bulb-feeling-an-interview-with-clay-spinuzzi/.
McNely, Brian. 2013b. "Visual Research Methods and Communication Design." In *Proceedings of the 31st ACM International Conference on Design of Communication—SIGDOC '13,* edited by Michael J. Albers and Katherine Gossett, 123–32. New York: Association for Computing Machinery. https://doi.org/10.1145/2507065.2507073.
McNely, Brian. 2015a. "Taking Things Seriously with Visual Research." *Communication Design Quarterly* 3, no. 2: 48–54.
McNely, Brian. 2015b. "Instagram, Geocaching, and the *When* of Rhetorical Literacies." *Kairos* 19, no. 3. https://kairos.technorhetoric.net/19.3/topoi/mcnely/index.html.

McNely, Brian. 2016. "Circulatory Intensities: Take a Book, Leave a Book." In *Rhetoric, through Everyday Things*, edited by Scot Barnett, and Casey Boyle, 139–54. Tuscaloosa: University of Alabama Press.
McNely, Brian. 2017. "Moments and Metagenres: Coordinating Complex, Multigenre Narratives." *Journal of Business and Technical Communication* 31, no. 4: 443–80.
McNely, Brian. 2018. "El Paso, Plastic Bags, Aesthetics." In *Inventing Place: Writing Lone Star Rhetorics*, edited by Casey Boyle, and Jenny Rice, 220–31. Carbondale, IL: Southern Illinois University Press.
McNely, Brian. 2019. "Lures, Slimes, Time: Viscosity and the Nearness of Distance." *Philosophy and Rhetoric* 52, no. 3: 203–26.
McNely, Brian, Paul Gestwicki, Bridget Gelms, and Ann Burke. 2013. "Spaces and Surfaces of Invention: A Visual Ethnography of Game Development." *Enculturation* 15. https://www.enculturation.net/visual-ethnography.
McNely, Brian, and Nathaniel A. Rivers. 2014. "All of the Things: Engaging Complex Assemblages in Communication Design." In *Proceedings of the 32nd ACM International Conference on Design of Communication CD-ROM—SIGDOC '14*, edited by Kathie Gossett, Brian McNely, and Dave Jones, 1–10. New York: Association of Computing Machinery. https://doi.org/10.1145/2666216.2666222.
McNely, Brian, and Christa Teston. 2015. "Tactical and Strategic: Qualitative Approaches to the Digital Humanities." In *Rhetoric and the Digital Humanities*, edited by Jim Ridolfo and William Hart-Davidson, 111–26. Chicago: University of Chicago Press.
Mead, Margaret, and Francis Cooke Macgregor. 1951. *Growth and Culture: A Photographic Study of Balinese Childhood*. New York: Putnam.
Micciche, Laura R. 2004. "Seeing and Reading Incest: A Study of Debbie Drechsler's 'Daddy's Girl.'" *Rhetoric Review* 23, no. 1: 5–20.
Miles, Matthew A., A. Michael Huberman, and Johnny Saldaña. 2013. *Qualitative Data Analysis: A Methods Sourcebook*. London: Sage.
Mitchell, Claudia. 2011. *Doing Visual Research*. London: Sage.
Mol, Annemarie. 2002. *The Body Multiple: Ontology in Medical Practice*. Durham, NC: Duke University Press.
Morris, Errol. 2011. *Believing Is Seeing: Observations on the Mysteries of Photography*. New York: Penguin.
Morton, Timothy. 2012. "An Object-Oriented Defense of Poetry." *New Literary History* 43: 205–24.
Morton, Timothy. 2013. *Realist Magic: Objects, Ontology, Causality*. Ann Arbor, MI: Open Humanities Press.
Muckelbauer, John. 2020. "The Human Problem (Part I)." *Philosophy and Rhetoric* 53, no. 3: 293–98.
Muncey, Tessa. 2010. *Creating Autoethnographies*. Los Angeles: Sage.
Nehamas, Alexander, and Paul Woodruff, eds. 1995. *Phaedrus: Plato*. Indianapolis: Hackett.
Nelson, Maggie. 2015. *The Argonauts*. New York: Graywolf.
Nietzsche, Friedrich. 1974. *The Gay Science: With a Prelude of Rhymes and an Appendix of Songs*. Translated by Walter Kaufmann. New York: Vintage.
Olson, Christa. 2009. "Casta Painting and the Rhetorical Body." *Rhetoric Society Quarterly* 39, no. 4: 307–30.
Orelus, Pierre Wilbert. 2013. "The Institutional Cost of Being a Professor of Color: Unveiling Micro-Aggression, Racial [In]Visibility, and Racial Profiling through the Lens of Critical Race Theory." *Current Issues in Education* 16, no. 2: 1–11.
Owens, Derek. 2014. "Critical Expressivism's Alchemical Challenge." In *Critical Expressivism: Theory and Practice in the Composition Classroom*, edited by Tara Roeder and Roseanne Gatto, 69–77. Fort Collins, CO: WAC Clearinghouse.
Packer, Martin. 2011. *The Science of Qualitative Research*. Cambridge: Cambridge University Press.

Pelias, Ronald J. 2007. "Jarheads, Girly Men, and the Pleasures of Violence." *Qualitative Inquiry* 13, no. 7: 945–59.
Pender, Kelly. 2008. "Negation and the Contradictory Technics of Rhetoric." *Rhetoric Society Quarterly* 38, no. 1: 2–24.
Pender, Kelly. 2011. *Techne, from Neoclacissism to Postmodernism*. Anderson, SC: Parlor Press.
Pilsch, Andrew. 2017. "Invoking Darkness: *Skotison*, Scalar Derangement, and Inhuman Rhetoric." *Philosophy and Rhetoric* 50, no. 3: 336–55.
Pink, Sarah. 2006. *The Future of Visual Anthropology: Engaging the Senses*. London: Routledge.
Pink, Sarah. 2007. *Doing Visual Ethnography: Images, Media, and Representation in Research*. London: Sage.
Pink, Sarah. 2011. "Multimodality, Multisensoriality, and Ethnographic Knowing Social Semiotics and the Phenomenology of Perception." *Qualitative Research* 11, no. 3: 261–76.
Pink, Sarah. 2012a. "Advances in Visual Methodology: An Introduction." In *Advances in Visual Methodology*, edited by Sarah Pink, 3–16. Los Angeles: Sage.
Pink, Sarah. 2012b. *Situating Everyday Life: Practices and Places*. Los Angeles: Sage.
Pink, Sarah. 2012c. "Visual Ethnography and the Internet: Visuality, Virtuality, and the Spatial Turn." In *Advances in Visual Methodology*, edited by Sarah Pink, 113–30. Los Angeles: Sage.
Pink, Sarah, László Kürti, and Ana Isabel Afonso, eds. 2004. *Working Images: Visual Research and Representation in Ethnography*. London: Routledge.
Pinney, Christopher. 2003. "Introduction: 'How the Other Half.' " In *Photography's Other Histories*, edited by Christopher Pinney and Nicolas Peterson, 1–16. Durham, NC: Duke University Press.
Pinney, Christopher. 2011. *Photography and Anthropology*. London: Reaktion Books.
Pollini, John. 2012. *From Republic to Empire: Rhetoric, Religion, and Power in the Visual Culture of Ancient Rome*. Norman: University of Oklahoma Press.
Poulos, Christopher N. 2008. *Accidental Ethnography: An Inquiry into Family Secrecy*. Walnut Creek, CA: Left Coast Press.
Prior, Paul, and Jody Shipka. 2003. "Chronotopic Lamination: Tracing the Contours of Literate Activity." In *Writing Selves, Writing Societies: Research from Activity Perspectives*, edited by Charles Bazerman and David R. Russell, 180–238. Fort Collins, CO WAC Clearinghouse.
Pruchnic, Jeff, and Kim Lacey. 2011. "The Future of Forgetting: Rhetoric, Memory, Affect." *Rhetoric Society Quarterly* 41, no. 5: 472–94.
Reed-Danahay, Deborah. 1997. *Auto/ethnography*. New York: Berg.
Rice, Jenny. 2012. *Distant Publics: Development Rhetoric, and the Subject of Crisis*. Pittsburgh: University of Pittsburgh Press.
Richter, Gerhard. 2010. "Between Translation and Invention: The Photograph in Deconstruction." In *Copy, Archive, Signature: A Conversation on Photography*, edited by Jacques Derrida, ix–xxxviii. Stanford, CA: Stanford University Press.
Rickert, Thomas. 2013. *Ambient Rhetoric: The Attunements of Rhetorical Being*. Pittsburgh: University of Pittsburgh Press.
Rickert, Thomas. 2016. "Afterword: A Crack in the Cosmic Egg, Tuning into Things." In *Rhetoric, through Everyday Things*, edited by Scot Barnett and Casey Boyle, 226–31. Tuscaloosa: University of Alabama Press.
Rickert, Thomas. 2017. "Tuning: A Brief on Rhetoric, Relationality, and Attunement." *Rhetoric Society Quarterly* 47, no. 5: 448–54.
Ridolfo, Jim. 2015. *Digital Samaritans: Rhetorical Delivery and Engagement in the Digital Humanities*. Ann Arbor: University of Michigan Press.
Rivers, Nathaniel A. 2014. "Tracing the Missing Masses: Vibrancy, Symmetry, and Public Rhetoric Pedagogy." *Enculturation* 17. https://enculturation.net/missingmasses.
Rousseau, Jean-Jacques. 1953. *The Confessions*. Translated by John Michael Cohen. New York: Penguin.

Ruby, Jay. 1995. *Secure the Shadow: Death and Photography in America*. Cambridge, MA: MIT Press.
Rule, Hannah. 2018. "Writing's Rooms." *College Composition and Communication* 69, no. 3: 402–32.
Rule, Hannah. 2019. *Situating Writing Processes*. Fort Collins, CO: WAC Clearinghouse.
Russell, David R. 2009. "Uses of Activity Theory in Written Communication Research." In *Learning and Expanding with Activity Theory*, edited by Annalisa Sannino, Harry Daniels, and Kris D. Gutiérrez, 40–52. Cambridge: Cambridge University Press.
Ryan, Susannah. 2018. "*Rhetoric and the Gift: Ancient Rhetorical Theory and Contemporary Communication* by Mari Lee Mifsud (Review)." *Philosophy and Rhetoric* 51, no. 1: 91–97.
Safranski, Rüdiger. 1998. *Martin Heidegger: Between Good and Evil*. Translated by Ewald Osers. Cambridge, MA: Harvard University Press.
Safranski, Rüdiger. 2017. *Goethe: Life as a Work of Art*. Translated by David Dollenmayer. New York: Liveright.
Saldaña, Johnny. 2009. *The Coding Manual for Qualitative Researchers*. Los Angeles: Sage.
Selzer, Jack, and Sharon Crowley, eds. 1999. *Rhetorical Bodies*. Madison: University of Wisconsin Press.
Serres, Michel. 2016. *The Five Senses: A Philosophy of Mingled Bodies*. Translated by Margaret Sankey and Peter Cowley. London: Bloomsbury Academic.
Shaviro, Steven. 2014. *The Universe of Things: On Speculative Realism*. Minneapolis: University of Minnesota Press.
Shipka, Jody. 2011. *Toward a Composition Made Whole*. Pittsburgh: University of Pittsburgh Press.
Shove, Elizabeth, Matthew Watson, Martin Hand, and Jack Ingram. 2007. *The Design of Everyday Life*. New York: Berg.
Smith, Patti. 2015. *M Train*. New York: Random House Vintage.
Smith, Shawn Michelle. 2014. "Photography between Desire and Grief: Roland Barthes and F. Holland Day." In *Feeling Photography*, edited by Elspeth H. Brown and Thy Phu, 29–46. Durham, NC: Duke University Press.
Solnit, Rebecca. 2000. *Wanderlust: A History of Walking*. New York: Penguin.
Solnit, Rebecca. 2005. *A Field Guide to Getting Lost*. New York: Vintage.
Sontag, Susan. 2004. *Regarding the Pain of Others*. New York: Picador.
Sorapure, Madeleine. 2006. "Text, Image, Code, Comment: Writing in Flash." *Computers and Composition* 23, no. 4: 412–29.
Sorapure, Madeleine. 2010. "Information Visualization, Web 2.0, and the Teaching of Writing." *Computers and Composition* 27, no. 1: 59–70.
Sparrow, Tom. 2015. *Plastic Bodies: Rebuilding Sensation after Phenomenology*. Ann Arbor, MI: Open Humanities Press.
Spencer, Stephen. 2011. *Visual Research Methods in the Social Sciences: Awakening Visions*. London: Routledge.
Spinuzzi, Clay. 2003. *Tracing Genres through Organizations: A Sociocultural Approach to Information Design*. Cambridge, MA: MIT Press.
Spinuzzi, Clay. 2008. *Network: Theorizing Knowledge Work in Telecommunications*. Cambridge: Cambridge University Press.
Spinuzzi, Clay. 2010. "Secret Sauce and Snake Oil: Writing Monthly Reports in a Highly Contingent Environment." *Written Communication* 27, no. 4: 363–409.
Springgay, Stephanie, and Sarah E. Truman. 2017. *Walking Methodologies in a More-than-Human World: Walkinglab*. London: Routledge.
Stazs, Clarice. 1979. "The Early History of Visual Sociology." In *Images of Information: Still Photography in the Social Sciences*, edited by Jon Wagner, 119–36. Beverly Hills, CA: Sage.
Stewart, Kathleen. 1996. *A Space on the Side of the Road: Cultural Poetics in an "Other" America*. Princeton, NJ: Princeton University Press.
Stewart, Kathleen. 2007. *Ordinary Affects*. Durham, NC: Duke University Press.

Stewart, Kathleen. 2008. "Weak Theory in an Unfinished World." *Journal of Folklore Research* 45, no. 1: 71–82.

Stewart, Kathleen. 2011. "Atmospheric Attunements." *Environment and Planning D: Society and Space* 29, no. 3: 445–53.

Stewart, Kathleen. 2013. "An Autoethnography of What Happens." In *Handbook of Autoethnography*, edited by Stacy Holman Jones, Tony E. Adams, and Carolyn Ellis, 659–68. Walnut Creek, CA: Left Coast Press.

Stone, Jonathan W. 2015. "Listening to the Sonic Archive: Rhetoric, Representation, and Race in the Lomax Prison Recordings." *Enculturation* 19. https://www.enculturation.net/listening-to-the-sonic-archive.

Stormer, Nathan. 2020. "Rhetoric by Accident." *Philosophy and Rhetoric* 53, no. 4: 553–76.

Tillmann, Lisa M. 2009. "Body and Bulimia Revisited: Reflections on 'a Secret Life.'" *Journal of Applied Communication Research* 37, no. 1: 98–112.

Tindle, Hannah. 2018. "The Instagram Account Celebrating Over-Plucked Eyebrows." https://www.anothermag.com/fashion-beauty/10520/the-instagram-account-celebrating-over-plucked-eyebrows.

Trapani, William C., and Chandra A. Maldonado. 2018. "Kairos: On the Limits to Our (Rhetorical) Situation." *Rhetoric Society Quarterly* 48, no. 3: 278–86.

von Amelunxen, Hubertus. 2000. "Afterword." In *Towards a Philosophy of Photography*, edited by Vilém Flusser, 86–94. London: Reaktion Books.

Wagner, Jon. 2011. "Seeing Things: Visual Research and Material Culture." In *The Sage Handbook of Visual Research Methods*, edited by Eric Margolis and Luc Pauwels 72–95. London: Sage.

Wagner, Roy. 1975. *The Invention of Culture.* Englewood Cliffs, NJ: Prentice-Hall.

Walsh, Lynda, Nathaniel A. Rivers, Jenny Rice, Laurie E. Gries, Jennifer L. Bay, Thomas Rickert, and Carolyn R. Miller. 2017. "Forum: Bruno Latour on Rhetoric." *Rhetoric Society Quarterly* 47, no. 5: 403–62.

Walters, Shannon. 2014. *Rhetorical Touch: Disability, Identification, Haptics.* Columbia: University of South Carolina Press.

Wang, Wayne, dir. 1995. *Smoke.* Paul Auster, screenwriter. Miramax Films, New York.

Watts, Vanessa. 2013. "Indigenous Place-Thought and Agency amongst Humans and Non Humans (First Woman and Sky Woman Go on a European World Tour)." *Decolonization: Indigeneity, Education, and Society* 2, no. 1: 20–34.

Wickman, Chad. 2010. "Writing Material in Chemical Physics Research: The Laboratory Notebook as Locus of Technical and Textual Integration." *Written Communication* 27, no. 3: 259–92.

Wickman, Chad. 2012. "Rhetoric, *Technê*, and the Art of Scientific Inquiry." *Rhetoric Review* 31, no. 1: 21–40.

Winsor, Dorothy. 1990. "Engineering Writing / Writing Engineering." *College Composition and Communication* 41, no. 1: 58–70.

Wrathall, Mark. 2011. *Heidegger and Unconcealment: Truth, Language, and History.* Cambridge: Cambridge University Press.

Wysocki, Anne Frances. 2005. "Awaywithwords: On the Possibilities in Unavailable Designs." *Computers and Composition* 22, no. 1: 55–62.

Yancey, Kathleen Blake. 2004. "Made Not Only in Words: Composition in a New Key." *College Composition and Communication* 56, no. 2: 297–328.

Yarbrough, Stephen R. 2018. *The Levels of Ambience: An Introduction to Integrative Rhetoric.* Lexington, KY: Intermezzo.

Yusoff, Kathryn. 2015. "Geologic Subjects: Nonhuman Origins, Geomorphic Aesthetics, and the Art of Becoming Inhuman." *Cultural Geographies* 22, no. 3: 383–407.

# INDEX

Page numbers followed by *f* indicate a figure.

absent presences, 24, 27–57
*Academic Writing as a Social Practice* (Brodkey), 30
actor-network theory, 59, 78, 206
Adams, Tony E., 155
adoration chapels, 81, 119–23, 120*f*, 138–42, 145–46, 210
affect/affective, 8, 25–26, 40, 43–44, 49, 58–60, 64, 81–82, 118–90
affective rhetorics, 9, 13–16, 21, 41, 83, 117–48, 207
Alfonso, Ana Isabel, 72
agency, 10–11, 18, 21–22, 30, 63–64, 66, 70, 77–78, 97, 118, 129–30
Ahmed, Sara, 59
ambient dwelling, 25, 117–48, 208
"Analytic Autoethnography" (Anderson), 156
Anderson, John, 165, 167–68
Anderson, Leon, 156–57, 161
anti-epistemist methodologies, 35–36, 39–41
apprehension, 10–12, 33, 44, 53–54, 151
*Argonauts of the Western Pacific* (Malinowski), 68
Aristotle, 42, 47, 127, 144, 183
Arnold, Jeanne E., 77
Arola, Kristin L., 43
Asen, Robert, 17
Ashmore, Malcolm, 94
*Asymmetry* (Halliday), 70
@dearcatcallers, 201–2
atherosclerosis, 17–18
@historyofoverplucking, 201
attunement, 23, 52–53, 62, 96–97, 115, 121, 127, 129–31, 142, 149–200, 208
autoethnography. *See* ethnography: autoethnography
*Autumn* (Knausgaard), 5, 55–56, 192

Backman, Jussi, 127
*Balinese Character* (Bateson and Mead), 69
Banks, Marcus, 72
Barad, Karen, 5, 12, 22–24, 30, 58, 63, 66, 70, 78, 122
Barnett, Scot, 5, 11, 15–17, 22–23, 118, 206–7

Barrios, Barclay, 43
Barthes, Roland, 13–14, 44, 75–76, 196–99, 202
Bateson, Gregory, 68–69
Beauvoir, Simone de, 183
Becker, Howard S., 72
being, 118, 126, 168–70, 183, 194. *See also* ontology
*Being and Time* (Heidegger), 144–45, 166–67
being there, 19, 23, 29, 36, 64, 144, 207. *See also* presence
Benjamin, Walter, 46, 180
Bennett, Jane, 78, 122, 176–77
Berger, John, 14, 44, 46, 87, 205
Bernhardt, Steven, 43
Bezemer, Jeff, 43
Black Lives Matter, 203
Blair, Carole, 61–64
*Blind Spot* (Cole), 15
Boas, Franz, 68–69
Bochner, Arthur P., 155
bodily movement and posture, 81, 117, 119, 122, 132–37, 171
Bødker, Susanne, 31
*Body Multiple, The* (Mol), 17
Bogost, Ian, 23, 56, 78
Bourdieu, Pierre, 31
Boyle, Casey, 5, 11, 15–16, 22, 118, 206–7
bracketing, 9–10, 127. *See also* unbracketing
Brighenti, Andrea Mubi, 43, 45, 49
Brodkey, Linda, 30, 32–33, 205–6
Brown, James J., Jr., 15
Brown, Roger, 74
Bryant, Levi R., 23, 78, 122
building, 25, 52, 124–46
"Building Dwelling Thinking" (Heidegger), 125, 129
Burke, Ann, 17, 28, 65, 137
Burke, Kenneth, 117

calculative thinking, 125, 129, 163–65, 169
Caldwell, Kate, 46
Carter, Michael, 42

Catholicism, 26, 81–82, 117–148, 119f, 120f, 121f, 132f, 133f, 134f, 207
cats, 149–40, 153–54, 161–62, 174–75
Ceraso, Steph, 15, 204
Changchun, China, 177–80
Chaplin, Elizabeth, 73, 158
Chauvin, Derek, 203
Chávez, Karma R., 15, 17
Christensen, Igner, 48
Clary-Lemon, Jennifer, 171
clearing, 194, 205–8
Clifford, James, 72
Cole, Teju, 15
collaborative writing. *See* writing: collaborative
color, 14–15, 29, 40
communication practices, 87–116. *See also* writing practices
comportment, 5–6, 9, 11–12, 25–26, 33, 42, 52, 59, 60, 66, 81, 88, 90, 111, 119, 123, 127, 130, 141–42, 144–47, 150–70, 186, 199, 203
concealment, 130, 137–43, 145, 198
*coniunctio*, 34–35
"Conversation on a Country Path about Thinking" (Heidegger), 166
Coole, Diana, 78
*Cost of Living, The* (Levy), 24
Crowley, Sharon, 61

Daniels, Inge, 76–77
Darwin, Charles, 176–77
*Dasein*, 144–45
*das Geviert*, 52, 125, 127–31, 136, 141, 146, 193
data collection and analysis, 34, 37, 61, 66–67, 94–96, 103–5, 110, 112, 114–15, 123–24, 157, 160–61, 205
Davis, Diane, 16, 23, 55, 118, 131
de Certeau, Michel, 31, 180–81
Deleuze, Gilles, 14
DeLieto, Nick, 202
Denzin, Norman, 155
Derrida, Jacques, 44–46
desks, 5–6
Dickens, Charles, 183
Dickinson, Greg, 64
digital privacy, 79–80, 88, 90–115, 115f, 100
digitization, 203
disclosedness, 46, 125
*Discourse on Thinking* (Heidegger), 129, 145, 163, 167, 170, 185, 192
distance, 15, 56, 68, 82, 168–70, 180–82, 186, 200
Dixon, David E., 117

documenting, 19–20, 22–23, 28, 39–40, 61, 66–70, 72–73, 80, 93–94, 114, 122, 132, 137, 159, 200–3
*Doing Visual Ethnography* (Pink), 72, 203
Dourish, Paul, 144–45
Duns Scotus, 54–55
dwelling, 15, 25, 33, 119, 122, 124–90, 207–8. *See also* ambient dwelling
Dyer, Geoff, 71

El Guindi, Fadwa, 72
Ellis, Carolyn, 155–56
embodiment, 15, 185–86, 202
Emig, Janet, 44
Enos, Richard Leo, 117
environments/environs, 5, 19–20, 25 30–34, 51, 78, 82, 89–90, 93–94, 96–98, 107, 114–48, 155, 168–69, 203–7. *See also* spaces
epistemist approaches to rhetoric, 35–37, 39, 42, 48, 93–94, 118. *See also* ant-epistemist methodologies
*ereignen*, 193, 195
Erwitt, Elliot, 202
ethnography, 17–21, 72–149, 155–58; auto-ethnography, 25, 82, 153–91, 208; visual, 25–96, 107, 113–48, 153, 207
Eucharistic Adoration practices, 25, 81–82, 117–53, 119f, 121f, 132f, 133f, 207, 210. *See also* Catholicism and spirituality
Evans, Jessica, 75
excessive inclusion, 24, 67–69, 78–79
extra-discursive rhetorics, 81, 117–48, 204

factorial rhetorics, 25, 80, 83, 96–116, 158, 162, 206–7
Faigley, Lester, 66
feeling, 5, 11–15, 33, 46, 56, 59, 62–66, 81–82, 87, 117–48, 157–58, 174, 184, 197–200, 206
feminism, 201–2
Fernheimer, Janet, 205, 208
fieldwork, 19, 28, 33–43, 45, 49–50, 61, 75–79, 81–82, 88, 93–95, 107–8, 114, 123, 153–54, 163, 170–71, 207–8; visual fieldwork, 24, 66–69, 72–74, 77, 157–61
Finnegan, Cara, 43
Fleckenstein, Kristie S., 43
Floyd, George, 202–3
Flusser, Vilém, 50
focus groups, 30–31, 79–80, 87–88, 90–91, 93, 97–106, 99f, 100f, 110, 112
fourfold. *See* das Geviert
Frazier, Darnella, 202–3
Freedman, Aviva, 65
Frost, Samantha, 78

Gallagher, Victoria J., 43, 45
Gandhi, Mahatma, 183
gathering, 11, 25, 52, 119, 124–46, 150, 165, 199–200, 207
*Gay Science, The* (Nietzsche), 186
*Gelassenheit*, 25–26, 83, 149–87, 208
Gelms, Bridget, 17, 28, 65, 137
Genet, Jean, 191
geological forces, 171–72
George, Diana, 43
Gestwicki, Paul, 17, 28, 65, 137
Goethe, Johann Wolfgang von, 13, 46
Goodall, Bud H. L., 155
Gorkemli, Serkan, 46
Graesch, Anthony P., 77
Graham, S. Scott, 20
Graves, Michael, 117
Greece, 194–95
Gries, Laurie E., 16, 21–23, 63, 118, 162, 207
Griffiths, Alison, 67–68
Gros, Frederick, 186
*Growth and Culture* (Mead), 68
Gruber, David, 35–36

Hall, Stuart, 75
Halliday, Lisa, 70
Handa, Carolyn, 43
haptic stimuli, 14–15, 66, 75, 81, 83, 90, 103, 130, 135–139, 204. *See also* touch
Haraway, Donna, 40
Hariman, Robert, 43, 59–61, 64, 69, 197
Harman, Graham, 23, 58–59, 78, 93, 127
Harper, Douglas, 73
Hashimov, Elmar, 37
Haskins, Ekaterina V., 43
Hawhee, Debra, 15–16, 25, 65, 118–119, 121
Hawisher, Gail E., 43
Hawk, Byron, 15, 48–49, 204
hearing, 13, 15, 17–18, 55, 66, 117, 137, 140, 149–50, 173, 179–82, 199
Heidegger, Martin, 9–13, 24–26, 31, 33, 44, 46–49, 52–56, 81–83, 125–31, 142–46, 150–53, 163–70, 185–86, 191–200
hermeneutic methodology, 76–78
heuristic methodology, 76, 88
Hocks, Mary E., 43
Hofstadter, Albert, 191, 193, 198
Holliday, George, 203
Houck, Davis W., 117
Howard, Robert Glenn, 17
Huberman, A. Michael, 66, 96
Hurt, William, 71

"Idea of Philosophy and the Worldview Problem, The" (Heidegger), 10–11
imagination, 9, 24–25, 45, 48, 59–61, 64, 200

im Thurn, Everard, 67–68
Indiana State Museum, 36–37
indigenous materialisms, 171–72
ineffable, 8, 81–82, 117–48, 150, 207
Ingold, Tim, 16, 31, 122, 152
Ingraham, Chris, 15, 118
interstitial writing genres, 64–65, 80, 102–6, 102f. *See also* writing
Investigation and Foresight, 88–97, 104f, 114, 124, 132, 207
invisibilities, 24, 27–57

Jacknis, Ira, 68
Jewish Kentucky Oral History Collection, 206
Jones, Madison, 16

Kalin, Jason, 35–36, 57
Kant, Immanuel, 78, 183
Keitel, Harvey, 70–71
Kierkegaard, Søren, 183–85
King, Rodney, 202–3
Knausgaard, Karl Ove, 5, 8, 51, 53, 55–57, 192
kneeling, 81, 117, 119, 122–23, 132f, 132–37, 139
knowing, 18–19, 33–36, 44, 47–48, 52–57, 65, 75, 80–81, 118, 143–44, 168
knowledges, 18–20, 35, 41–42, 48–49, 65, 72–74, 80–81, 90, 101–2, 110, 115, 155, 171
knowledge-making, 35–36, 45, 72–73, 80–81, 102, 105, 118, 131, 154–57, 208; collaborative, 75, 80, 98–106, 124
Knowles, Caroline, 73
Kostelnick, Charles, 43
Krell, David Farrell, 125
Kress, Gunther, 43
Kürti, László, 72

Lacey, Kim, 118
Latour, Bruno, 78, 94, 101, 206
Lauer, Janice M., 71
Law, John, 21
Lefebvre, Henri, 180–81
Levy, Deborah, 24
Lewis, Camille, 117
Lexington, Kentucky, 171–79, 181–83
LGBTQIA+ rights, 202
*lichtend*, 193–94
Liggett, Helen, 32
lightening, 54, 193–95, 198–99, 205–8
literalisms, 24, 59–60
Lucaites, John Lewis, 43, 59–61, 64, 69, 197

## INDEX

MacDougall, David, 72
Macgregor, Francis Cooke, 68
Malcolm, Janet, 191
Maldonado, Chandra A., 54
Malinowski, Bronislaw, 68
Marback, Richard, 62–64, 162
Marcus, George E., 72
Markel, Mike, 43
material cultures research, 24–25, 71–78
materiality, 10, 17–19, 23–24, 31, 44, 46–48, 61–64, 69, 77–80, 83, 93, 97, 127, 129, 130–31, 142, 160, 196, 207
material rhetorics research, 25, 58–87, 162
Maxwell, Anne, 68
McKinnon, Sarah L., 17
McNely, Brian, 17, 28, 32, 37, 52, 65, 93, 101–2, 137, 143, 153, 159–60, 203, 206
Mead, Margaret, 68–69
media research industry, 25, 45, 80, 90–97, 102–3, 110–16
mediated actions, 64–67, 93–94, 99–102, 107
meditative thinking, 26, 82–83, 119, 121, 125, 129–30, 139–45, 150, 163–69, 183–86, 191–210
memory, 70–71. *See also* unforgetting
Meno, 179
Micciche, Laura R., 43
Miles, Matthew A., 66, 96
Mitchell, Claudia, 73
Mol, Annemarie, 18–22, 50, 62, 78–79, 81, 93
monstrance, 81, 120–22, 121*f*, 130, 133–37, 134*f*, 139, 146, 207
mood, 6, 21, 31, 33–34, 83, 112, 117–48, 151–54, 163, 197, 200
Moraski, Brittney, 43
Morris, Errol, 60
Morton, Timothy, 23
*M Train* (Smith), 199
Muckelbauer, John, 36
Muncey, Tessa, 155–56
music, 117, 121, 138–39, 160
mutual vulnerability, 62–63, 83–84, 149–89, 199, 208
*Mythologies* (Barthes), 14

nearness, 11, 15, 53–55, 82, 152–53, 169–71, 181, 200. *See also* proximity
Nehamas, Alexander, 183
Nelson, Maggie, 46
new materialism, 5–210
Nietzsche, Friedrich, 183, 186
non-discursive rhetorics, 64, 82, 131
Nylandsted Klokmose, Clemens, 30

objectivity, 68–69, 147, 154; myth of, 9–10
object-oriented rhetoric, 204
objects, 16, 18–23, 35, 44–45, 52, 57, 59, 62–66, 74–80, 127, 147–48, 162, 165, 168–69, 199, 207
Ochs, Elinor, 77
olfactory sensations, 12, 16–17, 48, 55–56, 66, 75, 81–83, 117, 119*f*, 123, 125, 137–39, 145–46, 149, 152–53, 160, 194
Olson, Christa, 43
ontography, 56–57
ontology, 16, 18–24, 36, 64–69, 79–80, 142–48, 156, 159; object-oriented ontology, 22–23, 58–59, 93–94
oppression, 200–202
*Ordinary Affects* (Stewart), 157
Orelus, Pierre Wilbert, 46
"Origin of the Work of Art, The" (Heidegger), 194, 196
Ott, Brian, 64
Owens, Derek, 34

Packer, Martin, 33, 65
pain, 124, 140, 146
painting, 14, 33, 87, 196–97
participatory rhetorical acts, 25, 117–48
Pearson, Melissa, 43
pedestrian commuting, 149–90
Pelias, Ronald J., 155
Pender, Kelly, 42, 47–51, 53
perception, 70, 74, 81–82, 114; visual, 11–14, 43–45, 59–62, 186, 196–97, 204
*Phaedrus* (Plato), 183
photo-elicitation, 25, 80–81, 89–90, 95–96, 106–48
photography, 13–14, 26, 32–33, 35, 39–42, 45–46, 48, 50, 56, 59–61, 67–83, 87, 93, 158–59, 191–204
"Phototrails" project, 205
picturing writing, 24, 27–57, 87–116, 205
Pilsch, Andrew, 5
Pink, Sarah, 31, 39, 45, 72–76, 123, 161, 203
Pinney, Christopher, 24, 45, 57, 67–69, 79, 114, 159
Place-Thought, 171–72
*Plastic Bodies* (Sparrow), 82
Plato, 183
*Poetry, Language, Thought* (Heidegger), 191–93
*poiesis*, 9, 24–58, 60–61, 79, 96–97, 100–27, 158, 198–207; contingent forms of, 80, 91, 101, 105, 111–13, 152
police brutality, 202–3
political activism, 201–3
Pollini, John, 117
Poulos, Christopher N., 155

practical approaches to the study of rhetoric, 21, 24–26, 54, 65–67, 90, 127, 153, 163, 169
*Practice of Everyday Life, The* (de Certeau), 180–81
praxiography, 18–24, 46, 50, 58, 65, 79–83, 90, 93–96, 159, 163, 166, 206
prayer, 134, 140–42
presence, 25, 82, 119–124, 127, 130, 133–47, 150, 180, 198
presencing, 48–49, 61
Prior, Paul, 32
proximity, 26, 169–71, 200
Pruchnic, Jeff, 118
*punctum*, 14

Ragazzini, Enzo, 77
reading, 82, 119, 139–40, 164
realisms, 22–24, 30, 58–61; agential, 22–23; speculative, 23
realist rhetorics, 61–64
Reed-Danahay, Deborah, 155
relationality, 23, 44–45, 50, 66, 152
releasement, 25–26, 83, 153, 163, 165–71, 181, 186, 199, 208. *See also Gelassenheit*
religious rituals, 117–48, 119*f*
*Rhetorical Bodies* (Selzer and Crowly), 61
rhetorical enactments, 17–25, 28, 30–31, 34, 36, 39–40, 44, 47–49, 51–52, 58, 60, 63–64, 66, 70, 79–80, 83, 87–189, 195
*Rhythmanalysis* (Lefebvre), 180
Rice, Jenny, 15, 118, 147–48, 155, 162
Richter, Gerhard, 45
Rickert, Thomas, 8, 16, 21, 25, 33, 52, 66, 81, 93, 96–97, 115, 118, 124, 127–31, 137, 142, 144–45, 147–48, 151–53, 155, 163, 166, 170, 199, 207
Ridolfo, Jim, 206, 208
Rilke, Ranier Maria, 125, 129
Rimbaud, Arthur, 183
Rivers, Nathaniel A., 22, 206
"Roman Elegies" (Goethe), 13
Ronan, Alex, 201
Rousseau, Jean-Jacques, 183–85
Ruby, Jay, 73
Rule, Hannah, 17, 101
Russell, David R., 37, 93
Ryan, Susannah, 39, 50

Safranski, Rüdiger, 10–13, 51, 54–55, 192, 195, 197
Saldaña, Johnny, 66, 96
salience, 8–15, 18, 20–24, 33–36, 39, 41, 64, 70–71, 75, 127, 161
Sander, August, 46
Selfe, Cynthia L., 43

Selzer, Jack, 61
sensory artifacts, 25, 81–83, 117–53, 207–8
sensory engagements, 5, 25, 31, 58, 62, 66, 72, 75, 81–83, 97, 117–53, 158, 160–62, 170–71, 198–210
sensory rhetorics, 25, 56, 58, 74, 81–83, 117–90
Serres, Michel, 12, 14
sexual harassment, 201–2
shaping, 51–52
Shaviro, Steven, 12, 23, 66, 78, 165, 207
Shipka, Jody, 32–33, 64, 93
*Shoes* (Van Gogh), 196
Shove, Elizabeth, 77
sight, 12–15, 43–44, 62, 117–48, 197. *See also* perception: visual
situational variables, 66–67
Smart, Graham, 65
smell, sense of. *See* olfactory sensations
Smith, Patti, 199
Smith, Shawn Michelle, 14\
*Smoke* (Wang), 70–71
social media, 37, 39, 76, 80, 87–116, 164, 201
Socrates, 179, 183
Solnit, Rebecca, 179, 183–86
Sontag, Susan, 13, 59–60
Sorapure, Madeleine, 43
sound, 15, 18–19, 28, 48, 55, 65–66, 81–83, 139, 149–51, 160–61, 177–83. *See also* hearing
soundscapes, 160, 178–81, 201, 204, 208
spaces, 6, 31–32, 34, 72–73, 77–79, 81, 83, 92, 94–95, 97–115, 104*f*, 117–48, 161–62, 164, 203, 205–8
Sparrow, Tom, 58, 82
spectatorship, 61, 63–64
speculative middle, 40–42
speculative realism, 23, 59
Spencer, Stephen, 74
Spinuzzi, Clay, 16–17, 37, 65, 78, 93, 204
spirituality, 117–148, 207
Springgay, Stephanie, 22, 40–41, 45, 56, 171
Stazs, Clarice, 73
Stewart, Kathleen, 19, 24, 31, 52, 58, 62, 79, 122, 157–58, 198
Stone, Jonathan, 204
Stormer, Nathan, 16
Strand, Paul, 46
suasion, 5, 25, 62–64, 83, 94, 96–98, 115, 123, 145, 147–55, 206
subjectivity, 10–12
Sweetman, Paul, 73
systematic approaches to the study of rhetoric, 17, 21, 24, 41, 64–65, 77, 92, 112, 153

tabernacle, 119–22, 120f, 130, 135, 137–41, 207
tactile interactions, 66, 75, 83, 87, 117, 139, 204
*technes*, 9, 24, 26–58, 60–61, 66, 69–70, 79, 113, 115, 198–210
Teston, Christa, 32
theoretical studies of rhetoric, 17, 20–26, 30, 32–33, 36, 47, 67, 76, 78–79, 93, 117–48, 153, 163, 168, 204–8
theory/empirical practice bifurcations, artificiality of, 20–21
there Being, 144–45, 148, 152, 162, 165–66, 194, 200. *See also* Dasein
*Thief's Journal, The* (Jenet), 191
things, 5–25, 34–35, 45–46, 50–52, 55–56, 58–63, 70, 77–81, 87, 97, 107–13, 117–53, 161–66, 179–80, 192–95, 199–200, 206–10
this-now-here-ness, 25, 27–58, 82, 90, 127, 148, 153, 198
Thompson, Roger, 117
Tillmann, Lisa M., 155
Tindle, Hannah, 201
touch, sense of, 13–15, 117, 135–36, 139. *See also* haptic stimuli; tactile interactions
*Toward a Composition Made Whole* (Shipka), 32
translation, 191–94
*Transmedia Indiana*, 36–39
Trapani, William C., 54
Truman, Sarah E., 22, 40–41, 45, 171

unbracketing, 10–11, 15, 24–26, 50
un-concealed, 53–54, 198, 200
unforgetting, 24–26, 39, 31
universe of things, 12, 207

Van Gogh, Vincent, 196
*Vibrant Matter* (Bennett), 176–77
videos/videography, 32, 35, 38, 45–46, 50, 68–69, 73–81, 83, 91, 93–94, 122, 160, 203
violence against women, 201–2
visibility, 9, 13, 27–63, 66, 80, 87–116, 195–96, 198, 200, 205–6
visuality, 9, 27–63, 196, 205–6
visual and material cultures research, 74–79, 201
visual anthropology, 24–25, 68, 71–75, 78
visual data, 33–34, 39, 66–69, 72–74, 82, 87–15, 99f, 100f, 102f, 106f, 115f, 159–60

visual ethnography. *See* ethnography: visual
visual rhetorics, 13–15, 32–33, 39, 43, 45, 58–87, 201
visual sociology, 24–25, 58–87
Voices, 4, 202
von Amelunxen, Hubertus, 50

Wagner, Jon, 46
Wagner, Roy, 59
WAGR (writing, activity, and genre research), 37, 80, 93–94
waiting upon, 25, 167–71, 194
walking, 183–86
Walsh, Lynda, 15–16, 20, 23, 118, 131, 147–48, 151–53, 155, 162, 205
Walters, Shannon, 204
*Wanderlust* (Solnit), 183
Wang, Wayne, 70
Watts, Vanessa, 171
Wickman, Chad, 47–48, 65, 101
Winogrand, Gary, 56
Winsor, Dorothy, 101
withdrawal, 25, 82, 119, 124–48, 150, 198
Witte, Stephen, 66
Wittkower, Rudolf, 69
Woodruff, Paul, 183
Woolf, Virginia, 183
Wordsworth, William, 183
worlding, 10–15, 26, 52, 149–210
Wrathall, Mark, 127
writing, 6, 82–83, 101–2, 124, 139–40 157–58, 164, 191–4; collaborative, 25, 28–38, 31f, 80–81, 90, 93–116, 99f, 100f, 102f, 106f; technologies of, 18; topography of, 87–116, 142, 205; writing with light, 200–4. *See also* picturing writing
writing, activity, and genre research. *See* WAGR
writing practices, 6–8, 27–57, 64–65, 87–116. *See also* communication practices
written artifacts, 28, 81, 87–116, 99f, 100f, 102f, 106f, 115f
Wysocki, Anne Frances, 43

Yancey, Kathleen Blake, 43
Yarbrough, Stephen R., 16
Yusoff, Kathryn, 171

Zagacki, Kenneth S., 43, 45
Zappen, James, 43

# ABOUT THE AUTHOR

**Brian McNely** is associate professor in the deparment of Writing, Rhetoric & Digital Studies at the University of Kentucky. He studies everyday affects, sensations, aesthetics, and environments and their relationships to rhetorical theory, and he teaches courses in visual rhetorics and cultures, rhetorical theory, technical and professional writing, and creative nonfiction. He also races bikes.

www.ingramcontent.com/pod-product-compliance
Lightning Source LLC
Chambersburg PA
CBHW052137070526
44585CB00017B/1857